WHERE YOU GOIN' WITH THAT GUN IN YOUR HAND?

THE TRUE CRIME BLOTTER OF ROCK 'N' ROLL

KEITH ELLIOT GREENBERG

D1198288

Backbeat Books

Guilford, Connecticut

Published by Backbeat Books
An imprint of The Rowman & Littlefield Publishing Group, Inc.
4501 Forbes Boulevard, Suite 200, Lanham, Maryland 20706
www.rowman.com

Distributed by NATIONAL BOOK NETWORK

Copyright © 2019 by Keith Elliot Greenberg

Book design and composition by UB Communications

Library of Congress Cataloging-in-Publication Data is available

ISBN 978-1-61713-685-6

☺™ The paper used in this publication meets the minimum requirements of American National Standard for Information Sciences—Permanence of Paper for Printed Library Materials, ANSI/NISO Z39.48-1992.

Printed in the United States of America

WHERE YOU GOIN'
WITH THAT GUN
IN YOUR HAND?

CONTENTS

Acknowledgments

Aside from those already quoted in this book, the author wishes to thank the following people: Bernadette Malavarca, senior editor at Backbeat Books, and John Cerullo, group publisher at Hal Leonard/Backbeat Books; the crew at Giovanni's Brooklyn Eats, including Giovanni Tafuri, William "Reggie" Ruggerio, and Peter DePasquale, for helping me brainstorm at the beginning of the project; my family Jennifer, Dylan, and Summer; Tom Stephen, who was always ready to hang out during my L.A. excursions; my cousin, Barrie Waldman Marker, who lobbied on my behalf a close relative of one of the prime subjects; and Alex Shipman from *GloucestershireLive* and Richard Lovett, who assisted me in the UK. Also, *tack så mycket* to Scott Lakey, Eva Thomasson Lakey, Barbara Dernhagen, Erik Palmkrantz, and Emil—the guy who refused to charge me at the gym—for adding some light to a dark winter visit to Stockholm.

Introduction

There was always supposed to be something transgressive about rock 'n' roll. That was the point. The driving music and suggestive lyrics were intended to lower inhibitions, to fill listeners' minds with thoughts about lust, upheaval, and liberation. The music of each generation has been characterized as revolutionary, an impetus for society to stare down its ugliness and emerge under a more daring banner, marginalizing the ordinary and normalizing the misunderstood.

Invariably, the backlash decries the replacement of time-honored values with those venerating carnality, drug abuse, and violence. While teens were assigned much of the blame for the transfigurations in the 1950s, since the '90s, parents have also been targeted for raising their children in an atmosphere of licentiousness, based on the music that might have been playing at the moment of conception.

Which is why the topic of crime and rock 'n' roll is such an exciting one. Whether authentic or manufactured, the rock-star disposition was intended to be dangerous. When Mick Jagger, Jimi Hendrix, David Bowie, and Jay Z stood before police cameras to pose for their mug shots, the public was simply getting what it wanted. Critics could rave about the role models anointed by a generation of deluded youth, while fans imagined themselves staring back at their jailers, just as cool and fearless.

It was all fun. After all, it's not like anyone got murdered.

This book focuses on those rare times when rock 'n' roll and homicide have intersected. Sometimes the personalities have been the perpetrators; at other times, they've been the victims. John

Lennon, Selena, and Dimebag Darrell were all literal casualties of their fame, assassinated by fans whose names will forever be linked to the performers. Phil Spector's celebrity, on the other hand, allowed him to operate outside the boundaries of acceptable behavior—until he waved a gun around one last time, killing an actress inside the home that he referred to as his "castle." Tupac Shakur, Notorious B.I.G., and Norwegian black-metal guitarist Euronymous all but sacrificed themselves to maintain the integrity of the movements they represented. Sid Vicious has been mythologized as the punk rocker who flamed out after fatally stabbing his girlfriend. But was he really the perpetrator? And although history views Brian Jones and Jim Morrison as pampered rock stars whose excesses led to their early deaths, there's a strong possibility that they might have had help.

Both the famous—Michael Jackson and Marvin Gaye, for instance—and the not so famous—Mia Zapata and Sammytown McBride, among others—are included in these pages. But readers should note that not every music industry murder case is covered here. Rather, this is a snapshot of the underside of rock 'n' roll, a lifestyle known for spectacular climbs and catastrophic crashes.

1

As Tears Go By

Did Someone Drown Brian Jones?

Pat was around near the beginning, and Anna was there at the very end. Both loved the musician known as "the Golden Stone" and wanted to spend the rest of their lives with him. But Brian Jones's life was a short one and as the years stretched on, neither woman ever faltered in her conviction that Brian didn't just drown in his heated pool in the British countryside. Rather, they believed, he was murdered.

For decades, Anna Wohlin, the Swedish model who was living with Brian at the time of his death, tried building a chasm between herself and the incident—even after she lived long enough to become the only surviving person who'd been at the estate on the night he died. When asked about her relationship with the founding member and, in his words, the "undisputed leader" of the Rolling Stones, she was quick to point out that she was very young at the time, just twenty-one, and a lot had happened since then.

"I tell you, I've never been a Stones fan," she told me forty-eight years after the incident, over pike and salmon roe at Sjöpaviljongen, a waterfront restaurant in Stockholm's Bromma section, a short distance from the boutique she'd run for decades. "I like David Bowie and T. Rex, Mark Bolan. Everyone expects me to be a Stones fan. I don't even know all their songs."

What she did know was that Brian was not a doomed rock star bent on his own self-destruction—even if he was the first member of the "27 Club," a fraternity that would come to include Janis Joplin, Jimi Hendrix, Jim Morrison, Kurt Cobain and Amy Winehouse.

Although he'd parted ways with the Stones just three weeks before he died, Anna insisted that Brian was content, and had aspirations that could have redefined rock 'n' roll. "Every day, he talked to John Lennon," she said of a collaboration that might have included Hendrix. "Every day, he went to his music room. He wanted to go back to the beginning" before the celebrity, squabbles, and drug busts. "He wanted to play the music he loved with different musicians."

Despite the scarves, lace shirts, gold caftans, and velvet Edwardian frocks, Brian was still very much the stocky, sensitive kid who'd worn glasses, gone trainspotting, and learned the keyboards from his rigorous mother in the placid town of Cheltenham, some ninety miles from London.

"What I remember about Brian was his heart," Anna said. "Very good heart. Big, big, big heart. Worrying about everybody. The older I get, sometimes, I get very funny flashbacks."

The day before, Pat Andrews—who bore Brian a child when she was just sixteen—relaxed in Prezzo, an Italian restaurant franchise in Cheltenham, shaking her dyed red hair back and forth and laughing, as she gestured through the picture windows at a building across the street. "That over there was the Regal Cinema," she pointed out. "That place played a significant part in my life."

Every Saturday morning in the 1950s, the theater showed a medley of films to an exclusively juvenile audience, starting with cartoons, then a serial like *Superman* or *The Lone Ranger* and, finally, a children's movie. The only adult Pat remembered attending the screenings was Uncle Len, who led sing-alongs on the accordion as the words to the various tunes appeared on the screen.

Pat attended the Cinema Club, as it was known, once or twice a month. But Brian's family never sent him. "It probably would have been too frivolous for them," she said. "I don't want to be derogatory, but they were very austere. They were [of] a certain background. You didn't cook on a Sunday. You didn't have fun."

Brian's parents, Louisa and Lewis, were of Welsh ancestry and predisposed to music. Although Lewis was an aeronautical engineer, he found time to play the piano. Louisa taught the instrument; she also played organ and led the choir at church.

Cheltenham was a proper sort of town. "When you walked outside, you'd say, 'Good morning. Lovely day today,'" Pat said. "It wasn't done out of habit. It was *meant*. If you were a child, you could raise your voice in the park when you were playing with your friends. The rest of the time, you kept yourself dignified. There was a gentility about it."

Reportedly, Brian developed asthma at age four, a factor that would later be cited as a possible reason for his drowning. Yet a far more traumatic incident, in terms of the family dynamic, was the death of his two-year-old sister of leukemia when Brian was three and a half.

"His mother was nice," Anna recalled, "but Brian stood closer to his father. When his sister died, his mother shut him out. In those days, if you had feelings, you kept them inside. Now—only now—I understand his mother's pain."

The strained bond with his primary caregiver may have contributed to Brian's temperamental nature. That and the fact that, from early on in his life, he exhibited an artist's disposition.

With two US military bases within driving distance of Cheltenham, Brian was exposed to the American records and music magazines that the soldiers traded locally for cash. As a teen, he convinced his parents to buy him a saxophone after he became fascinated with the jazz saxophonists Cannonball Adderley and Charlie Parker. He'd also shown a preference for bluesmen Elmore James and Robert Johnson, and added the guitar to his growing repertoire of instruments.

All of this made Brian a fairly interesting character. At sixteen, he impregnated his fourteen-year-old girlfriend Valerie, who was sent to France to give birth, while Brian was dispatched to family friends in Germany until the scandal subsided. He'd recently returned to Cheltenham when he met fifteen-year-old Pat, who was working at the Boots pharmacy chain and hoping to save money for college.

"One of my friends said, 'I know this boy who just came back from Germany and doesn't know a soul,'" she said. As soon as Pat entered the Aztec coffee bar and saw the forlorn-looking blond kid, she was smitten. "He sort of walked me home that night, and it went from there."

The two spent hours at teen clubs, listening to tunes like "Chantilly Lace" and "Running Bear." While the girls line-danced, most of the boys lingered near the wall. "But Brian and I were like Fred Astaire and Ginger Rogers."

Brian took Pat out for her first Chinese meal, but was primarily absorbed in his music. There were long bus rides to a place called the South London Jazz Club in the town of Bishops Cleeve. Sometimes they'd wander into a department store, where consumers were allowed to listen to a record while deciding whether to purchase it. "We spent a lot of time in the record booth."

Once they went with a group of friends to a bar and dared each other to order drinks. When they were actually served, Brian held up the glass, then set it down on the counter. "What are we going to do with this?" asked the then-sober teen.

A similar experience would occur later when the young couple was in a nightclub and "these boys came around, selling black bombers and purple hearts. And not the sort you'd get from the army. Brian didn't take anything."

Brian didn't like discussing the reason he'd been sent abroad but, when he did, Pat thought he might be inventing a fiction. "He was a great storyteller, and I didn't even know how babies were born," she said. "I thought only old women had babies."

Indeed, it was hard to imagine the seventeen-year-old boy changing nappies or wheeling a pram, when all he wanted to do was perform. At thirteen, he'd played washboard in a band specializing in skiffle, a British-accented blend of jazz, ragtime, and folk music. Alexis Korner was an older guy who'd recorded a skiffle record, and recruited Brian into a group called Blues Incorporated. "Eric Clapton and the rest of them can eat their bloody hats," Pat said. "No one in this country—no white person anyway—ever played slide guitar before Brian. I went with him to the garage when he had a piece of pipe cut out for his finger."

Although Brian's parents appreciated his musical talents, they didn't particularly understand the genres the teen had chosen to explore. And after the incident with Valerie, they worried about the choices that he was starting to make. When Pat was introduced to the Jones family, Lewis and Louisa were pleasant enough—until she mentioned her job at the drugstore. "His mother's mouth dropped. They didn't know I wanted to go to university. To them, I was just a shopgirl."

On another occasion, Louisa came home to find Pat ironing her boyfriend's shirt before a gig. "She went ballistic," Pat said. After fathering a child with one teenager, Brian appeared to be setting up house with another. While Louisa didn't blame Pat personally, she did fault rock 'n' roll, grabbing her son's guitar and attempting to smash it.

"Brian got the guitar away from her," Pat said. "And she was screaming, 'My son's assaulting me!' The way the world was going was too much of a shock for a lot of parents back then."

What no one knew at this time was that Brian had fathered a second child—with a married woman with whom he'd had a one-night stand. She and her husband had chosen to raise the baby without telling the aspiring musician. Either way, the next time that Brian returned home, his house was in darkness and his suitcase was on the lawn. From that point forward, he crashed with Alexis Korner and other musicians, shifting his focus from Cheltenham to the London music scene.

In the midst of all that, though, Pat became pregnant. "I told everyone I had a tumor and they'd be sorry for saying I was pregnant," she said. "I don't know what Brian's parents thought. They'd be the last people I'd tell."

Yet Brian appeared excited about the situation. When Pat gave birth to a son—although he's been named elsewhere, Pat asked that his privacy be respected—Brian showed up at the hospital cradling armfuls of flowers. He sold two of his cherished Cannonball Adderley albums to buy Pat a skirt and top to wear home. From London, he wrote Pat twice a week, and tried to incorporate her into the life he was trying to forge there.

It was a life that neither would be able to control. Brian Jones, after all, was about to become a Rolling Stone.

By Pat's assessment, had Brian Jones never crossed paths with Mick Jagger—a student at the London School of Economics at the time—the lead singer of the Rolling Stones would have enjoyed a judicious career as a banker.

It was 1962 when Mick and Keith Richards went to the Ealing Jazz Club in west London to see another friend, Charlie Watts, play drums with Blues Incorporated. When twenty-year-old Brian— billed as "Elmo Lewis"—sat in for a rendition of Mississippi bluesman Elmore James's "Dust My Broom," the pair was astonished.

They'd never seen a person play slide guitar before.

Although Brian preferred the blues to rock 'n' roll, he agreed to begin playing with the duo. But it was very much his band. He handled management and PR chores, and cut himself an extra five pounds for every performance. Inspired by the Muddy Waters tune "Rollin' Stone," he christened the combo "Brian Jones and the Rollin' Stones." By January 1963, bassist Bill Wyman and Watts had been admitted into the group, along with pianist Ian Stewart. Appealing largely to art-student types, the Stones occasionally drew crowds as large as four hundred.

Soon, Brian was living with Mick and Keith in a flat at 102 Edith Grove in a run-down section of Chelsea. While Mick's and Keith's mothers occasionally cooked for the boys, Brian expanded his partners' musical tastes with different albums he'd found and arranged rehearsals. One day, Keith returned home to discover that Brian had taught himself how to play the blues on a mouth harp while his flatmate was out.

For a while, Alexis Korner's friend Giorgio Gomelsky—a writer and club manager—oversaw the Stones' business affairs, inviting members over his home to listen to records and eat his wife's chicken soup. But the boys were still broke, and in 1963, Andrew Loog Oldham and a partner signed a management contract with the band, hoping to market them as a gritty alternative to the Beatles. According to Pat, Oldham arranged a photo session one afternoon in London's Battersea Park and noticed the Golden Stone paying attention to his girlfriend and young son. Calling Brian over, Oldham laid down the law. As a teen idol, he was no longer to be seen in public with his child.

Although Jones and Richards had enjoyed some musical cama-raderie, Oldham encouraged Mick and Keith to begin writing originals, restricting the number of blues covers Brian favored. Furthermore, the manager limited Brian's influence by promoting the flamboyant Jagger as the group's front man.

"Brian didn't have an ally," Pat said. "He didn't have his family. He didn't have anyone who knew him prior to when he joined the Rolling Stones."

Still, Oldham contended that it was Brian who made himself an outsider, traveling separately from the group to their gigs at British church halls, staying at different hotels, and demanding extra money. To Wyman, Brian was a split personality: deep and artistic, as well as needy and volatile. "He pushed every friendship to the limit and way beyond," Wyman said in his autobiography, *Stone Alone*.

Nonetheless, Pat thinks that Brian could have learned to coexist with Wyman, Richards, and Watts. "If Mick hadn't been there, it would have been all right."

By Pat's recollection, it was Mick who played a significant role in the couple's breakup, fabricating a story about having slept with Pat—a rumor repeated over the years in Stones biographies and profiles. Fame was encroaching on the boy from Cheltenham, and the tale—along with a confession from one of Keith's girlfriends about a night spent with Brian—obliterated the three-and-a-half-year relationship. Raising their son at her parents' home, Pat only saw Brian one more time, when the Stones came to Cheltenham a few months later to play a show there.

It was a bizarre scene. In the time that Pat had been away, the Stones were even bigger than when she'd left. "All these girls were screaming," Pat said. "And I thought, 'Why are they screaming? They wouldn't scream if they'd seen these boys, down and out, in their flat at Edith Grove.'" With fans packing the sidewalk outside the Odeon Theatre, Pat was dispatched to buy cigarettes for the band. "Of course, I got the money first. With them, you had to get the money."

As Pat returned to the venue, she noticed a curious sight: Lewis Jones furtively purchasing a ticket to see his son in concert. Pat was surprised, because Brian had arranged for her to attend the show for free. She also wondered if Brian's mother knew where her husband was going that night.

When the group returned from its tour of the British Isles, Brian promised to call Pat. He never did. Over the next two years, two young women would give birth to children said to be fathered by Brian. Pat would receive nominal support for the maintenance of her son—payments that ended after Brian's body was scooped out of the pool.

She never got to know the Brian Jones described in popular lore as a drug-addled peacock. "He was very into drugs, too much into drugs," Anna said, "especially acid. He was terrible on acid. I don't think he was made for it."

Nor was he equipped to handle the cocktail of uppers, downers, amyl nitrate poppers, alcohol, and marijuana, that he was regularly consuming by 1966. He was paranoid—both from substance abuse and on account of legitimate plots against him in the band. "I do believe that I behaved in a very childish way, but we were very young and, in some ways, we picked on him," Mick told *Rolling Stone* in 1995. "But, unfortunately, he made himself a target for it. He was very, very jealous, very difficult, very manipulative and, if you do that in this kind of a group of people, you get back as good as you give."

Brian launched into an intense, often caustic relationship with model Anita Pallenberg, but lost her to Keith Richards. On one occasion—fed up with his bandmates—he is said to have hurled himself from a window, only to land in the bushes. Regardless, he had become one of the most creative individuals on the planet. He was asked to join Bob Dylan's band, and was reportedly the inspiration for Dylan's song "Like a Rolling Stone." Jimi Hendrix—whom Brian would introduce at the Monterey International Pop Festival—began mimicking the overstated fashions favored by the Englishman. So did Jagger. Merging his knowledge of English Renaissance composer John Dowland and the Delta blues, Brian composed "Ruby Tuesday" on the recorder and played lead sitar on "Paint It Black," marimba on "Under My Thumb," and dulcimer on "Lady Jane"—instruments that had heretofore been alien to rock 'n' roll.

It was an awful lot for a kid to experience, and the bad came with the good. "Things like LSD were all new," Jagger said in *Rolling Stone*. "No one knew the harm. People thought cocaine was good for you." With everyone indulging, trouble was always close by. Brian was busted for hash, cocaine, and methamphetamine in 1967, and provoked a raid that netted Jagger, Richards, and art dealer Robert Fraser—at whose gallery John Lennon met Yoko Ono—after boasting about drugs to two strangers who turned out to be tabloid reporters. Another bust at Brian's home only yielded a lump of cannabis inside a ball of wool, but Brian was convinced that he and the rest of the Stones were being set up by authorities who wanted to diminish the band's influence on British youth.

By now, the Rolling Stones had a fixer on staff. Tom Keylock had met Mick and Keith in 1965 when he was hired to drive them to Heathrow Airport. He was so adept at keeping the paparazzi and fans away that he was given a permanent position in the Stones' organization. One of the many tasks assigned the man Richards dubbed "Mr. Get-It-Together" was periodically cooking for the Stones; he also sneaked the boys out of hotels and utilized decoy cars and unpredictable routes to shuttle the band to various venues.

Whenever members found themselves in a legal predicament, it was Keylock who accompanied them to court.

They also acquired a manager who could conservatively be described as a racketeer. Allen Klein was initially hired by Oldham to oversee the group's business affairs; by the end of the decade, he'd buy out Oldham and be working with the Stones and Beatles simultaneously. Klein looked through record company documents and unearthed thousands of dollars in royalties due the Stones. But he also maneuvered to acquire the rights to the band's recordings and publishing—apparently without informing members of the scheme—retaining control of all Rolling Stones music written before 1971. The band would also accuse him of neglecting to pay its taxes for five years, forcing the Stones to "exile" themselves from England to France to protect their assets. He would serve two months in prison in 1979 for tax fraud.

By and large, the band was oblivious to Klein's machinations because of their musical obligations and drug and lifestyle experimentation, and because of the tensions surrounding Brian. Between 1967 and 1969, as the group created such albums as *Their Satanic Majesties Request* and *Beggars Banquet*, Brian's influence within the Stones waned. As a blues enthusiast, he appeared to resent performing pop music. In his autobiography, Wyman noted, "He formed the band. He chose the members. He named the band. He chose the music we played. . . . He was very influential, very important, and then slowly lost it . . . and blew it all away."

After Brian's death, Anna would repeatedly hear that his discontent had been motivated by his antipathy toward Mick. "He wasn't jealous of Mick," she argued. "If you see the videos, Brian doesn't want to be in front. He has his back to the audience. He cared about the music. He didn't want to be in Mick's position."

By the time she and Brian became lovers, Anna had been on the same circuit as the Stones for several years. She'd landed in London as a teen, fleeing Sweden for spots like the 100 Club on Oxford Street, and the Speakeasy Club and Ad Lib. She modeled on and off, she admitted, but "mostly, my parents supported me, to be honest. What I wanted to do was go to the best clubs, and if you get home early in the morning, you don't want to have to wake up to go to work."

Through her wanderings, she'd become acquainted with Paul McCartney, John Lennon, and Ringo Starr. "I knew everybody," she said. "But Brian was the one I fell in love with."

The first time he noticed her, he was in the Marquee Club: he made eye contact and started to approach. But as he crossed the room, he was mobbed by fans and turned back. On another occasion, he drunkenly asked Anna to come home with him and was turned down. When they started dating seriously, in 1969, Brian subjected Anna to an extensive background check. "He telephoned everyone to see if I wasn't a groupie," she recalled. "Then he said he'd live with me."

A year earlier, he'd purchased Cotchford Farm in the village of Hartfield in East Sussex, a scenic estate of landscape gardens, woodlands, and a two-chimney brick mansion previously owned by *Winnie the Pooh* author A. A. Milne. Although he continued to drink, he cut down on his drugging and tried to fit in with the locals, riding his scooter to the Dorset Arms pub, where he lingered by the fireplace and made amiable conversation.

"He didn't like the life of a rock star," Anna said. "He hated it. Everyone was always pulling on you and taking from you. There were girls hiding in wardrobes and bathrooms. You couldn't sleep. He wanted to live a proper life, a good life.

"Brian was quite happy to be smelling flowers. We had five dogs. He wanted horses. I asked if he could ride. He said no, but he wanted the full experience."

There were other incentives, as well. Brian believed that it would be more difficult for the police to plant drugs at Cotchford Farm than at an apartment in London. And he was still seeking his parents' approval. "He wanted to be good enough for them," Anna said. "When he started the Rolling Stones, they told him, 'You can't live off this. You're wasting your life.' When you saw his name in the press, the word *drugs* was always used. He wanted to get that off his back, and for his parents to be proud of him, to see he had made it."

Hoping to earn enough to pay off their massive tax bills, the Stones were planning an extensive tour of the United States—their first in three years. But Brian's two arrests could have prevented him from acquiring a work visa. Plus, the band didn't particularly want him along.

One night at Keith's country home, Brian reportedly raged at Mick for rejecting the dinner on the table and leaving with Marianne Faithfull to eat in a restaurant. According to folklore, Brian swiped at Jagger with a steak knife, then dove into a moat outside. When Mick went to save him, the story goes, Jagger discovered that the trench was only four feet deep, and that Brian was bending his knees to pretend to be submerged.

Already, Mick Taylor had filled in for Brian on the recording of "Honky Tonk Women." After mixing the song in the studio, Mick, Keith, and Charlie drove to Cotchford Farm to discuss Brian's status. In the kitchen, Brian mentioned his visa problems, then said that he was not only skipping the US tour, but leaving the band for good.

"I'm out," he apparently said. "I was dealt out a long time ago."

They all shook hands, and appeared to part as friends.

In a public statement, Brian was quoted as saying, "We no longer communicate musically. The Stones' music is not my taste anymore. I have a desire to play my own brand of music rather than that of others."

The popular mythology is that Brian was kicked out of the band, then went on a self-abusive bender that culminated in his death. But Alexis Korner, who visited Brian after the meeting with his former bandmates and knew him better than they did, described him as "happier than he had ever been." Likewise, Anna—who was with Brian on the last day of his life—was adamant that he was excited about various musical possibilities.

Although Brian was technically out of the Rolling Stones, he was still entangled in their organization. When he needed renovations to Cotchford Farm, Tom Keylock arranged for his friend Frank Thorogood—who'd previously worked on Keith Richards's Redlands estate—to organize a team of three laborers. Thorogood was allowed to bill the Stones' office for his expenses, and the fees would be reimbursed by Brian. The workmen also kept an eye on Brian, and reported their findings back to Keylock.

It was not a happy arrangement. The laborers were resentful of the opulence they saw, and Brian's humor could be biting and condescending. But they were in no rush to finish the job. Although his official residence was in London, Thorogood stayed on the property, where the workers drank Brian's liquor, ate his food, picked vegetables from his garden, and brought their girlfriends.

By Anna's estimation, Thorogood was terrible at his job. "He was paid very well for very bad work."

At least once, Anna said, Thorogood put his arm around the model and tried to seduce her. "Keylock would come by and say, 'Why are you staying here? I can get you such a good job in London.' I never told Brian any of this, and I still don't know why they wanted to hurt him."

In addition to the toxic atmosphere, construction was way behind schedule. And whatever work was completed had been done carelessly. When Anna reached for a ringing telephone one day, a beam snapped out of the ceiling and tumbled toward her. "Brian pushed me out of the way before it could hit me," she said. "Brian was very mad. He started talking about it all the time. 'It could have killed you. It could have killed you.' Then, he called the Stones' office and said he didn't want Frank Thorogood to get paid."

Anna remembers being with three other people at Cotchford Farm on the night of July 2, 1969: Brian, Thorogood, and Janet Lawson, a twenty-six-year-old nurse who was romantically involved with Keylock. Although some accounts place Keylock on the grounds, he always insisted that he was commuting between the Olympic recording studio in London and Richards' estate to return a forgotten guitar. Reports that Paul McCartney and Princess Margaret stopped by the property earlier in the day are tantalizing but almost certainly false.

"Frank was not doing the building work properly," Janet told the *Daily Mail* in 2008. "Brian had sacked him that day." Allegedly, Thorogood was agitated over £8,000 that he believed was owed him. "There was something in the air. Frank was acting strangely, throwing his weight around a bit."

Yet Brian and Anna still had dinner with the other two—steak-and-kidney pie, according to Janet's recollection.

"Brian and I wanted to go to bed quite early after we watched this American show that he loved," Anna said. She was talking about *Rowan & Martin's Laugh-In*, a sketch comedy program with a counterculture edge, which aired during the summer on BBC Four. "But he didn't like that Keylock's mistress was over. He went upstairs, then came back with Frank Thorogood and Janet Lawson. We sat down for a drink." It was the first drink Anna remembered Brian consuming that day. She suspects that Frank spiked Brian's beverage; published reports would mention a sleeping pill in the rock star's system.

"Why were they downstairs with us when we were ready to go to bed, and the lights to the pool were already out?" Anna asked. "But Frank wanted to have a swim."

Anna changed into her suit and entered the pool. As she immersed herself in the warm water, she became agitated about the forced activity, exited, and quickly toweled off. "We were ready to go to bed. Why were we swimming?"

Inside the house, Anna took a call from a friend phoning from London. Janet later said that Brian sent her inside to retrieve his asthma inhaler. "I went to look for it by the pool, in the music room, the reception room, and then the kitchen," she told the *Daily Mail*. "Frank came in in a lather. His hands were shaking. He was in a terrible state." She rushed outside, she said, and saw Brian at the bottom of the pool. She claimed that she shouted for Frank, who went outside and dove in. "But I had not said where Brian was. I thought, 'How did he know Brian was at the bottom of the pool?'"

She said that she ran back into the house and tried to call emergency services. "But Anna was on the phone and would not get off it."

Anna's memory was different: "Janet came in and said, 'Anna, Anna, something happened to Brian.' I ran out to the pool. But first I met Frank in the kitchen, still in his swimming trunks. Why wasn't he outside, helping Brian?"

Anna remembered jumping into the pool and trying to pull up her boyfriend's body. "He was heavy, and he slipped away from me. I had to dive deeper and pull him up again. When I came to the surface, I shouted to Frank and Janet, 'Can you help me?' Frank walked very slowly. Janet said she couldn't swim. Nobody was really helping."

She'd conclude that Thorogood and Brian had had a dispute about the £8,000 being withheld from the builder. "Frank knew that Brian was a very good swimmer. He could swim under the water from one end to the other. I think Frank held his head under to scare Brian because he wanted the money. But Brian went down. And that's why Frank was in the kitchen. Because he didn't really want to kill Brian, and he didn't want to be there when we found him."

The first officer on the scene arrived at 12:10 a.m., while emergency medical technicians were still trying to resuscitate Brian, confiscating bottles of pills and alcohol and any other substance that might have caused the rock star's death. Another constable searched Thorogood and discovered five black bomber capsules. "I look after them for Brian," Frank explained, "so that he won't take too many at a time."

Although the British police were engaged in a vigorous war on drugs, a senior officer opted to take Thorogood at his word, and the finding was never reported to the coroner.

Pat Andrews eventually became a teacher, deriving particular joy from helping children deemed "unteachable." When a friend called to say that she'd heard about Brian's death on the radio, Pat was dismissive. "Don't be so silly," she said. "People don't die that young."

She'd remembered Brian talking about being a lifeguard, and found it difficult to fathom that he'd drowned in a pool. When she read about the possibility of an asthma attack, she was incredulous. "In all the time I knew him, he never talked about having asthma. And [later] when I went to Cotchford Farm to see for myself, that pool was the size of a bathtub."

In the immediate aftermath of Brian's death, Anna remembered being ferried from one spot to another by Stones management. Despite the friction with his former bandmates, all of the Rolling Stones appeared stunned, saddened, and even frightened by the turn of events.

As a gesture of good faith, Brian had planned to attend the Stones' concert in London's Hyde Park on July 5, 1969, featuring the onstage debut of his replacement, Mick Taylor. Instead, the event turned into a memorial for the Golden Stone. Jagger—standing barefoot in a white frock with a gold-studded leather collar—read a poem written by Percy Bysshe Shelley upon learning that John Keats had passed away: "He is not dead, he doth not sleep. . . . He hath awakened from the dream of life."

As the words reverberated off the trees, arches, and statuary, some three thousand butterflies were released. These had been stored in boxes on the side of the stage for hours, and many were weakened. Some never made it into the air. Other flapped their wings a few times and plummeted from the sky.

Anna had the sense that her knowledge of what had transpired at Cotchford Farm was threatening to Stones management; one neighbor reported seeing documents hurled into a bonfire hours after Brian's death. After the show ended, Anna said, Keylock and a group of men stormed into her London hotel room and ordered her to pack her bags. "They took me to another hotel with a person I didn't know, and I was not allowed to go out." A short time later, she was brought to Allen Klein.

"He came into the room and said, 'Is £50,000 all you want?' I said, 'No, I don't want any money.' I was in love with Brian. I was so young and naïve. I should have said a hundred [thousand].

"I went back to my hotel. Then they came and said, 'Get ready.' I thought I was going to Brian's funeral. Instead, they took me to the airport."

Anna boarded a plane for Stockholm. She had the impression that she was no longer welcome in England.

Stones management was unaware that Anna was pregnant. She was expecting a girl, and Brian had been looking forward to giving her the Swedish name Johanna. But in all the stress, Anna soon lost the baby.

She never modeled again. She was done with that phase of her life, and with the British rock scene. Within a year, she was married to a Swedish businessman. There were no calls to the house from John Lennon or conversations about composing music with Jimi Hendrix. But Anna didn't feel like she was sacrificing anything. In fact, when she read about the stabbing death of a Stones fan by the Hells Angels at Altamont Speedway five months after Brian's death, she was relieved to be away.

True to form, Tom Keylock arranged Brian's funeral in Cheltenham. When Lewis Jones saw his son's sumptuous bronze coffin, he was enraged. The Jones family was subdued, not brassy. But

Keylock prevailed. "Brian was a star," he argued, according to the *Independent.* "He lived like a star and he died a star."

Bob Dylan apparently paid for the elaborate casket, which was carried into the church past an eight-foot high collection of red and yellow flowers sent by the Stones. No one is certain who was responsible for bleaching Brian's hair white during the embalming process, or for engraving the wrong date of death on his tombstone.

At the memorial, the assembled journalists noticed that Mick and Keith were nowhere in sight. But Charlie Watts was prominently in attendance, bursting out in laughter when a group of policemen saluted the hearse containing the rock god whose next arrest might have put him away for years.

The cause of Brian's demise was officially listed as "death by misadventure," although the amount of barbiturates and alcohol in his system was as potent as three and a half pints of beer. While chief investigator Bob Marshall described the incident as "a simple drowning," numerous conspiracy theories quickly emerged.

The most credible centered on the ownership of the Rolling Stones' name. Since Brian had started the band, was he considering using the moniker for his next group? According to one story, Jagger and Richards had confronted Brian about the plan at Cotchford Farm, and the ensuing conversation had become so heated that Keith menaced his former bandmate with a knife. Police took the claim seriously enough to file an internal report, ultimately concluding that the tale was ludicrous.

Another scenario had a group of killers holding Brian under the water while Keylock stood at the edge of the pool, supervising.

Had this occurred, though, Anna would have known about it. Still, police files reveal that three weeks after Brian's death taxi driver Joan Fitzsimons—a former Thorogood girlfriend—was attacked and left for dead. If she'd harbored any thoughts of going public with whatever Frank had confided, Joan—who died in 2002—apparently changed her mind after the assault.

Indeed, Keylock himself told the British show *Crimewatch* that while Thorogood was on his deathbed in 1993, he confessed to his old friend, "It was me that done Brian."

Keylock died in 2009—almost forty years to the day of Brian's drowning.

The same year, Sussex police reviewed the case again, focusing their suspicions on Frank Thorogood. But in 2010, authorities announced that there just wasn't enough evidence to renew the inquiry.

As afternoon turned to dusk in Cheltenham, Pat Andrews finished dessert, spoke about her weakness for dark chocolate, and urged every fan of her teen boyfriend to view his passing with cynicism. "There's a lot of money to be made in rock 'n' roll, so I question every rock 'n' roll death—Jim Morrison, Mama Cass, Sam Cooke. You know who managed Sam Cooke, of course? Allen Klein."

And, just as Klein profited from the Stones, she pointed out, he ended up owning the rights to Cooke's recordings after the singer was killed in 1964.

"Some people might say I can't let go of a relationship that ended a long time ago," Pat said. "But I believe in doing what's right. And when I'm speaking out, I'm doing it for Brian, myself, and my son, who deserves the truth after all this time."

She pointed out the window at the graying English sky. "The Brian Jones you saw was the Brian Jones who walked these streets right here. What changed was the perception. He was almost too good to be on this earth. That's why God wanted Brian up there with him. And if I'd been there that night, it would have been Frank Thorogood in the swimming pool."

2

DEATH IN PHIL SPECTOR'S CASTLE

The chauffeur watched the slight, bewigged man emerge from the back door of the thirty-three-room mansion, framed by cylindrical turrets, on the edge of a hill in Alhambra—a suburban pocket of Los Angeles County named for the fortress and palace complex built by the Moors in thirteenth-century Spain. Bug-eyed during even his lucid moments, Phil Spector was particularly spooked, as he shuffled toward Adriano De Souza, wielding a .38 Colt Cobra. The heralded musician, songwriter, and record producer's ears rang, his nostrils twitched, and his head spun from a night of consuming liquid intoxicants. In a muddled, confused voice, he looked at the Brazilian-born driver and uttered an admission that he'd later try to deny.

"I think I've killed someone."

It had been close to three decades since Spector had produced a hit, but the pop visionary once dubbed the "Tycoon of Teen" still commanded attention. The moment police radios began crackling with news that Spector—who'd been waving guns at both friends and strangers for much of the past thirty years—had finally pulled the trigger, news helicopters began buzzing the estate marked by a sign outside reading, "Phil Spector's Pyrenees Castle," while civilians—who'd perhaps once recognized something of themselves in the Crystals' "He's a Rebel," the Ronettes' "Be My Baby," Darlene Love's "(Today I Met) The Boy I'm Gonna Marry" and the Righteous Brothers' "You've Lost That Lovin' Feeling"—mashed their faces against the gate.

While the notion of owning a "castle" just eight miles from downtown Los Angeles was nouveau riche and pretentious, in the studio, Spector had been the real thing, writing and selecting songs, hiring and conducting musicians, overseeing arrangements, supervising the entire recording process. The self-professed "mad genius of rock 'n' roll" would be as prolific with bona fide superstars in the early 1970s—producing the Beatles' "Long and Winding Road" and George Harrison's "My Sweet Lord" the same year, and the former mop top's Grammy Award–winning album, *Concert for Bangladesh* the next—as he had been a few years earlier with the deeply talented girl groups he'd plucked from obscurity and sometimes deposited back there.

His calling card had been the richly layered "Wall of Sound," a production style that merged violins, bass, guitars, and rhythm sections into a symphony that made it difficult to distinguish the individual instruments, but created a mood that grabbed listeners through the jukebox or AM radio. As late as 1980, he was applying his masterful touch to the music of the Ramones, in an effort to expose the punk rockers to a more eclectic audience. But the relationship didn't end well, with group members spewing forth tales about Spector throwing drunken tantrums, pulling a weapon, and forcing the four to listen to him bang on the piano and sing his old hits.

"People tell me they idolize me, want to be like me," he told the *Telegraph*'s Mick Brown weeks before B-movie actress Lana Clarkson was found dead in Spector's home. "But I tell them, 'Trust me. You don't want my life.' Because it hasn't been a very pleasant life. I've been a very tortured soul. I have not been at peace myself. I have not been happy."

Harvey Phillip Spector was born in the Bronx in 1939, the son of Ben Spector—the family name had originally been spelled *Spekter*—a Ukrainian-born Jewish ironworker who'd fought in World War I for his adopted homeland. Phil's mother, Bertha, had been born in Paris, but her roots were in the same part of

Eastern Europe as her husband's. In fact, Phil would later tell *The Telegraph* that his parents were first cousins: "I don't know, genetically, whether or not that had something to do with what I am or who I became."

Certainly, there seemed to be a strain of mental illness in the household; Phil would later bestow songwriting credits on his sister, Shirley, to ensure that she could support herself, despite this affliction. "My sister's in an asylum," he once told singer-songwriter Gene Pitney, "and she's the sane one in my family."

On April 20, 1949, Ben Spector left for work, pulled up in front of an abandoned building in Brooklyn, connected a water hose to his exhaust pipe, coiled the other end into the car, rolled up the windows, and restarted the engine. A coroner would list his cause of death as suicide from carbon monoxide poisoning.

In a possible effort to flee the demons that were always lurking, Bertha Spector moved her children to West Hollywood, where the family had relatives. While she worked as a seamstress, taking the bus early each morning to a sweatshop in downtown Los Angeles, Phil stayed in his room, studying the songs on the radio and learning how to play them on piano and guitar. At Fairfax High School, he and three friends formed a singing group called the Teddy Bears. As he schooled himself in record production at Gold Star Studios in Hollywood, the Teddy Bears released a tune based on the epitaph on Ben Spector's tombstone: "To Know Him Was to Love Him." In December 1958, it reached number one on the *Billboard* Hot 100 chart. Phil headed back east, not as the asthmatic kid who'd taken flight after his father's suicide, but as a rising star. After the quartet appeared on *American Bandstand* in Philadelphia, the song sold more than 1.4 million copies.

Possessing neither the looks nor the personality of a pop idol, Spector felt most comfortable in the studio, producing a string of hits: "Corrina, Corrina" by Ray Peterson, "Pretty Little Angel Eyes" by Curtis Lee, "I Love How You Love Me" by the Paris Sisters. "He's a Rebel" was attributed to the Crystals—who toured the country to perform and promote it—although the actual singers were the Blossoms, headed by the astounding Darlene Love.

It was one of several ghost projects for the minister's daughter, whose voice could also be heard in the background of "Be My Baby," and "You've Lost That Lovin' Feeling," although her name was usually omitted from the liner notes.

Through the efforts of Love and other equally unheralded musicians, Spector had managed to become a millionaire by age twenty-two. "Rather than develop his artists' careers," music journalist-turned-production pioneer Jerry Wexler told Mick Brown, "Phil developed himself."

Ronnie Bennett was different than the others. Raised in Spanish Harlem—the daughter of an Irish father and a mother of African American and Cherokee ancestry—Ronnie began singing in the lobby of her grandmother's building at age eight, drawing a small audience as her voice echoed off the high ceilings. With her mother's encouragement, Ronnie appeared on amateur night at the famed Apollo Theater in Harlem, then formed a group with her sister Estelle and their cousin Nedra Talley. Wearing tight dresses with fringes on the back, the teens were an enthralling trio. But they needed to get to the next step. So in 1963, Estelle boldly called Phil Spector's office.

Ronnie's life would never be the same.

Packaging the group around Ronnie, Spector guided the newly branded Ronettes to a number-two hit within months: "Be My Baby," a flirtatious tune that elicited erotic thoughts even before fans had a chance to view the lead singer's pouty portrait. When the three toured England in 1964, Ronnie attracted the attention of both the Beatles and the Rolling Stones. But the British musicians were unusually discreet around the exotic visitor from New York. Ronnie was Phil's girl—and no one in the industry wanted to piss him off.

"I fell in love with his coolness," Ronnie told the *Telegraph*'s Hermione Hoby. "He was very cool. Always had one hand in his pocket. . . . Here's a guy, 24 years old, yet he's telling married men with children what to do? That turned me on so much. I fell in love with that power."

Yet, just as Spector easily discarded singers after they'd fulfilled their purpose, the business seemed to be on the verge of tiring of him—and his Wall of Sound—when his most elaborate production, Ike and Tina Turner's "River Deep—Mountain High," failed to generate a hit in 1966. His insecurities—always bubbling below the surface—overtook him, and in 1968 he married Ronnie and pulled her inward. Threatened by his wife's sultriness as well as by her success, he derailed the career he'd aggressively promoted, forcing her to stay home with him and repeatedly watch the movie *Citizen Kane*. His reaction to the classic was invariably the same, she said: tears shed over the burning of Rosebud, the sled that the lead character cherished as a boy.

If Phil was crying for Ben, he left it up to Ronnie to guess.

Oblivious to the dynamics of a functional family, Spector persuaded Ronnie to adopt three children, isolating her further. As the former singer—now known as Ronnie Spector—pined to return to the stage, Phil imposed a strict set of rules on his spouse, hiding her shoes so she'd stay indoors, and restricting her outside excursions to monthly runs to purchase feminine hygiene products.

"The last year of my marriage, I didn't talk at all," she told Hermione Hoby. "Because if I said anything, he'd yell at me. So why say anything? I was a scared little girl from Spanish Harlem, living in this mansion with five servants, not knowing what to do with any of it. I cried every night I was married."

Ronnie claimed that Spector had threatened to murder her if she ever left. But in 1972, while Ronnie's mother was visiting California, the older woman convinced her daughter that she'd die if she stayed. After formulating a plan for several days, the pair escaped together.

What ensued was a fifteen-year legal battle, not just over the terms of their divorce, but over unpaid royalties that Ronnie insisted that she was owed by her ex-husband. Although she won, she experienced the full force of Spector's vindictiveness; at one stage, he delivered a support payment in nickels. Up until the time of the murder of Lana Clarkson, Phil refused to utter Ronnie's name out loud.

The Beatles resurrected Spector's career, at least for a while. As the band was going through its death throes, he was commissioned to transform the abandoned tracks from an album tentatively titled *Get Back* into the group's twelfth and final studio LP, *Let It Be*. Unhappy with the overdubbing on "The Long and Winding Road," its composer, Paul McCartney, later released a raw—or "naked"—version of the tune. John Lennon and George Harrison, however, were impressed with Spector, and allowed him to apply his grandiose style to their solo projects, including Harrison's multiplatinum triple album, *All Things Must Pass* and Lennon's most popular LP, *Imagine*.

Yet, even in professional settings, Spector made no effort to soften the personality that caused Ronnie to live in fear of him at home. In 1973, Lennon had separated from Yoko, relocated from New York to Los Angeles, and gone on a lengthy bender that he later characterized as his "lost weekend." It was during this period that he decided to make his *Rock 'n' Roll* album, a collection of covers of the songs that had inspired him to become a musician. Spector was brought on to the produce the project, and the problems started instantly. Exerting the power that his now-estranged wife knew only too well, Spector demanded that security bar the former Beatle from the studio unless Lennon specified that he was there to work with Phil Spector. While both John and Phil were drunk much of the time, Spector took the dysfunction to a new level by wearing a holstered gun to sessions. Lennon suspected that the weapon was nothing more than an unloaded prop—until Spector grew frustrated one day and blasted a shot into the ceiling.

"Phil, if you're going to kill me, kill me," John reportedly responded in his Liverpudlian accent. "But don't fuck with my ears. I need them."

More and more, Spector was becoming as well known for his eccentricities as for the Wall of Sound. After a 1974 car wreck that nearly claimed his life, he began appearing in public with ridiculous wigs, reportedly to cover the scarring to his head, face, and scalp. Perennially armed, he showed up at restaurants and parties in Hollywood flanked by intimidating bodyguards and starting incidents. "I'm probably relatively insane," he admitted to Mick Brown. "I have devils inside that fight me. And I'm my own worst enemy."

Visitors to Spector's mansion were often intrigued by his stories and memorabilia *until* they expressed a desire to leave. At that point, Spector habitually had security lock the doors, while boasting about his guard dogs' capacity to maim.

A frequent, but unsubstantiated, story he told involved showing up at Bob Dylan's hotel room after the troubadour expressed hesitation about appearing at George Harrison's fabled Concert for Bangladesh. In Spector's telling, he rapped on Dylan's door with a gun and threatened to shoot through the portal until the singer agreed to perform at the event.

While recording with Canadian musician and poet Leonard Cohen, Spector is said to have stomped around the studio, swigging from a bottle of Manischewitz kosher wine while shoving a pistol into the singer's neck.

"Leonard, I love you," Spector apparently whispered.

"I hope you do," Cohen is said to have replied, gently pushing the barrel away.

During rare moments, though, he was capable of introspection. In 2002, while discussing possible plans to work with Coldplay and the Vines, he told Mick Brown about his concern for his daughter Nicole's psychological health: "Even if she, genetically, was well, I worried that, as she grew up, by seeing me as an example, she would become unwell herself and be attracted to men like that—manic-depressive or psychotic or cuckoo. . . . I wanted her to look up to me and say, 'This is what a reasonable man is like.'"

But as night fell on Los Angeles on February 2, 2003, he seemed to have pushed these worries away. The evening started in Studio City, where Spector had his driver, De Souza, pick up a woman named Rommie Davis—a caterer who'd worked at several of Phil's events—then proceed to a Beverly Hills restaurant called the Grill on the Alley. Spector and Rommie dined for two hours, during which time the producer also made the acquaintance of a waitress named Kathy Sullivan. When Rommie was dropped off, De Souza was instructed to return to the Grill, where Kathy was waiting outside.

She and Spector were whisked to Trader Vic's in Hollywood, a Polynesian-themed restaurant whose founder took credit for inventing the mai tai. Spector instead chose Navy Grog, made with 150-proof rum. After an hour, the pair continued to one of Spector's preferred hangouts, Dan Tana's restaurant in Santa Monica, where another dinner was ordered—along with more alcohol. At about 1 a.m., Spector left a $500 tip for a $55 check—musicians had been known to gripe that he had a penchant for overtipping servers while underpaying artists—then asked the driver to continue to the nearby House of Blues on Sunset Strip.

Tall, blonde Lana Clarkson was the hostess that night. But when Spector stepped off the elevator and arrived at the entrance of the exclusive Foundation Room, Clarkson thought the odd character with the bizarre wig and frock coat might be a homeless woman, and refused to seat him. Spector exploded, and the manager rushed over to investigate the disturbance. When he recognized Spector, he scolded Lana and informed her of the producer's exalted status in Hollywood. Spector, the manager specified, was to be treated "like gold."

Lana apologized profusely. It was a busy night—Judas Priest singer Rob Halford was performing on the ground floor—but a placated Spector emphasized that he was interested in quiet. Clarkson led the couple to a darkened spot called the Buddha Room, where Spector ordered rum.

He expected his date to imbibe with comparable gusto. When she didn't, he demanded, "Get a fuckin' drink." Kathy still demurred, and Spector flew into a rage. "That's it," he proclaimed. "You're going home." Lana was summoned to escort Kathy to the car, while Spector stayed behind and focused on the hostess.

Just short of her forty-first birthday, Clarkson had been knocking around Hollywood since her teens, working as an actress and model and scoring bit parts on television shows like *The Love Boat*, *Fantasy Island*, and *Hill Street Blues* and in such movies as *Scarface* and *Fast Times at Ridgemont High*. Producer Roger Corman used her in five fantasy films, including *Barbarian Queen*, in which she portrayed the lead character, a sword-fighting warrior who, in one memorable scene, is bound, topless, to a torture rack. After a number of other B-movie roles—including one in *Vice Girls*, a 1996 movie about a trio of female police officers who masquerade as strippers to catch a serial killer—she pondered the possibilities of marketing herself as something other than an on-screen sex kitten, and had been working on a stand-up comedy act.

As her acting roles dried up, Lana struggled financially, relying on her mother to pay for head shots and shoes. Hence, the job at House of Blues. According to some, she'd been despondent over a recent breakup, as well as over the changing landscape in Hollywood, but her mother said that Lana was adapting, and looking forward to a photo shoot for a phone advertisement, as well as a fitness company infomercial for which she'd be compensated in personal training.

As the night wound down at House of Blues, she returned to Spector's table and again apologized for the earlier misunderstanding. With her manager's approval, she sat down and agreed to accompany the odd-looking legend for a nightcap.

Climbing into Spector's Mercedes S430 limousine, she felt the need to tell De Souza, "This will be quick. Only one drink."

In an indication of what was to come later, the producer snapped, "Don't talk to the driver."

De Souza had been waiting in the car about an hour, napping while listening to music, when he heard a boom. It is likely Clarkson was given a quick tour past the two suits of armor in the foyer, the John Lennon print, the white grand piano, and the chandeliers shaped like candelabras. Then, like so many others, she must have hesitated when Spector made an advance—police would find her in a black slip, her dress having been removed—igniting his insecurities about being abandoned and prompting him to pull his .38. After Spector emerged through the back door, the driver peeked into the foyer, where he saw Lana—the bottom of her mouth blown off—slumped in an ivory brocade chair, still clad in her shoes and the nylon jacket she'd worn when she left the restaurant. Blood was splashed on the floor, walls, and stairway. Pieces of her broken teeth had scattered from the corpse.

"What happened, sir?" De Souza asked.

Spector answered with a shrug.

De Souza rushed back to the limo and tried to call 911, but his hands were shaking too much. As he peered at the doorway and watched Spector study his victim's body, the chauffeur feared that the producer might feel tempted to eliminate a witness. Pulling away, De Souza parked outside the front gate so he could view the house number as he called 911.

It was an act Spector apparently hadn't considered. Instead, he tried wiping the blood off Lana's face. Blood would also be found on a rag later next to the toilet, leading investigators to speculate that Spector had dipped his hands into the bowl to wash away evidence.

When police arrived, Spector walked directly toward them with his hands in his pockets. Wielding a three-and-a-half-foot-high bulletproof shield, an officer ordered Phil to put his hands up. Spector briefly acceded to the demand, then placed his hands in his pockets again.

"You've got to come see this," he said, gesturing at the house.

Once again, he was told to raise his hands. But Spector was the one who usually gave the orders, and he ignored the command.

After repeated warnings, he was tased. The first dart that struck him yielded little reaction, so police fired another time, zapping Spector with two 50,000-volt jolts. The impact was powerful enough to blacken both of Spector's eyes. As he fell to the marble floor, a knee was wedged into his back, and police rifled through his clothes. Satisfied that he was unarmed, the officers attempted to determine what had transpired.

"What's wrong with you guys?" Spector admonished in slurred speech. "I didn't mean to shoot her. It was an accident."

A tape recorder was produced, capturing Spector hurling obscenities at his visitors and jumping illogically from one topic to another. But he managed to repeat his claim that the whole incident had been an accident, and mention that Clarkson worked at House of Blues.

When police pondered Lana's body, they noticed that her purse strap was draped over her shoulder, but the bag itself was upside down—as if she'd been hastily posed after the shooting. Spector's .38 also happened to be resting under her left leg.

It wasn't until Spector arrived at police headquarters that he began to formulate an alibi. "I don't know what her fuckin' problem was," he complained to detectives, "but she certainly had no right to come to my fuckin' castle [and] blow her fuckin' head open."

Spector remained free on $1 million bail, and conducted himself as if his acquittal was a given. In an interview with *Esquire*, he proclaimed that Clarkson's death was an "accidental suicide" that occurred when she "kissed the gun"—suggesting, perhaps, that she might have been trying to excite the firearm-happy producer by fellating the revolver. After his murder indictment in 2004, he seemed to paint himself as a victim of anti-Semitism by denouncing the "Hitler-like DA and his stormtrooper henchmen."

The buildup to and proceedings of Spector's first trial were as tumultuous as his recording sessions. He switched lawyers several times, starting with O. J. Simpson "Dream Team" member Robert

Shapiro, then Bruce Cutler—best known for representing New York "Dapper Don" John Gotti—followed by Linda Kenney Baden, who was the lead attorney for closing arguments. On September 26, 2007, Judge Larry Paul Fidler declared a mistrial after two of the ten jurors refused to go along with the majority decision to convict.

Prosecutors immediately called for a second trial. In the interim, Phil undermined his own cause by showing up at the funeral of Ike Turner in December 2007 and verbally attacking the bandleader's ex-wife Tina, whose story about having survived her former spouse's violent rages had become one of the most inspiring in rock 'n' roll. "Ike made Tina the jewel she was," Spector said in a eulogy that oozed with misogyny. "When I went to see Ike play . . . there were at least five Tina Turners on the stage performing that night. Any one of them could have been Tina Turner."

The retrial began on October 20, 2008. While his wardrobe remained flamboyant, Spector made an effort to downplay the size of his wigs as well as that of his entourage, turning up at court with a single bodyguard, along with his wife, Rachelle—an aspiring singer and aviator who'd married the producer in 2006.

Just twenty-seven years old, Rachelle drew attention not just with her blond, wholesome looks, but with her arguments to the press that the system—particularly the media, who she insisted continuously perpetuated the myth that Spector wore wigs—was persecuting her spouse.

The defense contended that De Souza, the prosecution's most reliable witness, had misunderstood the producer's admission about killing someone—since the chauffeur was not a native English speaker and a fountain had been burbling close by. Clarkson's emotional frailty, the argument went, had been aggravated by her diminishing acting prospects and financial pressure, and the sight of Spector's gun induced her to finally act on her suicidal impulses. "Despite the fact that science shows this to be a self-inflicted wound," Linda Kenney Baden told jurors, "the government wanted this tragic death to be a murder."

But prosecutors pointed out that, while men tend to end their lives dramatically—through gunfire, hanging, or leaping off buildings—women are more inclined to intentionally overdose. For females, suicide is rarely a spontaneous decision—or one committed in a stranger's home. And, in this case, that stranger was standing extremely close to the victim as she held the revolver. Blood spatter on Spector's dinner jacket and Lana's slip placed them within three feet of each other when the weapon fired.

On the witness stand, five separate women reminisced about their own frightening encounters with Spector. The stories were relatively consistent: a female was invited to the Pyrenees Castle, only to find herself staring at the barrel of the gun after spurning Phil's sexual overtures and attempting to leave. According to prosecutor Truc Do, Spector had "a history of playing Russian roulette with women—six women. Lana just happened to be the sixth."

On April 13, 2009, jurors returned from a thirty-hour deliberation with a unanimous guilty verdict. In addition to the second-degree-murder penalty, Spector would receive an additional four years for using a firearm in the commission of a crime. The next month, the sixty-nine-year-old rock 'n' roll trailblazer—slouching in a dark suit and bright red tie—was sentenced to the maximum of nineteen years to life. As part of the court-ordered sentence, Phil's lawyer handed Clarkson's family a $17,000 check to pay for her funeral expenses.

Ronnie Spector had pointedly avoided the trial. "My heart goes out to the woman and her family," she said in a statement after her ex-husband's arrest. "I don't know what the circumstances are. I can only say that when I left in the early '70s, I knew that if I didn't leave at that time, I was going to die there."

Ringo Starr, who'd witnessed both Spector's brilliance and his mania in the studio, and who once lived across the road from him in Beverly Hills, had a more basic reaction to the episode: "The problem with being a fuckin' gun nut," he told documentarian Vikram Jayanti, "is that sooner or later, someone gets shot."

3

At First I Thought It Was Infatuation

The Nocturnal Blast That Killed Sam Cooke

After Sam Cooke's murder, Beach Boy Dennis Wilson purchased the crooner's red Ferrari 250 GTL Lusso. The only actual surfer in the Beach Boys, Dennis appeared to be the embodiment of the "California myth" idealized in the group's songs, a privileged kid for whom opportunity could be discovered at the end of every ride down the Pacific Coast Highway. Yet he deeply related to Cooke, a black man from Mississippi who'd started on the gospel circuit and recorded the civil rights anthem "A Change Is Gonna Come" shortly before his death. Just as Cooke could be fond of cruising through the lower precincts of Los Angeles, pushing his luck by cavorting with undesirables, Wilson battled substance abuse, regularly lost physical altercations, and once invited the Manson family to live in his house.

Obviously, Wilson was primarily attracted to Cooke as an artist. With an innate ability to tell a story through both his prolific songwriting and his smooth, expressive voice, Cooke has been credited as the inventor of soul music. Despite his deep roots in the African American community, Cooke was a true crossover performer, with twenty-nine Top 40 hits on the pop charts, including "Twistin' the Night Away," "Chain Gang," "Wonderful World," and "You Send Me." As one of the first black performers to transition to the business end of the industry, Cooke founded a record label and publishing company, and supervised many of his songs in the studio.

Wilson was regularly sighted driving around Los Angeles, blasting Cooke's music and singing the lyrics aloud. Even as everything else in his life was falling apart—Dennis was banned from the Beach Boys for, among other things, encouraging his troubled brother Brian's drug use—the drummer took great comfort in the sounds generated by the "King of Soul." But the music could only sustain him for so long. On December 28, 1983, after a day of drinking, Dennis drowned in the waters off Marina Del Rey. Sam Cooke's Ferrari was found parked nearby.

The presence of the vehicle was yet another perverse addition to the saga of Sam Cooke, a man who exceeded the circumstances of his upbringing and early career, yet seemed to have a ridiculously toxic impact on many who let him in.

Sam's father was a minister at the Church of Christ (Holiness) in Clarksdale, Mississippi, which was known for both its music and civil rights activism. John Lee Hooker, Muddy Waters, and Ike Turner had roots in the area, while Robert Johnson regularly appeared in the town's blues clubs. In 1937, the "Empress of Blues" Bessie Smith died after a car accident near Clarksdale on the same Highway 61 that would later be immortalized in the eponymous 1965 Bob Dylan song. During the struggle against segregation, Dr. Martin Luther King Jr. visited Clarksdale twice, urging African American residents to boycott local businesses that enforced discriminatory policies.

In 1933, when Sam was two, the Reverend Charles Cook—when he became a performer, Sam would add an *e* to the end of his surname—moved the family to Chicago from the Mississippi Delta, as part of the Great Migration that saw some six million blacks respond to the decline of the cotton industry by emigrating from the Deep South.

At age six, Sam was singing gospel music with his father and siblings at churches and events in the Chicago area; eventually, he moved from backup to the front of the stage. Even before he entered Wendell Phillips Academy High School—named for the nineteenth-century abolitionist—in south Chicago, Sam had his own group, specializing in renewing listeners' Christian faith through song. A few years earlier, Nat King Cole had also graduated from Wendell Phillips, and Sam began to consider his musical options. Although *Billboard* still ranked black-oriented music ratings under the category of "race records," King's success demonstrated that an African American performer could appeal to white Americans not only as an R&B artist but as a genuine pop star.

As it was, Sam was being treated like a celebrity when he toured with his gospel group, the Soul Stirrers, attracting a younger crowd than many in the genre, particularly teenage girls drawn to both Cooke's voice and looks. Tentatively, he released a secular record under a pseudonym, hoping not to antagonize his gospel audience. After the Soul Stirrers were signed to a Los Angeles label, though, he boldly shopped around a disc recorded under his actual name—featuring Sam singing the Gershwin Brothers' composition "Summertime," from the opera *Porgy and Bess*. On the B side was a tune cowritten by Sam and his brother L. C. Once disc jockeys learned about the record, they began paying greater attention to the secondary song, "You Send Me," enabling Sam to hit number one on both the *Billboard* R&B and pop charts.

At this point, there was no turning back. To the great consternation of those who insisted that a man of Sam's talent should concentrate solely on spreading the word of God, Cooke had emerged as a pop idol—one of the first to incorporate the spirit of the black church into rock 'n' roll.

Aware that his new listeners didn't want anything "too black," Sam was discreet about the degree of soulfulness he infused in his recordings. There were some concessions, however, that he wouldn't make. Despite his popularity, and the money being offered, he refused to perform in any club that banned black patrons.

In 1961, Sam and two partners started their own label, producing, among other acts, singer-songwriter Bobby Womack and the group he'd formed with his brothers, the Valentinos. The next year, Allen Klein—a controversial figure who would later manage the Beatles and Rolling Stones—brokered a distribution deal with RCA, cutting himself a percentage of the rights. Still, Sam received a then-substantial $100,000 bonus, and appeared to have complete artistic control over his songs.

Reportedly, RCA had been in the market for a "black Elvis," and the string of hits that followed appeared to meet the company's expectations: "Cupid," "Sad Mood," "Another Saturday Night," and "Bring It on Home to Me," this last with Lou Rawls.

Rawls and Sam had known each other since they were rivals in teen gospel groups. The pair had been in the same car in 1958 when an accident killed the driver and left Rawls in a coma for five days. Their "Bring It on Home to Me" collaboration introduced the call-and-response of the black church into a pop song, with Rawls responding to Sam's hearty "Yeah!" with a "Yeah!" of his own.

As he did Rawls, Sam knew Womack from the gospel scene, spotting Bobby and his brothers at a revival concert and playing a role in arranging a national tour for them. In addition to having Bobby tour with Sam's band, Cooke produced and arranged the Valentinos song "Lookin' for a Love" in 1963. Although the song sold a million copies, Womack said that the group received minimal compensation. "We didn't know that we were supposed to get paid," Womack was quoted in the *Telegraph* as saying. "We were just honored to be with Sam Cooke's company, and we didn't get no royalties. He said, 'Well, that car you bought was your royalties. You stayed in a hotel. You know what that cost me? We took care of you guys, paid for the session. You may be getting screwed, but I'll screw you with grease. James Brown, he'd screw you with sand.'"

The Valentinos fared better when the Rolling Stones recorded their song "It's All Over Now." "Man, the amount of money rolling in shut me right up," Womack recounted. To no one's surprise, Sam managed to own a piece of the song's publishing, as well.

When Sam first heard Bob Dylan's "Blowin' in the Wind" in 1963, he was both excited and disappointed. With the civil rights movement igniting around the United States, Cooke believed that the song was a portrait of the times, an accurate window into the way that society was slowly transforming. At the same time, Sam wished the erudite statement had come from a person of color who'd experienced persecution, and could express rage as well as idealism.

On tour, Cooke included a cover of the song in his performances. At the same time, he began conceptualizing his own musical contribution to help move the revolution along.

On October 8, 1963, Sam was traveling through Louisiana when he was denied lodging at a Shreveport Holiday Inn. He argued and refused to leave, then stomped outside and repeatedly honked the horn. When the police arrived, he shouted at them and continued to stand his ground, until they placed him under arrest for disturbing the peace.

In his prison cell, he mused about the best way to channel the experience into song. Later, on the same tour, he encountered a group of civil rights demonstrators at a sit-in in Durham, North Carolina, and stopped to talk to them. The two incidents combined led to Sam writing "A Change Is Gonna Come." So passionate was Sam about the cause that, he'd later relate, the words flowed out easily:

> *"It's been a long, a long time coming*
> *But I know a change gonna come."*

Although white fans were growing comfortable with the image of Cooke's smiling face on album covers and television, Sam was willing to take the political risk that came with the authorship of the song. As the tune flows through the listener's mind, Sam's voice conveys sadness and hope, and the strings and horns seem more suited to a symphony than to a pop song. When he appeared on *The Tonight Show* on February 7, 1964, producers expected Sam to perform a more palatable hit. Instead, he daringly went into the activist anthem.

By and large, though, the country seemed to be in sync with the message. Three days later, the US House of Representatives voted in favor of what became known as the Civil Rights Act of 1964.

Women were always cycling in and out of Sam's life. He fathered at least three children out of wedlock and was married twice. His first wife, singer-dancer Dolores Milligan, was killed in a Fresno, California, auto crash in 1959. He had three children with his second wife, Barbara Campbell: Linda, Tracy, and Vincent. Then, in 1963, two-year-old Vincent drowned in the family's Hollywood swimming pool. Reportedly, the accident tormented and embittered Sam—he blamed Barbara for the death—and may have contributed to the reckless behavior that he exhibited on December 10, 1964.

Earlier in the day, he'd stopped by Lou Rawls's home. Rawls claimed that the moment Sam passed through the door, the baby started crying and the dog ran outside. According to Rawls's superstitious grandmother, the combined actions suggested imminent doom.

At 9 p.m., thirty-three-year-old Sam was having dinner with producer Al Schmitt and his wife, Joan, at Martoni's Italian restaurant on Sunset Boulevard. Even in Hollywood, Sam's presence drew attention. One after another, fans and music industry insiders stopped by the table to pay homage. A live album of Sam's performance at New York's Copacabana nightclub had recently been released, and many complimented the singer on both the sound and the record's success.

When Sam disappeared from the table for a lengthy stretch, Al Schmitt went looking for him and found Cooke at the bar, laughing, regaling people with stories and buying drinks with a large roll of money. Al informed Sam that the food had just been brought to the table. But Sam seemed in no hurry to return, telling Al to eat without him.

As his eyes scanned the restaurant, he noticed a pretty young woman sitting with a group of fellow musicians. Immediately, Sam ambled over to introduce himself. Elisa Boyer was twenty-two years old, part English and part Chinese. A police source would later describe her as "the perfect little China doll." Clearly, Sam approved of the way she presented herself. He began to focus on Elisa to the exclusion of everyone else, until they repaired to a private booth.

The Schmitts told Sam that they were going to continue their night at P.J.'s, a Santa Monica Boulevard nightclub commonly referred to as the first discotheque in Los Angeles, and made plans to meet up later on. At around 1 a.m., Cooke escorted Elisa to his Ferrari and drove her there. But when they arrived, the couple had already left. That was when the mood of the night turned. Allegedly, Sam became irate when another man began flirting with Elisa, and a loud argument ensued. According to Elisa, she asked to be taken home.

"He took the freeway," she'd tell police. "I was very frightened because he was driving so fast." When Elisa again demanded to be taken home, she said, Sam assured her that that was where they were going. But he appeared to be driving in the wrong direction. "He kept talking to me, saying how he thought I was such a lovely person, and I had such long, pretty hair. . . . I said, 'Please Mr. Cooke, take me home.'"

Instead, she maintained, Sam turned onto South Figueroa Street in a run-down section of the city and drove up to the office at the three-dollar-a-night Hacienda Motel. Elisa stayed behind as Sam entered and stood at the glass partition, registering under his own name. When manager Bertha Franklin looked over Sam's shoulder and spotted Elisa sitting in the passenger seat, the singer was instructed to sign "Mr. and Mrs." on the registration card. At one point, Elisa is said to have entered the office, as well, but she reportedly remained silent.

A short time after the couple repaired to a room, Franklin claimed that she was on the phone with the motel's owner, Evelyn Carr, when Cooke screeched up in the Ferrari outside—naked but for a sports jacket and single shoe. Furious, he demanded entrance to the office that also served as the manager's apartment, insisting that she disclose Elisa's whereabouts. "I told him to get the police if he wanted to search my place," Franklin told authorities. "He said, 'Damn the police.'"

After briefly storming into the parking lot and reentering his car, Sam came back to the office, the fifty-five-year-old manager contended, using his shoulder as a battering ram until the door frame broke and the latch popped. "When he walked in," Franklin said, "he walked straight to the kitchen and then . . . into the bedroom. Then, he came out . . . and he grabbed both of my arms and started twisting them and asking me where was that girl."

Once again, Franklin said, she told the enraged singer that she had no idea where Elisa had gone. "He fell on top of me," the manager recounted. "I tried to bite him through that jacket, biting, scratching and everything."

After kicking Sam out, Franklin alleged that she scrambled to her feet and reached for the pistol that she kept on top of the television for her protection. Fearing for her life, she said, she fired three times. The first two shots missed. The third passed through Sam's left lung, entered his heart and pierced the right lung.

"Lady, you shot me," the singer apparently uttered before marshaling his strength to lunge at Franklin again.

Snatching a broomstick, Franklin said that she beat Cooke over the head until he no longer posed a threat.

Hearing the gunshot from the other end of the telephone, Evelyn Carr remembered hanging up and reporting the shooting. After police arrived at the crime scene, Elisa Boyer suddenly appeared and provided her own version of events.

According to Elisa, after checking in at the Hacienda, Sam drove to the rear of the motel and dragged her into the room. "I started talking very loudly," she told police. "'Please take me home.' He turned the night latch, pushed me on the bed. He pinned me on the bed. He kept saying, 'We're just going to talk.' . . . He pulled my sweater off and ripped my dress. . . . I knew he was going to rape me.'"

Elisa said that when she asked permission to use the bathroom, Sam consented. There, she claimed that she attempted to flee, but the window was "painted down" and would not open.

However, she said, Sam now needed to use the bathroom himself. When he did, "I picked up my clothes, my shoes and my handbag." In her rush to flee the scene, she claimed that she inadvertently included Sam's clothes and wallet in the pile. Clad in only a slip and bra, she recalled, she ran to the motel office and banged on the door. But she said that Bertha Franklin was on the phone, and took too long to answer. Frightened that Sam might pursue her, Elisa said that she raced around the corner and up the street, where she dumped Sam's possessions, hastily dressed, and called police from a pay phone.

"Will you please come down to this number?" she asked. "I don't know where I am. I'm kidnapped."

By the time that she returned to the motel to meet the police sirens, she continued, the "King of Soul" was dead.

Blood testing showed that, at the time of the shooting, Sam had a blood alcohol level of .16, or twice the legal limit for drivers—explaining, in the eyes of some members of law enforcement, his peculiar behavior on the final night of his life. Despite the wad of cash that he'd displayed at Martoni's, only $108 remained in the money clip found in his sport coat. Because both Bertha Franklin and Elisa Boyer passed lie detector tests—and Evelyn Carr's recollection of what she heard over the phone matched the story told by the motel manager—a coroner's inquest determined that the killing had been a "justifiable homicide."

For three days, fans in Los Angeles filed past Cooke's glass-topped coffin. The body was then flown to Chicago, where twenty thousand people lined up in the freezing weather to pay their respects before a service was held. This was followed by a second funeral back in Los Angeles, where Ray Charles, the Staple Singers, and Billy Preston all sang. So did Lou Rawls, who performed a touching version of "Just a Closer Walk with Thee."

Within a month of the shooting, a new Sam Cooke album and two singles were rushed into stores. "Shake" reached the Top 10 on both the R&B and pop charts. On the B side was "A Change Is Gonna Come."

Conspiracy theories were rife. A jealous Barbara Cooke was blamed for orchestrating the attack. Sam was said to have been killed while intervening for a friend indebted to drug dealers. Racists had targeted Sam, some argued, because he was a black man with the audacity to dictate his own terms in the music business.

"All one has to do is read the autopsy report and coroner's inquest to know that Sam Cooke, a healthy man of 33, did not die at the hands of a 55-year-old, slightly overweight Bertha Franklin," the singer's nephew Erik Greene told the website *Inn the Basement*. "Sam had cuts on his face and forehead, a broken rib and a large lump on the back of his head. . . . Family members remember both of Sam's hands being broken, with the skin on his knuckles almost gone completely. Whomever Sam encountered in his last hours, it wasn't this middle-aged woman who didn't have a scratch on her."

Singer Etta James, who viewed the body before the funeral, maintained that she observed a mashed nose, crushed hands, and a head practically separated from the shoulders. Many viewed the mangling as signs of a mob-related hit, perhaps engineered by manager Allen Klein, whose company was still warring over proceeds with members of the Cooke family more than forty years later. According to another Mafia theory, Sam was actually killed at an entertainment executive's mansion before being dumped in South Central.

The problem with the underworld suspicions is that mob-tied record executives and club owners interested in exploiting Sam were better off keeping him alive. After "Change Is Gonna Come," Sam's future looked limitless. Hence, it would have made better business sense for even the most parasitical figures in the industry to allow the singer to continue to excel for several more years.

As observers reexamined Elisa Boyer's narrative, a number of flaws stood out. Although Boyer claimed to have been frightened of Sam as he drove her to the Hacienda Motel, she made no effort to flee his Ferrari when he left her alone in the car to register. Indeed, she supposedly exited the vehicle to join Cooke when he filled out the registration card. And if Sam intended to rape Boyer, as she allegedly feared, what possessed the well-known singer to write down his real name? A witness noted that there did seem to be tension between the two as they entered the motel room, but emphasized that Cooke was not dragging the woman, as she described. And despite the contention that Boyer was essentially enslaved, Sam seemed to have no qualms about leaving her alone when he used the bathroom.

A more telling picture emerged a month after the shooting, when Boyer was arrested for prostitution. Given that the Hacienda was a popular spot for prostitutes to bring their tricks, it's entirely possible that Boyer directed Sam to the motel, then scooped up his clothes, wallet, and money when he went into the bathroom. Thus she would not only have robbed the singer, she would have prevented him from pursuing her.

When an undressed Sam thundered up to the office, he likely thought that Boyer and Bertha Franklin—an ex-madam with a criminal record—were working in tandem. In fact, Boyer may have actually been hiding in the apartment when Sam arrived, disposing of his clothes around the corner once the shooting occurred and she knew that the police were on the way.

As for Cooke's injuries, some believe they were inflicted not solely by Franklin, but perhaps by a group of goons who regularly collaborated with the two women after they robbed johns.

Following the killing, the Hacienda was bombarded with death threats, prompting Franklin to abandon her position at the motel. She sued Cooke's estate, blaming the singer for both physical injuries and mental anguish. With Boyer providing testimony on the manager's behalf, Franklin won the case in 1967 and was awarded $30,000.

Despite rumors that she'd moved to the Midwest, she remained in Los Angeles until her death in 1980. Just one year earlier, Elisa Boyer had been found guilty of second-degree murder after killing a boyfriend.

Three months after the murder, thirty-one-year-old Barbara Cooke remarried. The groom was Sam's former protégé, twenty-one-year-old Bobby Womack. Womack later said that the relationship started while he was comforting Barbara after the shooting. But no one seemed to celebrate the nuptials. Bobby's brothers and many fans shunned him. Barbara's brother beat him up. The marriage lasted until 1970, when Barbara discovered that Bobby was romantically involved with her eighteen-year-old daughter, Linda—Sam Cooke's biological daughter.

She fired a gun at her younger husband and missed.

Linda later married Bobby's younger brother Cecil. The new couple formed a group called Womack & Womack, with Bobby occasionally joining them in the studio. It was one of the few positives to emerge from the aftermath of Sam's murder. Although Womack would work with such revered artists as Aretha Franklin, Janis Joplin, and Sly and the Family Stone, his life was packed with tragedy. Vincent Womack, his son with Barbara, committed suicide at age twenty-one. A son from his second marriage died at four months old. Bobby's brother Harry was fatally stabbed by a jealous girlfriend. For much of his adult life, Womack battled drug addiction. Before his death from Alzheimer's in 2013, he struggled to remember the words to his songs.

But Sam left before all that. As the years passed, he was rediscovered by new generations, inducted into the Rock and Roll Hall of Fame, and awarded a star on Hollywood Boulevard. A half-century after his death, his music could be heard everywhere, his silky, inviting voice conjuring up feelings of optimism, rather than the decadence and disorder that led to the late-night slaying at the Hacienda Motel.

4

WHY DOES LOVE GOT TO BE SO SAD?

JIM GORDON AND THE VOICE THAT WOULDN'T STOP

They were a family of voices, headed by a patriarchal figure with a white beard. But there was also the pretty blonde, and the swarthy fellow who may have been Greek. They were affable at first, offering tips on cleanliness, personal hygiene, what to cook and eat. "I heard them all the time," Jim Gordon told *Rolling Stone* in 1985. "They would tell me if I was doing right or wrong. And I took it like a fool."

Some of the voices were more familiar. Jim could recognize those of his aunt and brother, along with that of his mother. Of all the sounds swimming through Jim's head, the voice of Osa Marie Gordon was the loudest and most persistent.

When Osa made observations about his behavior, she was critical, particularly about the size of the portions on his plate. Osa wanted her son to eat less. She commanded it. Often, Jim said, he'd acquiesce, starving himself for days, then retreating to a motel and gorging himself on fried chicken.

He knew he couldn't go on this way. At a certain stage, it was either going to be him or her. Yet, even after the murder, he never really excised his mother from his life. At one parole hearing, he claimed that Osa was still alive.

Furthermore, he wasn't exactly certain that he'd committed homicide. Rather, the death of Osa kind of "happened." "When I remember the crime, it's kind of like a dream," he told the *Washington Post* in 1994. "I can remember going through what happened in that space and time, and it seems kind of detached, like I was going through it on some other plane. It didn't seem real."

But Jim's delusions were real to his mother. In 1983, the seventy-one-year-old woman had avoided in-person visits with her son for two years. Nonetheless, Jim was certain that she was still manipulating him, getting in his mind, berating him when he was alone in his Van Nuys condominium, driving his Datsun 200SX, or sitting behind his drum kit, waiting to play.

And Jim was a guy who'd played with everybody: Eric Clapton, George Harrison, John Lennon, Art Garfunkel, Dr. John, Carole King, Frank Zappa, and Barbra Streisand. He was versatile, and could jump from one genre to another, backing up the Beach Boys on "Good Vibrations," Glen Campbell on "Wichita Lineman," and the Hues Corporation on the early disco hit "Rock the Boat." A sample of his drum break on the song "Apache" from Michael Viner's Incredible Bongo Band's 1973 *"Bongo Rock"* album would later become a staple of hip-hop.

Certainly, Jim was a little off. But this was an industry that embraced the peculiar and tended to overlook, and forgive, personal psychoses.

Anyway, no one thought he'd go so far as to kill his mother. Even the doctors who'd been treating him never warned Osa that her son might actually harm her. Then again, they'd been misdiagnosing his condition for years, blaming his misapprehensions on the d.t.'s, or delirium tremens, a confused state resulting from alcohol withdrawal. So on May 23, Osa wrote her son a letter, beseeching Jim to no longer blame her for his torment, and urging him to call if he needed love and support.

Jim never opened the envelope. But the contact apparently ignited something in the plagued drummer. On June 1, he phoned Osa, reproaching her for "bugging" him and vowing to take her life.

Osa hung up, then dialed the psych ward at the North Hollywood Medical Center, a place Jim had visited on a multitude on occasions. He'd been there earlier in the day, a nurse said, complaining about feeling violent and asking for the antipsychotic drug Thorazine. Before a doctor could speak to him, though, he left.

Concerned about where he might go next, Osa called the police. Since Jim wasn't anywhere near her property, she was told, there was no point in sending over an officer. But, if it made her feel better, maybe she should leave the lights on. The next day—after yet another frightening call from her son—she phoned the city attorney's office and inquired about a restraining order. The switchboard operator couldn't provide specific instructions and, as Osa knew all too well, these kinds of things took a while. Not wishing to spend any additional time on the phone, she hung up and hoped for the best.

It wasn't like she hadn't experienced this type of situation before. After all, Jim had been hearing voices since he was a child—those of imaginary friends, like many kids his age, as well as the demons who would torture him into adulthood.

Jim may have imagined his mother persecuting him over his weight because he'd struggled with the issue as a kid in the Sherman Oaks section of the San Fernando Valley. Still, he was so adept at music that few people noticed that the boy tended to be a little corpulent. He was eight when he fashioned a set of drums out of trash cans, impressing his parents so much that they registered him for music lessons. As his mastery revealed itself, they added an addition to their house so Jim could have a drum room. It was a wise investment. In high school, he performed with the Burbank Philharmonic Orchestra and in the Tournament of Roses parade, and toured Europe one summer. On weekends, he played weddings, bar mitzvahs, and dances. Upon graduation, he declined a scholarship to UCLA to work in the record industry.

In 1963, he accompanied the Everly Brothers on a British tour, earning a spot at the table where the L.A. studio musicians hung out at the A&B Corned Beef restaurant. His mentor during this period was Hal Blaine, arguably the most popular drummer on the scene. When Blaine was too busy to make a gig, he recommended Jim. Soon, Jim was doing two or three sessions a day, charging double time and specifying that he'd only play his own drum set. At one point, he was shuttling between Los Angeles and Las Vegas daily, finishing a session in Hollywood, then catching a plane for an evening show at Caesars Palace.

Jim was still in his teens when he married, but he and his spouse lived like adults, purchasing a Spanish-style house in North Hollywood, near his parents, as well as a Mercedes 220S. Both were featured on the television show *Shindig!*—a rock 'n' roll series featuring stars like James Brown, the Supremes, and Sonny and Cher, along with such British Invasion acts as the Who and the Rolling Stones. Jim played drums, while his wife's go-go dancing moves were admired by males all over the US.

At one point, he tried starting his own group, but the unit disbanded after the first album. By 1969, he was single again and touring England with Delaney and Bonnie, a soul-rocking troupe headed by singer/songwriter couple Delaney and Bonnie Bramlett. At various times, George Harrison, Eric Clapton, Leon Russell, Rita Coolidge, and Duane and Gregg Allman all played with the band. Drugs were plentiful. But for a guy who already heard voices, this was potentially troublesome. Jim later said that throughout his tenure with the group, he had a sense that somebody was watching him.

He was a real rock star now, not necessarily a household name, but a well-respected member of the fraternity. He and Coolidge—whose hits would include "(Your Love Has Lifted Me) Higher and Higher"—became a couple, and were regarded as equals, until he invited her into the hallway one day at New York's Warwick Hotel and slugged her in the eye. Coolidge called off the romance, but, in the often misogynistic music industry subculture, the outburst had little impact on Jim's blossoming career.

In fact, when the Bonnie and Delaney tour ended, Harrison recruited Jim to work on *All Things Must Pass*, a triple album largely comprised of material George had been writing during the waning days of the Beatles. With Phil Spector shepherding the project, *All Things Must Pass* instantly shot to the top of the charts. In the meantime, Clapton asked Jim to join a band he was starting with Duane Allman, Carl Radle, and Bobby Whitlock.

The group, Derek and the Dominos, produced arguably the most notable work of Clapton's career, *Layla and Other Assorted Love Songs*, a double album of soulful blues rock. While Jim tried keeping the voices in his head at bay, Clapton experienced his own anguish, working alongside his good friend Harrison on *All Things Must Pass*, then withdrawing and grappling with the deep affection he'd developed for the former Beatle's wife, Pattie Boyd. "When you heard (the title song) 'Layla,' you knew right away what it was all about," Whitlock told the *Telegraph*. "It was understood Eric was totally in love with Pattie. It was understood by everyone, but no one said anything."

When Clapton wasn't attempting to numb his feelings with various mixtures of alcohol and drugs, he and Jim were working magnificently in tandem. Clapton is credited with writing the driving first part of "Layla," while Jim is said to be responsible for the touching piano coda that enlivens the second half.

Although the emotionality yielded great art, the band is now considered cursed. A year after the album's 1970 release, Allman was killed in a motorcycle crash. Radle's substance abuse issues led to his own death in 1980. Following a successful American tour, Clapton took off his guitar one day in the studio and walked out while the Dominos were attempting to make a second LP. According to Whitlock, he stayed home for two years, shooting heroin.

In the midst of all this, Jim hit a creative roadblock. Lauded since the beginning of his career, he was frustrated in his efforts to realize his goal of becoming a songwriter. In fact, he was later accused of stealing the "Layla" piano coda from his old girlfriend, Rita Coolidge.

During more trying times, he admitted to Whitlock that he was struggling to blot out the voices that crept into his brain. Whitlock responded that Jim was just hearing his own "consciousness." But Jim knew that someone else was talking to him.

The truth was that Jim Gordon was a schizophrenic, a person who experiences auditory hallucinations, frequently in the form of voices that relentlessly criticize and issue decrees. Although antipsychotic drugs work with some sufferers, many choose alcohol and street drugs to moderate the symptoms. Unfortunately, the voices return, sometimes with greater force due to the user's altered state.

From his time in Derek and the Dominos, Jim had cultivated a taste for heroin. Like domestic violence, this was not viewed as a detriment, since Clapton and other rock luminaries shared the same predilection. John Lennon, who'd met Jim when they'd both played with Harrison and Clapton at a 1969 UNICEF concert, invited the drummer to perform on *Imagine*. He joined Traffic for the *Low Spark of High Heeled Boys* album and subsequent tour. Over the next few years, his drumming could be heard on Carly Simon's "You're So Vain," Maria Muldaur's "Midnight at the Oasis," and Steely Dan's "Rikki Don't Lose That Number." Despite his tastes for speedballs—cocaine/heroin combinations— even the unsullied Osmond family enthusiastically welcomed him into the studio.

By and large, he was regarded as being as responsible as he was gifted, never missing a session. Yet he was no longer the youthful, eager character Frank Zappa had once playfully nicknamed "Skippy." When he wasn't playing, he'd withdraw and mumble to himself—right in front of the other musicians. In Jim's mind, people were out to get him—the younger, real-life drummers lobbying to take his gigs, and imaginary figures who harbored grudges and demands that were not of this world.

Ultimately, the professional life he'd constructed for himself started to unravel. He beat his third wife, cracking her ribs while babbling about a "magic triangle." He choked another girlfriend while she was sleeping. During a recording session in 1977, he suddenly stopped playing and argued that his hands were involuntarily moving because of something a guitarist was doing from the other side of the room. That same year, he checked into Southern California Hospital at Van Nuys for psychiatric treatment.

"I couldn't cope with being outside anymore," he told *Rolling Stone*. "The voices were chasing me around, making me drive to different places, starving me. I was only allowed one bite of food a meal. And if I disobeyed, the voices would fill me with a rage, like the Hulk gets."

Although he told doctors during this period that his mother was his only friend, Osa's voice was louder than everyone else's. Even when he visited her home during weekend furloughs, he heard her in his head, goading him. When he eventually defied doctor's orders and checked himself out of the hospital, she found him, overdosed on psychiatrist-prescribed sedatives. The voices, he explained after he came to, didn't care if he lived or died.

Yet some people in the music business were still willing to give him a chance. During a tour with Jackson Browne in 1978, Jim appeared disciplined, jogging and playing racquetball with the singer. "It was pretty well known that he had a breakdown," Browne told *Rolling Stone*. "But I wanted him on the tour. You just wanted to root for him. . . . He was such a good drummer."

The tour was a success, but these were becoming fewer and farther between. On orders from his mother's voice, he hung up on Bob Dylan when the troubadour called about a spot on the tour that followed the release of *Slow Train Coming* in 1979. During a gig with Paul Anka in Vegas, Jim stood up after just playing a few beats. His mother, he maintained, had mandated that he leave.

Holed up at home, Jim went through stretches when he wouldn't bathe or change clothes. He stockpiled food, envisioning the end of the world. At times, he imagined his mother's collusion in the deaths of singer Karen Carpenter and comedian Paul Lynde.

Occasionally, he managed to get out and play the drums again. He even spoke about forming a band, then became concerned that he might die from lifting up his drumsticks. During a hospital stay in 1982, he fretted about killing himself or possibly slaying his mother.

On June 6, 1983, he drove to Osa's North Hollywood apartment, sure that his mother had directed him to take her life. Before leaving, he'd sharpened an eight-and-a-quarter-inch butcher knife and packed it with a hammer. The plan was to smash her with the mallet first and knock her out. When she was unconscious, and unable to register pain, he'd thrust the blade into her chest.

Osa wasn't home when Jim arrived, so he turned around and went back to his place. But now, he couldn't reverse course. At 11:30 p.m., he returned and knocked on the door. Osa appeared surprised to see him.

"Jim?" she asked.

He brought the hammer down hard, striking her four times as she crumpled to the ground. Then he stabbed her three times in quick succession. Leaving the knife in her chest, he exited, but made no effort to hide his crime.

After all, he wasn't really sure that he'd done anything wrong.

Predictably, once Osa was dead, Jim no longer heard her voice. He did, however, hear the taunts, pronouncements, and directives issued by others.

It wasn't until his 1985 trial that his condition was accurately diagnosed—acute paranoid schizophrenia. Even the prosecutors agreed with the five psychiatrists called to the stand by the defense. Because of the voices in his head, Jim really wasn't responsible for his actions. But recent changes to the insanity defense in the state of California inhibited his legal team from recommending a long stay in a sanitarium.

He had a fellow schizophrenic named John Warnock Hinckley Jr. to thank for that.

For most of the twentieth century, American defendants could be declared legally insane if they were incapable of distinguishing between right and wrong. Then, in 1962, laws were expanded to allow medical and psychiatric evidence to exculpate a suspect who, at the time of the crime, lacked the "substantial capacity either to appreciate the criminality of his conduct, or to conform his conduct to the requirements of the law." This distinction helped Hinckley after he shot President Ronald Reagan and three others in 1981 to impress actress Jodie Foster. Not only did he get Foster's attention—she provided videotaped testimony at his trial—but a jury found him not guilty by reason of insanity.

Conservatives were outraged. Indiana senator—and future vice president—Dan Quayle railed against "pampered criminals" permitted to murder "with impunity." The backlash resulted in the passage of the Insanity Defense Reform Act of 1984, which, among other measures, eliminated the diminished-capacity defense, limited the scope of expert testimony, and shifted the burden of proof from the prosecution to the defense.

In this atmosphere of reduced options, Jim was convicted of second-degree murder and sentenced to sixteen years to life. Working against his own interests, he maintained that his mental illness was not as chronic as others assumed. "I really don't feel that crazy," he told *Rolling Stone* several months after the trial. "I get along with people. I think I'm pretty normal."

An inmate/activist known as Boston Woodward concurred. In 1996, he was a music coordinator at the California Men's Colony, as well as the editor of the prison newspaper. When he first met Jim, the once-heralded drummer was standing in the prison yard, chain-smoking and shifting from foot to foot. "I learned later," Woodward wrote on the *Community Alliance* website, "that this is typical behavior [for] someone fighting the horrible effects of psychotropic drugs."

Because of the medication, Jim's mouth was constantly dry. But during a visit to the water fountain, he let Woodward and a fellow inmate engage him in a conversation about rock 'n' roll, and agreed to meet them a few days later in the prison's band room. "Despite all the stories that Gordon had lost interest in music, there he was behind a drum kit," Woodward said. "His drumming was so steady, dynamic, impeccably clean. The man was a human metronome. . . . He didn't talk much, but what he lacked in words, he made up for with each beat of the drum and crash of the cymbals."

In a photo from that era, Jim is surrounded by his strapping bandmates, a gaunt, shrunken, white-haired figure looking out at the world through thick spectacles, as Woodward rests a protective arm on him. "Week after week," Woodward said on the *Community Alliance* website, "Gordon progressively became more sociable, not only with the band members, but with other prisoners and the staff," telling stories about Joe Cocker, Joan Baez, and Derek and the Dominos. "My experience with Gordon showed . . . how music can create an island of respite and deep connection even for those of us locked away in prison."

To the authorities, though, Jim remained troubled and defiant, resistant to counseling and court-ordered medication, a "danger to society" who didn't bother meeting with an attorney before parole hearings because he'd resigned himself to being "institutionalized."

In 2013, Los Angeles deputy district attorney Alexis de la Garza recommended a conservator to safeguard Jim's substantial royalty payments. "The question is," De la Garza said at the hearing, "would people be preying on him on the outside, as they have on the inside, because of his finances?"

But authorities were likely unaware of the relationships he'd created in prison, a universe as fantastical as the one inhabited by the scolding, shrieking, and howling voices responsible for his incarceration. Woodward recalled an afternoon in the band room when Jim acceded to a request to play the long piano coda from "Layla." "Everyone in the room stopped," the inmate wrote, "mesmerized by a piece of music heard on every rock radio station . . . now being played before their eyes. It was surreal watching Gordon do his thing, but heartbreaking to watch him do it behind prison walls."

5

WHEN THE MUSIC'S OVER

HOW DID "THE END" REALLY COME FOR JIM MORRISON?

The headline in London's *Daily Express* told a story that many had been hearing for years.

Jim Morrison was still alive.

In this telling, he was alleged to be existing as a "homeless hippy" in New York. Pictured was a screenshot—from a widely disseminated YouTube video—of an older, heavyset man with a long, lush head of hair and a bushy gray beard, swinging his arms at his sides the way "the Lizard King" was known to do in concert. Reportedly, he was even overheard reciting a nonsensical stream of poetry that Morrison might have composed, had he spent the past four decades sleeping on fire escapes and below highway trestles.

According to some fans, Morrison faked his own death in 1971 to escape the rigors of fame. Friends said that he'd actually discussed this possibility, joking that he wanted to disappear somewhere on the African continent and assume the alias Mr. Mojo Risin,' an anagram of his surname that appears on the song "L.A. Woman." Over the years, there were Morrison sightings at a rodeo in the American Midwest, as well as deep in the Australian outback and Tibet. For a while in the 1970s, a man in San Francisco made the rounds dressed as Morrison and writing checks in his name. In 2016, Maurizio Gasparri, the vice president of the Italian Senate, was criticized for giving public credence to a hoax that a notorious criminal in his country was the man once called the "King of Orgasmic Rock."

The root of many conspiracy theories had much to do with the efforts made by Jim's common-law wife, Pamela Courson, to keep the death a secret. Only five people attended his burial at Paris's famed Père Lachaise cemetery. It wasn't until two days later—six days after the singer's death—that the news reached the American press.

"There was no service and that made it all the better," his manager, Bill Siddons, told *Rolling Stone*. "We just threw some flowers and dirt and said goodbye."

The casket containing Jim's remains was deliberately closed, prompting Doors keyboardist Ray Manzarek to question Siddons, "How do you even know Jim was in the coffin? How do you know it wasn't 150 pounds of fuckin' sand?"

Nor was there an autopsy. "We didn't want to do it that way," Siddons explained. "We wanted to leave him alone."

Officially, Morrison died from heart failure, perhaps complicated by a lung infection, in the bathtub of the apartment he shared with his Pam in Paris's Marais district—two years to the day that Brian Jones was discovered at the bottom of a swimming pool at his estate in southeast England, and some nine months after the deaths of Jimi Hendrix and Janis Joplin. All four were twenty-seven years old when they died, members of a morbid "club" that Kurt Cobain and Amy Winehouse would later join.

While the heart failure contention may be simplified, Doors drummer John Densmore, who'd slowly watched the singer destroy himself, never believed the notion that his friend had been spirited out of France to abscond from stardom. "I am sorry," Densmore stated decisively. "He's dead."

It's *how* Jim broke on through to the other side that's yet to be settled.

Depending on the hour you caught him, Jim Morrison had conflicting views about death. During one conversation, he spoke about living into his hundreds and waiting for medical science to create a formula ensuring his eternal existence. On another occasion, he drunkenly muttered the names of Hendrix, Joplin, and Jones to producer Paul Rothchild, concluding with, "You're drinking with number four."

A week before his death, he was walking through Père Lachaise, noting that Oscar Wilde, Edith Piaf, Honoré de Balzac, and other giants of the arts were interred there. Considering the brevity of his own time on earth, Morrison said that even if he died in Los Angeles, he liked the idea of joining those luminaries in the Paris burial ground.

In his writing, the topic of mortality was a regular theme. Once, while performing at Gazzarri's on the Sunset Strip, he was singing "When the Music's Over," when he suddenly screamed and threw his microphone on the ground. As he walked offstage, Pamela inquired about the motivation behind his tantrum—particularly since the place was practically vacant. "You never know when you're giving your last performance," Jim responded.

On a regular basis, Jim tested the limits of his impermanence. "We used to call him the Human Fly," Doors former secretary Kathy Lisciandro, who once watched an inebriated Morrison mimic a tightrope walker across the fifteen-inch-wide ledge on the roof of 9000 Sunset Boulevard in West Hollywood, the tallest edifice on the Sunset Strip, told *Rolling Stone*. "He'd have no regard for his physical body. He'd just abuse it. He'd fallen out of windows . . . just playing."

Those who bought the "natural causes" story speculated that accumulated injuries might have caused the internal damage responsible for Morrison's death. Lisciandro opined that Jim saw his body as "just a 'thing,' and he thought that non-physical things were more real."

He wasn't really supposed to turn out like that. But when James Douglas Morrison was born, in Melbourne, Florida on December 8, 1943, his parents, George and Clara, couldn't have anticipated the upheaval of the 1960s or their eldest child's role in it. Like his forebears, Rear Admiral George Morrison was a career navy man, who was working in the Office of the Chief of Naval Operations at the Pentagon when Jim died.

The family lived primarily in the DC suburbs—Alexandria, Arlington, Bethesda, and Falls Church—and, for a while, it looked like Jim might adhere to the clan's conservatism. While attending Alexandria's George Washington High School, he ascended to the rank of Eagle Scout, made the honor roll, and expressed fondness for the sounds of Frank Sinatra. But he tended to keep to himself, drifting off to a blues bar on the other side of Jefferson Davis Highway called the 1320 Club, taking comfort in and inspiration from the grimy environs. When the admiral began figuring out his son's predilections, there were clashes at home.

"I grew up in a different era," George Morrison told the *Washington Post*, "and I didn't like all [the] loud music. But I consider Jim a great writer and I like some of his songs."

Everyone agreed that the Beltway region wasn't quite the right place for a kid like Jim to find himself, so he went to college in Florida—St. Petersburg Junior College and Florida State—before shifting coasts and attending UCLA's film school.

In 1965, Jim was hanging out at Venice Beach and got into a conversation with a fellow UCLA student who had a side gig as a keyboard player in a pub rock band. When Morrison mentioned that he'd been writing a few songs himself, Ray Manzarek realized that he'd made a new friend. Curious about Jim's other artistic pursuits, Ray attended a screening of Morrison's plotless, stream-of-consciousness student film, digging the imagery on-screen while other classmates questioned its purpose. At the Maharishi Mahesh Yogi meditation center Manzarek befriended Densmore, convinced the drummer possessed the wisdom to help make Jim's songs come to life.

Ray loved the name Jim had chosen for their new band, a reference to a passage created by English poet William Blake: "There are things that are known and things that are unknown; in between are doors."

Rehearsal sessions took place in a Venice garage. For a while, Ray had his brothers, Rick and Jim, in the group, and a female bassist whose name appears to be lost to history. Then Robby Krieger, a guitarist with versatile music tastes and a unique finger-style approach, took their place. "When I think about the beginning of the Doors, it feels like a strange, beautiful, psychedelic dream that happened," Densmore told *Rolling Stone*. "I guess it happened."

Officially, the band played its first gig at a UCLA screening of one of Manzarek's films, followed by a private party at Hughes Aircraft, where his father worked. Working out their material on-stage, the group began playing six nights a week on the Sunset Strip, at a place called the London Fog. There was a go-go girl in a cage who was supposed to enhance the performance, but she was accustomed to shaking to tunes by groups like the Monkees, Young Rascals, and Tommy James and the Shondells. But, according to Densmore's observations, she never learned to dance to "The End."

When the London Fog stint ended, fans followed the Doors to other venues on the Strip, like Gazzarri's and the Whisky A Go Go. Under the lights, Jim was as much of a stage performer as a poet and musician, freaking observers out by falling all over the place and emitting piercing shrieks—while Krieger's trancey guitar playing and Densmore's accelerating drumbeats brought spectators to states of exhilaration and exhaustion. "As Jim explained it, he felt like his life up 'til that point was like a bow string being drawn back," Krieger told *Rolling Stone*, "and then, you finally let it go and all the creativity comes out."

In August 1966, the band went into the studio for five days and recorded its debut album, *The Doors*. The record quickly soared to number two on the *Billboard* charts, and Jim Morrison was officially a rock star. Five more albums followed, along with hits that virtually everyone in the Western world has heard: "Light My Fire," "Hello, I Love You," "Riders on the Storm," "People Are Strange," and "Love Me Two Times," among others. Breaking every convention regarding the length of radio-friendly tunes,

"The End" went on for eleven minutes and thirty-five seconds, the closest commercial rock had ever come to spoken-word. "Father, I want to kill you," an Oedipal Morrison recited. "Mother, I want to . . ." He completed the line with a primal scream.

According to bandmates, there was a genetic disposition to alcoholism in the Morrison household. While everyone on the scene was imbibing multiple substances regularly, Jim was a particularly difficult drunk. At the Doors' office, Jim's desk was always populated by bourbon and tequila bottles, alongside an ashtray brimming with old joints and cigar butts. He turned up at the studio drunk on a regular basis. Often, he'd stagger around and say that he didn't feel like recording that day.

Booze was bad, but Jim insisted that he could be doing worse. "There seem to be a lot of people shooting smack and speed now," Morrison said in an interview with the *Los Angeles Free Press*. "Alcohol and heroin and downers—these are painkillers. Alcohol for me—'cause it's traditional. Also . . . I hate the kind of sleazy sexual connotations of scoring from people. . . . I like alcohol. You can go down to any corner store or bar, and it's right across the table."

One day, in the midst of recording *Morrison Hotel*, Krieger and Densmore broached the subject of their singer's vulnerability to alcohol, while the three were relaxing by the pool. Jim conceded that he drank too much and wanted to dry out. Then he suggested going out and getting a good drink.

"That was Morrison," Krieger told *Classic Rock* magazine, "the romantic poet who wrote, 'I woke up this morning, got myself a beer.' . . . Unfortunately, that was the reality. Jim's attitude was always, 'Look out, man. I'm hell bent on destruction.'"

Morrison admitted that he took great pleasure in generating turmoil. "Who isn't fascinated with chaos?" he asked future biographer Jerry Hopkins. "More than that, though, I am interested in activity that has no meaning."

On March 1, 1969, that philosophy turned to action while the Doors were performing for twelve thousand fans at Miami's Dinner

Key Auditorium. Jim was in a particularly belligerent mood, and it was hard to figure out whether he was angry with his devotees or the role that society was forcing them to play. Throughout the show, he derided them with a choice selection of names and commentary, referring to his audience as "a bunch of slaves" who "love getting your face stuck in shit." Finally, he challenged, "You want to see my cock, don't you?"

The response was largely affirmative. Even if it hadn't been, Morrison was not to be dissuaded. He unzipped his pants and ran through the crowd. Four days later, the Miami-Dade State Attorney's Office charged him with "lewd and lascivious behavior in public by exposing his private parts and by simulating masturbation and oral copulation," along with profanity and public intoxication. Facing a sentence of more than three years in prison, he was found guilty of drunkenness and exposure following a two week trial.

The verdicts were under appeal when he died.

While no one would say it, Jim's mental health might have been declining. Physically, he was also beginning to transform into a caricature of a gourmandizing rock star. "Morrison looked ugly," Paul Rothchild told *Classic Rock*. "He was unhappy with his role as a national sex symbol, and after the Miami obscenity trial, he did everything in his power to obliterate that. He gained [an] enormous [amount of] weight. He grew a beard."

To those who questioned his appearance, he expressed contentment with his new look. "Why is it so onerous to be fat?" he asked a reporter from the *Village Voice*. "Fat is beautiful. I feel great when I'm fat. I feel like a tank."

But Jim's armor was rusting. During the recording sessions for the band's final album, *L.A. Woman*, he struggled with both his voice and his ability to write lyrics, while consuming three dozen beers a day. When the record was completed, the Doors posed for a cover photo. The picture was telling, Manzarek observed. In place of the "youthful poet" whom the keyboardist had first met a few short years earlier, Morrison appeared to be a man "on the way out."

A lot had transpired in six years. Stardom and gluttony had worn Jim down. For the time being, Los Angeles wasn't working for him. He needed a change—of both scenery and mind-set. In March 1971, a week after "Love Her Madly," the first single on *L.A. Woman*, was released, he left for Paris—where Pamela was already living, struggling with the vices that would claim *her* life three years later.

While traveling in Morocco to acquire djellabas, tunics, and other hippie fashions for her boutique at 947 North La Cienega Boulevard—a business that was closed more than it was open, and that was subsidized by Jim's royalty check from the *Strange Days* album—Pam had met Count Jean de Breteuil, a well-bred heroin dealer who was dating Marianne Faithfull. When Pam arrived in Paris, she and Breteuil began spending time together, due largely to his ample supply of her favorite narcotic, and may have been romantically involved. There were references to the distractions Pam was experiencing on a number of Doors songs. "Can't hear my baby, though I call and call," Jim sang on "Cars Hiss by My Window." On "Love Street," he spoke of a woman who "has robes and she has monkeys, lazy, diamond-studded flunkies."

In the original line of the song, Jim actually wrote, "junkies."

As *L.A. Woman* conquered the charts, Jim landed in Paris, hoping to rest and escape the expectations of American celebrity. He'd always had periods of lethargy followed by spurts of creativity, and believed the fresh atmosphere would lead to new realizations. The couple started out together at the sumptuous Hotel George V, moved on to L'Hôtel, on the rue des Beaux Arts—where Oscar Wilde, Salvador Dalí, and Princess Grace had passed before—and finally settled into an opulent, three-bedroom apartment—owned by French model and actress Elizabeth Lariviere—at 17, rue Beautreillis in the storied Marais district.

On a bench in the Place des Vosges, a square commissioned by "Good King" Henri IV in the early seventeenth century, Jim wrote poetry, and contemplated an album of verses that he hoped to record in an authentic, ambient setting. Seemingly rejuvenated, he called Densmore and spoke about returning to Los Angeles and embarking on new projects with the Doors. He even persuaded two buskers he'd met in a cafe to join him in a Paris studio and record a few tunes.

Depending on the source, Jim was either drinking less and trimming down, or worsening by the day. Some said that he gained more weight in Paris, and the city's poor air quality had worsened an existing asthmatic condition. Alain Ronay, who'd met Jim at UCLA's film school in 1965, recalled Morrison breathing heavily and sweating while walking up the stairs to his apartment. When Jim told Pamela that he was coughing up blood, she urged him to visit an American doctor, who wrote a prescription to alleviate pneumonia and respiratory issues.

None of this seemed to prevent Jim from going out, particularly to a number of clubs on the Left Bank of the River Seine, including the Rock 'n' Roll Circus, Alcazar, Le Sherwood, and La Bulle. War photographer Patrick Chauvel was a part-time bartender at the Circus—which featured trapeze artists and, occasionally, live circus animals—and had vivid memories of the era. "A lot of drugs, yes, a very free time for sex, a lot of jealousy and tension," he told *Ultimate Classic Rock*. "The nightclub scene was heavy—gangsters and very bad cops. There were a lot of fistfights inside, which wound up on the stairs and in the street. There was a gunfight outside the club. I used to carry a bayonet for protection."

By the time Morrison would arrive at the Circus, he'd usually be visibly intoxicated. "He'd be silent," Chauvel said, "then, he'd get up and say something really loud. You could see in his eyes, he had something important he wanted to say . . . but it wouldn't get past his mouth. It went through his eyes for a moment. . . . He was not in a good place."

One night, bouncers physically removed Morrison from the Circus. He and another patron, Gilles Yepremian, got into a taxi, but Jim rolled down the window and started hurling obscenities at nearby police. Yepremian ended up bringing Morrison to a friend's apartment to sleep it off. The next day, Jim took both men to a bar, where he consumed an entire bottle of Chivas Regal, among other drinks, and insulted the people at nearby tables. "When he was sober, he looked just like an American student on holiday," Yepremian told *Ultimate Classic Rock*. "Very quiet and shy. Once he became drunk, he was a madman."

For a reprieve, Jim and Pam took off for Andorra, Spain, and Morocco, where he shot some Super 8 movies and apparently managed to relax. But when the two returned to Paris, they instantly fell into their destructive habits.

On July 2, 1971, Morrison and Ronay spent several hours perusing shops and trying a restaurant specializing in food from the country's Alsace region. Before Ronay parted ways with the singer, he recommended that Jim and Pam see the movie *Pursued*, a Western starring Robert Mitchum. By one account, the couple followed the advice; by another, Morrison went to the movies alone. Pam would later say that she and Jim were home by 1 a.m., and watched home movies from their trip. Jim also sat at his desk, she said, sipping whiskey and writing in his journal.

"Regret for wasted nights & wasted years," he inscribed. "I pissed it all away."

It could have been taken as a sign that the end was near, if Jim hadn't always been writing—and saying—grim things. Pamela maintained that the night was uneventful, culminating with the two drifting off to sleep while listening to music.

Jim woke up coughing an hour or so later, Pam said, and threw up some blood. But the episode apparently passed. Pam suggested calling a doctor, she recalled, but Jim said that he felt better and asked her to run a bath for him. As he relaxed in the tub, she said that she went back to bed and quickly fell asleep.

It was just after 6 a.m., she claimed, when she noticed that Jim had never returned to bed. She called his name but received no reply. Entering the bathroom, she said, she saw Jim submerged in the water, his lips curled up into a smile. "He had blood in his nostrils," she'd tell police. "I tried to pull him out of the bath, but it was impossible for me."

At around 8 a.m., a hysterical Pamela phoned Ronay and film director Agnès Varda, begging them to get to the apartment right away. Agnès alerted the fire department, which had a unit of paramedics. Emergency medical technicians carried Jim from the bath to the bed and attempted to do cardiac massage, to no avail. The Varda family doctor, Max Vasille, also arrived. Allegedly, he expressed surprise that the victim was only twenty-seven years old. By Vasille's estimation, Jim appeared a good three decades older.

Yet the doctor wanted to avoid controversy—especially since his name was now linked to the death—hence his official conclusion that Jim had died of "natural causes," given the stomach ulcer and asthma attacks that had been plaguing the singer since his arrival in Paris.

Had police bothered to investigate further, they might have realized that Pamela's version of events changed several times. In 1991, Ronay and Varda said that Pam told them that she and Jim had done heroin that night, sniffing lines off his credit card. Doors manager Danny Sugerman claimed that Pamela had told him that Jim succumbed to a heroin overdose after snorting what he thought was cocaine. Since the heroin circulating on the French underground scene was said to be 86 percent pure, it's easy to deduce that Jim—who may not have dabbled in Pam's preferred pastime until they set up housekeeping in Europe—had yet to build up the tolerance needed to sustain the narcotic's potency.

Overcome by grief and guilt, Pamela allegedly blurted out that she'd "killed" her lover. Still, some absolve Pam of any blame, insisting that Jim wasn't even with his common-law wife when he consumed the fatal dose.

Sam Bernett, who'd go on to author a French-language book about Morrison's death and become a vice president of Disneyland

Paris, among other achievements, was managing the Rock 'n' Roll Circus when he said he saw Morrison after midnight July 3, 1971, ordering beer and vodka at the bar. "He'd come in to pick up heroin for Pam," Bernett told the *Daily Mail* in 2007. "He was always collecting drugs for her, and the club was full of dealers."

Eventually, Bernett said, Jim made a transaction with two men working for Count de Breteuil, and disappeared into the bathroom around 2 a.m. "Then, about half an hour later, a cloakroom attendant came up to me and told me someone was locked in one of the cubicles and wasn't coming out. It was then that I got a bouncer to smash the door down."

As he stood a few feet back, Bernett said that he saw Morrison—in a US Army jacket and cowboy boots—slumped over the toilet, head down and arms dangling. "We were certain he'd been snorting heroin because there was foam coming out of his lips, as well as blood. He was scared of needles, so never injected drugs. He just snorted them."

A doctor who frequented the club was summoned, and pushed back Jim's eyelids, checked his mouth, and listened to his chest for signs of a heartbeat. Pretty quickly, the doctor concluded that the rock star had died. But when the dealers materialized a few moments later, Bernett said, they argued that he'd merely fainted, and scooped up the singer and began to transport him down a staircase and onto a side street.

"I helped carry him in a blanket," bartender Chauvel told *Ultimate Classic Rock*. "I can't say 100 percent that he was dead, but he wasn't moving. . . . He was then put into the backseat of a Mercedes. . . . They took him home, is what they told me."

The staff was warned, Chauvel said, not to alert the police, the media, or anyone associated with the singer.

According to Bernett, the dealers carted Jim up to his apartment and placed him in the tub, hoping that the water would revive him.

The story sounds plausible, and may have actually occurred. However, some theorize that the Rock 'n' Roll Circus incident took place on another night, and that the resuscitation was successful. Regardless, the narrative goes, Morrison was on a downward spiral, and lost his life several days later.

Either way, in her autobiography, Marianne Faithfull wrote about Breteuil storming into their hotel room at 6 a.m. on the morning of July 3, "scared for his life" and demanding that she pack quickly. "Breteuil was Pam's dealer and had supplied the heroin" that killed Jim, Bernett said.

After disposing of his drugs, Breteuil whisked Faithfull to Tangier, she said, to ride out the incident. Within a year, he'd suffer a fatal OD, as well.

While Jim's body was wrapped in plastic and preserved in dry ice in the apartment, Pamela and Alain Ronay picked out the least-expensive coffin available—a casket worth about seventy-five American dollars. For three days, the corpse remained at 17, rue Beautreillis. Anyone who called was told that the singer was resting.

Even after the burial, the press was reporting that Morrison was battling fatigue and being treated in "a hospital or sanitarium." One tabloid included a recent photo, creating the illusion that Jim was still walking the earth. The death certificate itself was misleading, using Jim's middle name, Douglas, with the word *James* added later by someone with different handwriting.

On the Paris underground, though, rumors were rife. Morrison had been killed in a clash with Breteuil and his criminal associates, a Marseille hit man and the Corsican Mafia. Jim had sustained two bullet wounds to the head. He'd committed suicide. In its campaign to eradicate counterculture icons, the CIA had tracked Jim to Europe and arranged for an operative to administer a fatal dose of drugs. The night after Pam allegedly discovered him in the bath, Jim's death was announced by the disc jockey at a Paris night club. Within hours, the story was being repeated in London.

It wasn't until the next day that Doors manager Bill Siddons received a call from the London office of Elektra, the band's label, inquiring as to whether the rumors were true. It took several hours for Siddons to reach Pamela and confirm the news. Before arranging his flight to Paris, Siddons phoned the other members of the Doors.

"In one way, I wasn't surprised at all," Manzarek told *Ultimate Classic Rock*. "I thought his excesses would do him in. Of course, we were devastated. . . . It was like my brother had died."

None of the Doors were invited to the funeral. Nor was any member of the Morrison family; to avoid a conflict with Jim's parents over their preference for a specific type of ceremony, Pamela lied to the American embassy, claiming that Jim had no next of kin. But Siddons argued that the clandestineness wasn't weird at all. After witnessing the bedlam that surrounded the funerals of Joplin and Hendrix, both the manager and Pam wanted Jim to go out with dignity.

When the pair were back in the United States—six days after the singer's death—Siddons issued a succinct statement: "I have returned from Paris, where I have attended the funeral of Jim Morrison. I can say he died peacefully of natural causes."

For three months, the grave was unmarked—until it was discovered and made into a shrine.

Yet, the air of secrecy—coupled with the fact that no member of the Doors had actually seen Jim dead—led to the legends that Morrison was still alive. During the band's subsequent shows, Manzarek would periodically exploit these myths, announcing that the singer was somewhere in the venue and might take the stage at any moment.

"We don't know what happened to Jim in Paris," Manzarek wrote in his autobiography, *Light My Fire: My Life with the Doors*. "To be honest, I don't think we're ever going to know. Rumors, innuendos, self-serving lies, psychic projections to justify inner needs and maladies, and just plain goofiness cloud the truth."

6

IT'S LIKE THAT

THE MURDER OF JAM MASTER JAY

The neighborhood where Jam Master Jay lost his life bustles with excitement and a hint of danger. Jamaica, Queens, is a starting point for many, a dead end for others. Outside the subdivided private homes off Merrick Boulevard, tangles of cables crisscross through alleys, and aging satellite dishes teeter on worn shingles. A sign outside a doctor's office advertises a "vampire face-lift," offering services in Hindi, Urdu, Punjabi, Bengali, Spanish, and Russian. Across from the Islamic Circle of North America's Al-Markaz mosque, two signs are posted in the lobby window of a redbrick apartment building: "No Soliciting, Loitering, Smoking. Drug-Free Zone" and "No Piggybacking. Letting someone in the door behind you is against the rules." Then, just past the expansive concrete and marble Queens Public Library and the bus station, stands a series of two-story businesses—a storefront dentist, for example, topped by a print shop. And there, above the Sophisticated Beauties salon, is the studio where the hip-hop pioneer was gunned down by someone he almost certainly knew.

Like almost everyone else in this part of New York's largest borough, the killer was probably a fan.

When I asked a kid wearing a pair of green headphones if the studio upstairs was still operational, he evaded the question, insisting that he couldn't "be snitchin'." An older guy leaving the building was more cooperative, sending a quick text before a window popped open, and a smiling man with round, black spectacles waved me up.

I was buzzed in, the way Jay's killer was on October 30, 2002.

A number of studios occupied the space, adorned with paintings and posters of Run-DMC. As I navigated past a labyrinth of sound booths, mixing rooms, and hangout areas, work crews banged hammers and sawed wood. Alix Dontfraid, the owner of Signature Soundz, estimated that eight singers, ten songwriters, and five engineers were on the premises, along with poets and dancers. Some gathered around a fish tank watching a ravenous tiger oscar hold a small, struggling goldfish in its mouth before swallowing it.

Over the years, several guests have claimed to have heard footsteps and seen doors opening and closing, signs, they concluded, that Jam Master Jay was still around.

"This is where his spirit is," Dontfraid noted. "We feel his creativity all the time, and we're taking that energy and running with it. There's a lot more that happened here than him dying."

Jason Mizell grew up just about three miles away, in the Hollis neighborhood that figures so prominently in Run-DMC folklore (*"It's Christmas time in Hollis, Queens,"* goes one tune. *"Mom's cooking chicken and collard greens."*). Among other notables from this largely African American pocket of the city, which includes Jamaica, Queens Village, and St. Albans: A Tribe Called Quest, LL Cool J, Ja Rule, and 50 Cent and his G-Unit.

But Run-DMC—the group Chuck D of Public Enemy called "the Beatles of hip-hop"—came first.

Jay was not so much a DJ as a turntablist, treating his disc spinner like a musical instrument. Like the lead guitarist or drummer in a traditional rock band, Jay elevated his front man, using smooth, percussive scratches. With partners Joseph "Run" Simmons and Darryl "DMC" McDaniels, Jay was responsible for hip-hop's first gold album, *Run-DMC*, and platinum LP, *King of Rock*. Run-DMC was the first hip-hop group to be nominated for a Grammy and appear on the cover of *Rolling Stone*. They also managed to transcend the genre and draw in white audiences, particularly after the group and Aerosmith literally broke down barriers in their 1986 video for "Walk This Way."

"Back then, technology didn't interfere with the showmanship," observed Alix. "But what Jay did wasn't *just* showmanship. It was personal. The way he mixed a record, that was a performance."

Like Elvis in Memphis or the Beatles in Liverpool, Run-DMC is part of the folk culture of the area. On a brick wall behind a deli on 205th Street and Hollis Avenue is a tasteful mural, describing Jay as "the Best DJ in the US of A." Since 2009, the road has also been known as "Run-DMC JMJ Way." By the time it was given that name, Jay had been dead seven years. Yet—despite the alleged presence of five witnesses on the night of the murder—the case remained unsolved.

"In the minority community—and I can say this because I'm black—people don't talk unless they *have* to talk," Derrick Parker, told me. Parker is the former NYPD detective responsible for an intelligence unit that studied the infiltration of hip-hop by criminal elements, and author of the book *Notorious C.O.P.* "And the NYPD messed up the case. It was a bundle of errors."

Despite the exalted status he enjoyed with rappers more predisposed to idealize the gangsta life, Jason Mizell was anything but a thug. The themes of Run-DMC songs were generally positive, with the same types of messages that might be delivered in a high school civics class: stay smart, keep clean, treat yourself and those around you with dignity. A thirty-seven-year-old family man, Jay had been raised to rely on his abundant skills, and was never known to resort to violence. His criminal record was impeccable, even though, as a teenager, he had occasionally associated with kids who harbored less savory impulses.

Just across Hillside Avenue from Jamaica sits the upscale Jamaica Estates neighborhood, where Donald Trump grew up, and Eddie Murphy's fancy girlfriend was supposed to live in the movie *Coming to America*. From time to time, guys from Hollis would wander past the well-trimmed lawns and mini-mansions, breaking into a

Tudor or Cape Cod–style house. Jay had strict parents, so he tended to avoid these excursions. When he did finally accompany his friends, the news worked its way back to his family via the neighborhood grapevine. As Jay's mother cried and his father issued warnings, the future rap star decided to pursue more productive enterprises.

Jason was five, and the youngest of three children, when he started playing drums and singing in the young-adult choir at Brooklyn's Universal Baptist Church. He was ten when the family relocated to 203rd Street in Hollis. By the time he was in Andrew Jackson High School, he'd taken up the tuba, trombone, bass, and keyboards.

More than anything else, Jason wanted to be part of a band. He played with a few local units while cultivating his abilities as a DJ, practicing with headphones at night when his parents thought that he was asleep. By 1979, he was confident enough to begin performing publicly. As DJ Jazzy Jase, he'd set up his decks in parks and playgrounds, sometimes drawing hundreds of listeners, including Simmons and McDaniels. When Run-DMC finally formed, they had an advantage other Queens crews lacked: Run's brother, future mogul Russell Simmons, who began guiding the trio toward greatness.

With Russell Simmons's help, the group signed with Profile Records in 1982, selling 250,000 copies of "It's Like That," the small label's biggest single.

In the studio, the three managed to replicate the excitement people experienced when they heard the group perform in the park. To Jay, the record player was just one of the many musical instruments he'd conquered, but now, his cutting and scratching was responsible for a sound no one had really heard before. Chuck D of Public Enemy would later equate Jay's timing behind the turntable with James Brown's ability to suddenly stop, let the audience catch its breath, and start up at an even more frenzied pace.

Run-DMC was also a streamlined operation: one DJ and two vocalists. Rap was such an unknown commodity at the time that when the three would arrive at a venue, promoters regularly asked, "Where's your band?"

Invariably, Run and DMC pointed to Jay. "That's our band," they'd say in unison.

While other black music personalities of the day adorned themselves in brightly colored leather, Run-DMC's look was stark and urban, dark jackets and pullovers, supplemented with gold chains and laceless, shell-toed Adidas. During one Madison Square Garden concert, the legend goes, Run asked the crowd in to hold up their sneakers. Reportedly, an Adidas representative in the audience was paying close attention, and Run-DMC was soon the first hip-hop act to sign a lucrative endorsement deal.

In total, Run-DMC released seven studio albums, with Jay periodically playing drums, keyboards and bass in addition to the turntable. In 1989, he started his own label, Jam Master Jay Records, which would be followed by a fashion line in the early part of the next decade. Along the way, the group gained a reputation for helping aspiring performers like the Beastie Boys and Public Enemy.

"If Jam Master Jay and Run-DMC hadn't looked out for us way back when," Beastie Boy Adam "Ad-Rock" Horovitz told *Rolling Stone* shortly after the DJ's death, "I don't know where we'd be now."

South Jamaica product 50 Cent said Jay taught him how to "write and make rap records." Fitty signed with Jay's label in 1996. Three years before his murder, Jay helped arrange a deal between the budding superstar and Columbia Records.

On a superficial level, Jay appeared to be aging gracefully. He stayed in Hollis and looked after friends outside the music industry, paying bills when necessary. He encouraged his kids to play musical instruments, and taught them the art and philosophy of DJing. In the Hollis playground where he once performed, visitors grew accustomed to seeing the rap star playing chess with elementary school children.

In 2002, he opened the Scratch DJ Academy in Manhattan for aspiring turntablists and producers. Ten years later, there would be sister schools in Miami and Los Angeles, and a student body numbering fifty thousand annually.

Fans who ran into Jay came away telling stories about his soft-spoken graciousness and humility. "No one suspected Jay had problems with anybody," Parker said. "But Jay lived a different life."

Part of the problem was his spending. He owned a Lincoln Continental, a Toyota Land Cruiser, a Mercedes, a Jeep Wrangler, and a Lincoln Navigator, and purchased expensive cars for friends and relatives. Despite outward appearances, Jay was struggling. The IRS was demanding $500,000 in back taxes. The situation was so dire that he was forced to pawn his extensive jewelry collection, while his wife, Terri, took a job at Banana Republic because the family needed the paycheck.

Although Jay had no taste for hard drugs, he'd encountered enough dealers to know that they seemed able to come up with cash quickly. "What people don't realize is that Jay traveled all over the country and he knew people everywhere," Parker said. "And that includes drug dealers. So when he had money problems, those were the people he turned to."

It wasn't Jay's nature to peddle narcotics himself. But because of his wide network of connections, he was willing to act as a middleman, receiving a share of the profits. But just because Jay was well-liked didn't mean that some of his business associates were above swindling him. Reportedly, when he came home from a Milwaukee expedition without the funds he'd promised, he angered the wrong people.

"These guys thought that, because he was a rapper, he had money," Parker said. "So when he didn't pay what he owed, they thought he was ripping them off."

And the penalties were going to be harsh, he was warned. Parker claimed that Jay received a series of disturbing phone calls. He couldn't identify the caller, but understood the message.

"I'm gonna shoot you."

The year before the murder had been a fruitful one for Run-DMC. After an eight-year sabbatical, they had continued merging rock and hip-hop by including guest vocalists Kid Rock, Third Eye Blind's Stephan Jenkins, and Limp Bizkit's Fred Durst on the album *Crown Royal.* In early 2002, the group toured with Aerosmith and Kid Rock. Jay was scheduled to perform on Halloween in Philadelphia. The evening before, he packed some equipment and stopped to eat before heading to his 24/7 Studio.

A cold rain was falling on Merrick Boulevard as Jay parked his car and made his way up the stairs to the small lounge area, where he was eventually joined by old friend and business partner Randy Allen. Each had a personal stake in their ongoing project, a duo called Rusty Waters, slated to release their debut album on Virgin within days. The group featured a kid named Rodney Jones—aka Boe Skagz—who happened to be a nephew to both Jay and Randy. To further enhance the feeling of family in the studio, the facility's bookkeeper and business assistant was Randy's sister Lydia High.

A promotional tour had been scheduled to coincide with the release of the Rusty Waters album, so Randy dispatched Boe to a nearby barbershop to get groomed. But an associate of Randy's called Mike B. was hanging out in the room, along with Jay's friend Uriel "Tony" Rincon, who'd recently fallen on hard times and had been granted permission to crash at the studio. As Jay discussed his upcoming itinerary with Lydia, he and Tony sat on the sofa and played *Madden NFL* on Xbox on the wide-screen TV. All in all, it was a fairly typical night at 24/7, but for the presence of one item: a gun that Jay had taken to carrying because of the threats on his life. The pistol made Lydia uneasy, and she asked Jay to put it away. He complied, then stepped into another room with Randy to listen to demo tapes.

It was about 7:30 p.m., and Jay had been in the studio about an hour and a half when the bell rang. Lydia looked at the security monitor, apparently recognized whoever was at the bottom of the stairs, and pressed the buzzer. The monitor was situated next to the video game machine, and Jay likely glanced at the face as well, but displayed little reaction. Tony claimed that his cell phone rang at this point, and he looked down to retrieve it from the floor, hearing the sound of footsteps advancing toward the room. Depending upon who told the story, either one or two men entered the studio. Tony maintained that he was too distracted to pay attention, but assumed that Jay was familiar with whomever was dropping in.

"Had there been immediate animosity or if there was a problem . . . his gun was right there," Tony told *MTV News*. "He would've been blazing."

Randy would tell the New York *Daily News* that Lydia spotted a neck tattoo on one guest, a man in a black sweat suit, who stepped forward and greeted Jay with a hug.

Those who say that two men arrived that night claim that one hung back while the other wielded a .40-caliber pistol and demanded that Lydia look at the ground.

"Oh, shit," Jay yelled to his friends, as the weapon was pointed at his head. "Grab the gun."

Before anyone could intervene, Jay's assailant fired the pistol. Jay fell to the ground, a bullet having passed behind his left ear, leaving both an entry and exit wound. Because of the proximity of the weapon to Jay's skull, the rapper's shirt was both stained with blood and burned with gunpowder.

Fans would later dwell on the fact that the DJ died in his celebrated Adidas.

As he turned to leave, the assailant fell over a bowed Tony. A second bullet was discharged, ricocheting and striking Tony in the leg.

Producing another weapon, a .357 magnum, Randy is said to have chased the intruders out of the building. Somewhere along the way, he fired. But he supposedly lost the pair in a parking lot, leaving the gun behind.

The murder weapon was never found.

Later, when the case remained unsolved and every witness was viewed as a potential suspect, some speculated that the pursuit was a ruse designed to obscure Randy's alleged involvement in the crime. Gossip about an insurance policy leaving Jay's assets to Randy abounded. Investigators looked into the theory and determined that it was groundless.

"You can't believe everything you read," he told *MTV News*. "That's a cruel thing to do to Jam Master Jay."

As in so many cases involving the hip-hop community, police did nothing to endear themselves to witnesses. Instead of being treated with sensitivity, a traumatized Lydia High was handcuffed and badgered by detectives who asserted that she wasn't providing enough detail. Given this auspicious beginning, the inquiry was destined for failure.

When news of the shooting broke, fans materialized outside the studio, leaving behind flowers, notes, candles, and an Adidas sneaker with the slogan "RIP JMJ" written in marker. They were joined by some of Jay's hip-hop associates, including DMJ and Chuck D. Industry powerhouse Lyor Cohen, who had started his music career as Run-DMC's road manager twenty years earlier, lamented to the *Daily News*, "I'm trying to tell myself this isn't true." Within a week, celebrities like P. Diddy, Doug E. Fresh, Foxy Brown, and Busta Rhymes would offer their public support to Jay's family. But, according to Joseph "Run" Simmons, Run-DMC was disbanding. "We can't perform anymore," he said at a press conference. "I can't find a way to do it without three members."

Because of Jay's ties to 50 Cent, who'd survived his own shooting in 2000, many hypothesized that the emerging superstar was somehow linked to the murder. While others lauded Jay for helping Fitty broker his Columbia deal, the future Grammy winner complained that he'd been hustled by the elder statesman. "It was for $250,000," he told *AllHipHop*. "I got $65,000 in advance. Of that, $50,000 went to Jay and $10,000 went to the lawyers who negotiated the deal. I was left with $5,000. I was still selling crack."

Others said that Jay had been shot to send a message to his former protégé, whose battle rhymes had infuriated fellow rappers and their underworld associates. Convicted drug kingpin Kenneth "Supreme" McGriff, an associate of Murder Inc. label heads Irv and Chris Gotti, was alleged to be particularly angry over references to him in the song "Ghetto Qu'ran" (another unfounded rumor had McGriff engaged in an affair with Jay's wife). A 50 Cent show scheduled for the night after the murder in Manhattan was abruptly canceled after police cited a "credible threat" they'd uncovered. But the rapper's manager, Chris Lighty, dispelled the notion that the warning had anything to do with Jay. "There's a threat against everyone in this business every day," he told Fox News.

Indeed, over the following weekend, Kenneth Walker, a hip-hop promoter with a criminal record, would be gunned down just north of the city, in White Plains.

Jay's funeral, at the Greater Allen A.M.E. Cathedral on Merrick Boulevard, was an emotional affair, with friends and fans wearing his signature black bowler hat and white Adidas. "Jason helped build hip-hop," Run Simmons said during his eulogy, with stars like Queen Latifah, Grandmaster Flash, and LL Cool J seated alongside Jay's wife and children Jason Jr., TJ, and Tyra, "and his job is finished."

Randy Allen arrived with a bodyguard, but left early, telling a friend, "I can hardly breathe." Some investigators later theorized that the reason for Randy's distress was the presence of Jay's killer, boldly circulating throughout the church.

Just as shocking, Randy's sister Lydia was pulled over by detectives from the 103rd Precinct immediately after the ceremony. Now retired, Derrick Parker said that he was riding with her in the vehicle, offering support and protection while encouraging the witness to reveal the truth. "Every detective squad has a hard charger," Parker pointed out, "a guy who goes harder on people than others. The detectives thought she was holding back, but look how they were treating her. She was ready to talk, but they were making it hard."

With so many people in the small studio space, it seemed implausible that no one would have gotten a clear look at the killer's face. And the closed-circuit cameras should have provided a chronicle of the assassination. But there was no footage of the shooting. "The cops told me . . . somebody took all the cameras and turned them offline," Jay's brother Marvin Thompson told the television show *Crime Watch Daily*, "moved them so the monitors wouldn't show nobody coming in here."

In an interview with New York's *WPIX News*, NYPD detective Vincent Santangelo said, "It's not clear if [the security system] wasn't set up for recording—or tampered with. When we went to go and take that tape and view it, it was an old tape."

This led to the assumption that somebody inside the studio set Jay up for murder—or corrupted the footage because of the fear that the killer might return to take out any witness who cooperated.

"God knows who did it," Jay's mother, Connie Mizell-Perry, told WPIX. "Some other people know because they were in on it."

Or perhaps, people in the neighborhood theorized, the police were involved—either in the crime or the cover-up. "I know who killed him because I'm on the street," one resident told *MTV News*. "If I know, then I'm pretty sure they do, too."

The November 10, 2002, edition of the *New York Post* named Jay's longtime acquaintance Ronald "Tinard" Washington as a participant, describing him as a lookout who alerted the killers that Jay had arrived at the studio, then waited outside while the murder took place.

At one point, Lydia mentioned Tinard as well, telling authorities that he was the man who'd told her to put her head down before someone else fired the fatal bullet.

Tinard had been one of the kids in Hollis who went on burglary sprees in Jamaica Estates. While he and Jay remained friendly over the years, Tinard never left the criminal life, accumulating convictions—and prison time—for assault, drugs, and armed robberies. He was also suspected of participating in a car chase with Tupac Shakur associate Randy Walker in 1995, firing out the window and killing him. In 2007, Tinard denied involvement in the murders of Jay and Walker, contending that hostile detectives locked in on him and attempted to elicit confessions for both crimes.

Lydia would change her story several times, gradually disassociating herself from the investigation. "I knew Lydia knew," Parker said. "The problem was that she was afraid. What was the NYPD going to do to protect her? She wanted to move before she would talk. And she wanted maybe $15,000 for moving expenses. And the DA wouldn't do it. He wanted to have more. Jay was a big name, and the DA wanted a sure-win case."

Even if Lydia had cooperated, Parker said, there was a great deal authorities were doing to sabotage the probe. "In one case, the police couldn't find fillers [extra bodies] for a lineup. How can you not find a couple of guys to just stand there in a lineup? It was just embarrassing."

As of 2017, the murder of Jam Master Jay was still classified as a cold case—one of approximately fifty unsolved crimes in the United States involving rap music personalities, according to Parker's estimates. "The feds *should* take this case," the former detective said. "But they won't take it because it's so old."

In 2012, the surviving members of Run-DMC reassessed their decision to end the group. A reunion tour was organized, featuring Jason "Jam Master J Son" Mizell Jr. and his brother TJ "Dasmatic" Mizell. "They gave us a call like, 'You ready?'" Jason told *Rolling Stone.* "'You're up to bat now.'"

The DJ lessons that Jay had passed down to his offspring had not been wasted. Subsequent reunion tours exhilarated fans, due both to turntable timing and the sight of the Mizell brothers onstage with Run and DMC.

Nonetheless, in Jam Master Jay's old office, Von Seymour, aka VonSey, artist, producer, and owner of a company called Track House Recording, continues to despair over the absence of justice: "There's a bunch of anger over these pointless deaths, and they blame it on hip-hop. When a rapper gets killed, you can't get booked in the clubs. So what do kids do? They go out in the street and get into it with other kids."

Still, the vitality in the studio space was reminiscent of that which characterized Run-DMC's early recordings. And, like the legendary group, the place where Jay gave his life transcended cultural barriers. Although the majority of the people laboring in the studio were African American, guests included Hispanics, Asians, and a number of white Europeans who'd traveled to Queens specifically to follow in Jam Master Jay's footsteps.

"I can feel the creative energy," said Bret Beats, a producer from Athens crashing at Alix's home. "And the studio's in the heart of Queens, where so many people from so many places made music for the world."

When VonSey moved into the building, he decided to do some demolition work to make his space more accommodating to artists. "I was literally picking up pieces of carpet with Jay's blood on it," he said. "I thought about how one of the founding fathers of hip-hop passed away here, and I felt a responsibility. Hip-hop is a religion. I learned things from hip-hop my own father didn't tell me. So the message I wanted to go forth with is, 'Understand that wrong is wrong and right is right. You are what you put out.'"

7

SWEET SMELL OF DESTRUCTION
NORWAY'S BLACK-METAL DEATHS

"There is a saying," Varg Vikernes, the most infamous black-metal performer of all time, wrote on his blog in 2004: "'Show me your friends, and I can tell you who you are.' If that is the case, I most certainly and obviously was a complete idiot."

At first glance, the phrase implies that Vikernes regretted his standing in a scene so closely associated with Satanism, Nazism, and bloodletting. The reality is that "the Count"—as he labeled himself—wasn't particularly embarrassed by the way even followers of other metal genres were repulsed by the hateful rhetoric that accompanied the shrieking vocals, distorted guitar sounds, and irregular song structures on the albums that largely came out of Scandinavia in the 1990s. Nor did he find it silly or contrived that musicians affected corpse-like appearances, drenching themselves with animal blood and impaling the heads of pigs and sheep onstage. The whole point was to present as something less than human, and black-metal performers were vigilant about emphasizing that those who wanted in on the action would have to torch their bridges to the outside world.

Each band had a story more gruesome than the one that came before. According to myth, Nattramn of the Swedish group Silencer sliced off his hands while recording, then sewed severed pig's feet onto the stubs. He was also alleged to have planted an axe into the head of a five-year-old.

But Vikernes didn't need to live off half-truths or fiction. He despised his enemies and mistreated his friends—particularly one friend, Øystein Aarseth (better known by the pseudonym Euronymous), cofounder of the Norwegian black-metal group Mayhem. To outsiders, the two appeared to be tight. They recorded together, and Vikernes's band, Burzum, released its debut album on the label Euronymous owned. But people who live so far outside the margins generally don't partner well in business. Malicious rumors were started and threats made. "I have no problem with killing someone in cold blood," Euronymous boasted to a Finnish publication—appropriately called *Kill Yourself!!! Magazine*—in 1993. "Especially if I can get away with it. There are other people who are able to kill, too. It has already happened, but I'm not going to say more about that for obvious reasons."

One week after the interview, it was Euronymous who was murdered, discovered on the stairs outside his Oslo apartment with twenty-three knife wounds—two to the head, five to the neck, and sixteen to the back. At first, people on the scene suspected black-metal rivals from Sweden. But within two weeks, Vikernes was arrested for the slaying.

He had done it, he admitted, and he wasn't ashamed either. Still, he wanted people to understand, there was a lot to the story.

Before he adopted the stage name Count Grishnackh, Vikernes seemed destined for an average life in Norway's western coastal city of Bergen. He described his father as an electronic engineer and his mother as an oil company employee; at one point, the family lived in Iraq during the Saddam Hussein regime. While his father later became alarmed when he found a Nazi flag among Varg's possessions, Vikernes claimed that his parents also complained about immigrants breaking up the homogeneity of their town, and would not have approved of him marrying outside his race. The fixation with racial purity was apparently passed down. As he grew, Vikernes developed an admiration for Vidkun Quisling, Norway's German-installed president during World War II, but stopped short of calling himself a Nazi. Nonetheless, Vikernes became convinced that Jews had had a negative influence on

European society, popularizing a number of concepts he found reprehensible, including socialism, capitalism, urbanization, globalization, and even Christianity. In Vikernes's view, Norway was better off embracing the pagan philosophies that predated the Christian era.

By some accounts, Vikernes was a skinhead at one stage: he denied this allegation, explaining that he simply had short hair, liked weapons, and preferred German culture to that of the detestable Yanks and Brits.

After spending much of his childhood listening to classical music, he became enamored with Iron Maiden in 1985 at age twelve, feeling empowered by heavy metal's hard-driving rhythms. By fourteen, he was playing guitar; soon he was dabbling in other instruments, as he searched for a more vigorous sound. He was good enough to begin playing with local black-metal band Old Funeral, performing on an old Westone guitar—along with an amplifier rigged to his older brother's stereo—borrowed drum sets, and an inexpensive used bass. In 1991, at age seventeen, he started his own group, Burzum.

Burzum was one of the more prominent bands associated with black metal's second wave in the early '90s, along with Euronymous's group, Mayhem, as well as Immortal, Darkthrone, Gorgoroth, and Emperor in Norway, and Swedish units like Dark Funeral, Marduk, and Nifelheim.

With his fixation on Scandinavia's pagan era, Vikernes's songs included lyrics written in Old Norse. There was also an admiration for J. R. R. Tolkien's depictions of Middle Earth in *The Lord of the Rings*. The word *Burzum*, or "darkness," was inscribed on one of the fictional rings, while the name Grishnackh—as in Count Grishnackh—came from the book *The Two Towers*.

Because of the inspirations from Norse, Germanic, and Finnish mythology, among other sources, the *Lord of the Rings* books were compatible with black metal. Originally more thrash metal than it later became, black metal was largely activated by the English group Venom's second album, *Black Metal*, in 1982. Among the other groups in this first wave of black metal: Venom, Bathory, Hellhammer, and Mercyful Fate. From the beginning, Satanism and the dismantling of Christianity were consistent themes—Mercyful Fate singer King Diamond was a proud member of the Church of Satan—along with a reverence, in Scandinavia, at least, for the distant, Viking past. Unlike mainstream metal musicians, black-metal guitarists avoided solos, and drummers scorned efforts to adhere to technique. Earlier practitioners never aspired to commercial success. If you didn't automatically understand the spirit behind the noise emanating from the amps, the musicians had no desire to appeal to you.

If there was a black-metal impresario in Norway, it was Eurony-mous, whose Oslo shop Helvete (Hell) became the place to buy records, start bands, and rail against compromise. Downstairs was the headquarters of his independent label, Deathlike Silence Pro-ductions. During one of their early recordings together, Vikernes could be heard singing on what he described as the worst micro-phone he could find, while Euronymous pounded his fists on a large gong.

Arguably, Euronymous was black metal's most outspoken champion of Satanism. "I believe in a horned devil," he told *Kill Yourself!!!*, "a personified Satan. In my opinion, all the other forms of Satanism are bullshit."

His bandmates seemingly shared this hard-core attitude. Mayhem vocalist Per Yngve Ohlin used the pseudonym "Dead," and seemed dedicated to functioning as though his life had already ended. Before concerts, he reportedly buried his clothes in the ground in pursuit of a rotten "death scent." During one tour, he found a dead crow and stashed it in a plastic bag, sniffing it in order to perform with "the stench of death" in his nostrils. One fellow musician asserted that Dead even asked to be buried alive before shows, hoping that he'd arise with a milky, otherworldly pallor.

On April 8, 1991, Dead's fellow Mayhem members returned to the house they shared to find a note with the inscription "Excuse the blood." Venturing further into the residence, they discovered Dead with slit wrists and a shotgun wound to the head. Apparently he'd grown weary of the scene, describing it as inauthentic and commercialized, and this was a way to insert some purity into the genre. "Dead wanted to make evil music for evil people," Euronymous said. "But the only people he saw were walking around in jogging suits, caps and sneakers, and being into peace and love. He hated them so much, and no longer saw any reason to waste his time on them."

Later, two other Norwegian black-metal musicians would take their own lives: drummer Erik "Grim" Brødreskift in 1999, and bassist, keyboardist, and vocalist Espen "Storm" Andersen in 2001.

A photo of Dead's corpse would appear on the cover of Mayhem's bootleg album *Dawn of the Black Hearts*. Not one to miss a promotional opportunity, Euronymous had been fastidious about taking several pictures of the body with a disposable camera before notifying the police. He also spread rumors that he'd made a stew with portions of Dead's brain, and doled out necklaces made from pieces of the singer's skull to musicians whose dedication to the cause he deemed credible.

It's uncertain whether Vikernes was among those be honored with one of the trinkets. Either way, Euronymous held him in high regard. After Dead's suicide, Vikernes began playing with Mayhem.

It was certainly a strange time to be involved with the outlaw art form, and musicians not as possessed with the taking of blood would carry the stigma for decades. "A lot of journalists want to ask about shit that happened, that I wrote twenty years ago," Gylve "Fenriz" Nagell of the band Darkthrone, complained to *Complex* magazine in 2015. "I want to say, 'Let's see what you wrote twenty fuckin' years ago. Let's see what you wrote when you were twenty-one or eighteen. You feel confident in those things?' It's just I was stupid enough to put it out on vinyl."

But others on the scene were willing to do a lot more than simply crank out recordings. Between 1992 and 1996, more than fifty acts of arson directed at Christian churches were recorded by Norwegian authorities; Swedish black metallers began engaging in religious vandalism in 1993. In particular, the offenders focused on churches dating back to the Middle Ages, crafted from timber rather than limestone. The motive—besides attacking a structure representing the Judeo-Christian onslaught on Scandinavian culture—appeared to be revenge for the Viking burial mounds desecrated by adherents of the New Testament, starting in 793.

At the beginning, Vikernes's name was frequently linked to the church burnings. And he did nothing to dissuade this notion. A photo of the remnants of the damaged Fantoft stave church appeared on the sleeve of Burzum's *Aske* (Ashes)—album. Vikernes, Euronymous, and drummer Bård Guldvik "Faust" Eithun of the band Emperor were later accused of placing a homemade bomb on the altar of the Holmenkollen Chapel in Oslo, and detonating it with gasoline-soaked hymnals and Bibles. Vikernes and Faust were later convicted. Euronymous would have been, too, but he was already dead.

Vikernes—who'd also be sentenced for three more fires—claimed that much of his involvement in the arsons was heavily embroidered, the result of an interview he'd done with a reporter for the newspaper *Bergens Tidende* to promote Euronymous's shop, Helvete. "I exaggerated a lot," he wrote on his blog, "and when the journalist left, we . . . had a good laugh because he didn't seem to understand that I was pulling his leg. . . . Unfortunately, he went to the police the next day . . . and had me arrested."

Like Vikernes, Faust would become known for a crime far bigger than a church burning. In 1992, during a visit to Lillehammer to see relatives, he was leaving a pub when he met a man named Magne Andreassen. Andreassen was gay and, according to Faust, interested in repairing to the woods for a sexual encounter. "I agreed because, already then, I decided that I wanted to kill him,"

Faust was quoted as saying in the book *Lords of Chaos*, by Michael Moynihan and Didrik Søderlind.

Once they were alone, Faust stabbed Andreassen thirty-seven times. As the victim convulsed on the ground, the musician repeatedly kicked him in the head.

He'd later serve nine years of a fourteen-year sentence, describing the murder as "not a big deal." As with black metal, his goal had been "to get out some aggression. It's not easy to describe why it happened. It was meant to happen. And if it was this man or another man, that's not really important."

As Vikernes and Euronymous spent more time together, they found traits in one another that they started to dislike. Vikernes regarded Euronymous not as a fellow Norwegian, but as a Lap, as evidenced by the black-metal entrepreneur's short stature, fine, straight hair, and vaguely Asiatic facial features. When police began investigating the church burnings after the *Bergens Tidende* article, Vikernes said, Euronymous—on the advice of his parents—closed down Helvete. "So the 'evil' black-metal hero did what his mother and father told him to?" Vikernes wrote. "The customers came in droves, but to a closed shop! How stupid is that?!"

And while the Count decried the idea of capitalism, Euronymous apparently didn't. According to Vikernes, he loaned Euronymous the money to manufacture Burzum's record for Deathlike Silence Productions. When the albums sold out, Varg continued, Euronymous paid his private bills rather than reimburse his fellow musician.

"This is probably the reason why some people think I killed him," Vikernes said, "but certainly, I wouldn't have gotten my money back by killing him. Breaking his legs probably would have worked, but not killing him."

In fact, Vikernes argued that the only reason he committed homicide was that Euronymous planned to kill *him* first. The plan allegedly involved luring Vikernes to a location to discuss a new contract, zapping him with a stun gun, binding and confining him in the trunk of a car, and driving out to the country. There, Vikernes said fellow metallers had informed him, Euronymous intended to tie Varg to a tree and torture him to death—while capturing the entire incident on video.

Instead, Vikernes and recent Mayhem member Snorre "Blackthorn" Ruch—whose guitar playing, along with that of Euronymous, largely helped define the black-metal sound during the second wave—decided to drive to Oslo, where Varg could head off the plot. According to the Count, Snorre had no particular stake in the conflict. He considered both men his friends and only wanted to come along to play some new guitar riffs for Euronymous.

The pair arrived at Euronymous's building on Oslo's Tøyengata—or Tøyen Street—sometime between 3 and 4 a.m. on August 10, 1993. "You might think that visiting people in the middle of the night was a bit strange," Vikernes wrote, "but it was perfectly normal to us. A lot of people in the metal scene were nocturnal creatures."

While Snorre was outside smoking a cigarette, Vikernes confronted Euronymous at the door of his apartment. When Varg took a determined step forward, he said, Euronymous kicked him in the chest. The altercation spilled into the apartment, where Vikernes maintained Euronymous ran to the kitchen and grabbed a knife.

"I figured if he's going to have a knife," Varg wrote, "I'm going to have a knife, too."

Pulling out a pocket knife, Vikernes said, he jumped in front of Euronymous, who then spun around and raced toward the bedroom. Convinced that Euronymous was going to grab the shotgun Dead had used to kill himself, Varg began slashing.

Meanwhile, Snorre had lost his way on the dark stairwell, and was using his lighter to determine which was the proper apartment. Suddenly, Euronymous burst through his door, bleeding and screaming in his underwear. As Euronymous sprinted down the stairs, banging on the walls and doorbells of his neighbors, Vikernes kept pace behind him. By his estimate, Vikernes managed to stab Euronymous another three or four times in the left shoulder.

Euronymous stumbled and fell, then gingerly rose to his feet. Turning to his former friend, Euronymous gripped his shoulder and muttered, "It's enough." A moment later, though, Varg said, Euronymous attempted to kick him another time.

"I finished him up by thrusting the knife through his skull, through his forehead, and he died instantaneously," Vikernes wrote. "The eyes turned around in his head and a moan could be heard. . . . He fell down to a sitting position, but the knife was stuck in his head, so I held him up. . . . When I jerked the knife from his skull, he fell forward and rolled down a flight of stairs like a sack of potatoes, making enough noise to wake up the whole neighborhood."

Had he allowed Euronymous to live, Varg contended, the label owner would have recovered and attempted to kill his former bandmate another time. Confident in this certainty, Vikernes said, he felt not a modicum of sorrow: "I do not see any reason to pity a person who plans to torture me to death while videotaping it for his own amusement."

But there was no time to linger outside Euronymous's door, pondering the dead man's motives. Vikernes had to leave before the police arrived. He remembered sitting in passenger seat, observing a dazed Snorre navigating the car around Oslo. The pair pulled over by a lake, where Varg threw off his bloodied clothes, then donned a pair of dirty pants crumpled up in the backseat, a sweatshirt another musician had left behind and a T-shirt from a box of merchandise. Its slogan: "Pleasure to Kill."

A friend was crashing at Vikernes's apartment, and Varg wanted him to depart in case the police showed up. The car pulled over at a phone booth, and Vikernes dispatched Snorre to make the call. The telephone was broken. As fate would have it, a group of teenagers were smashing phones in the area, and when a passing police car spotted Varg and Snorre, the officer suspected that they might be the culprits. Not wishing to be detected so close to the crime scene, Vikernes instructed Snorre to take off. The two sped away and eventually lost the cruiser.

After the long drive back to Bergen, Varg was relieved to find the apartment empty when he returned home. He fell into a deep sleep, but twenty minutes later, the doorbell rang. It was a reporter who informed him that Euronymous's body had been found in Oslo. Did Vikernes have a quote that he wanted to share? The Count claimed that he was too tired to speak. But when the story was written, the implication was that Vikernes was so distraught over the death of his "best friend" that he was unable to articulate a sentence.

Yet, he quickly topped the list detectives were compiling of potential perpetrators. As they interviewed the various Mayhem members, investigators sensed that Snorre was acting a little strange and decided to push him for more information. It took a few days before he broke down and disclosed everything. Vikernes was leaving a nightclub between 2 and 3 a.m. when police placed him under arrest.

Inside Vikernes' home, police confiscated a stockpile of explosives and ammunition, along with an SS helmet that Varg claimed one of the officers took home as a souvenir. News reports speculated that Varg was planning to blow up an anti-fascist organization called Blitz House. In 2009, he told a reporter that he had been amassing the weapons in case Norway was attacked.

Some news sources reported that the murder was the result of a struggle for leadership in black metal's Satanic wing, ignoring Vikernes's dismissal of Satanism as a reactionary form of Christianity. But the stories resonated with certain factions of the black-metal community. One by one, followers came forward, blaming Vikernes, as well as other musicians, for offenses associated with the movement. "Because of them," he wrote, "the police solved almost all the crimes committed by black metallers in Norway from 1991 to 1993."

On May 16, 1994, Vikernes was sentenced to twenty-one years in prison—the maximum in Norway—for the murder, as well as three church arsons, the attempted arson of another sanctuary, and the cache of explosives found at his home. Snorre was given eight years because of his role as an accomplice in the crime.

In an apparent show of support for the Count, two churches were torched on the day of Vikernes's sentencing.

The same month, Mayhem released its album *De Mysteriis Dom Sathanas*, featuring Euronymous on guitar and Varg on bass. This greatly upset Euronymous's family, who asked the group's drummer, Jan Axel "Hellhammer" Blomberg, to remove the bass tracks. Hellhammer refused, telling the *Guardian*, "I thought it was appropriate that the murderer and victim were on the same record. I put word out that I was re-recording the bass parts, but I never did."

Because of the back story, the album is considered one of the most substantial records in black metal. The media sensation also opened up a new market for Vikernes's band, Burzum. In fact, the story of Euronymous's death all but mainstreamed the movement. Although there were copycat arsons for more than a decade in places as far away as Manitoba—where a church was ignited on Vikernes's birthday in 2006—black metal seemed to lose its edge. Christian bands were formed, as well as those specifically decrying National Socialism. Actors portraying black-metal musicians appeared in a Norwegian commercial for laundry detergent. When Gorgoroth vocalist Kristian Eivind "Gaahl" Espedal came out of the closet, he was feted as "Homosexual of the Year" in Vikernes's hometown. In 2016, Darkthrone's Fenriz was elected councillor in his town outside Oslo; his campaign poster depicted him holding a cat, alongside the words "Please Don't Vote for Me."

In prison, Vikernes wrote several books, primarily about ancient Scandinavian mythology, and continued to record, becoming irate when fans and the media discovered secret "Satanic" messages in the music. In 2003, while on leave, he attempted to escape, stealing a car at gunpoint, and had thirteen months added to his sentence. Even so, he only served fifteen years, and was released from prison on probation in 2009.

Eventually, he relocated to France. Now married, he raised a family, continued to record music, and supported the virulently anti-immigrant National Front. Authorities watched him closely, sentencing him to six months of probation and a fine of 8,000 euros in 2014 for using his writings to incite hatred against Jews and Muslims.

But in the Middle East, Islam's sons and daughters were sparking a black-metal revival. Sporting the same white face paint as their European counterparts, these blasphemers roared about burning the Quran, waging jihad against practitioners of the faith, and even having sex with the corpse of the Prophet Muhammad.

Given the consequences of those types of sentiments in that part of the world, the words once expressed by people like Faust, Euronymous, and Varg Vikernes practically seemed soft-core.

"They would kill me," an Iraqi singer named Anahita told the *Atlantic* in 2012 when asked about the way the religious authorities in her home country would react to her music, "and kill all of my friends by cutting off our heads."

8

People Always Told Me Be Careful What You Do

The Fall of the King of Pop

The autopsy revealed a horribly disfigured man who seemed far older than his fifty years.

Michael Jackson's hips, thighs, and shoulders were speckled with needle wounds, presumably scars acquired from his dependency on painkillers. Other marks divulged an addiction to plastic surgery. The most successful entertainer of all time had been wearing wigs to disguise the light layer of peach fuzz on his head. Above his left ear was an area that was completely bald and exhibited signs of the burns he'd sustained when a fire ignited his hair during a shoot for a Pepsi commercial in 1984. Although he was five foot nine, Jackson weighed just 112 pounds, his stomach empty except for several partially dissolved tablets.

"He was skin and bone, his hair had fallen out, and he had been eating nothing but pills when he died," a source told the London *Sun*.

Evidence of the frantic attempts to revive him exposed further damage: ribs broken while emergency medical technicians administered CPR, and four fresh injection marks around his heart from apparent efforts to save his life with adrenaline injections.

Within twenty-four hours, the Los Angeles Police Department began investigating the circumstances of Michael's demise at the mansion he was renting for $100,000 a month in the city's Holmby Hills section—and the actions of Dr. Conrad Murray, the six-foot-five-inch Grenada-born physician who discovered the singer's body on June 25, 2009, and claimed to love him as a brother.

"We were family," Murray told the *Daily Mail*, contending that Jackson felt the same way. "He looked at me and said, 'You know, for the rest of your life and my life, our names will become inseparable.'"

Through a career that saw him experience the pinnacles of success and misery—sometimes simultaneously—Michael Jackson spent some forty years in the public eye. While the fans who squealed for him as children grew up, Jackson remained suspended in perpetual preadolescence, collecting a menagerie of exotic pets, addressing visitors in a shy, falsetto tone, and engaging in roller-coaster rides and sleepovers with preteens.

Le Figaro columnist Yann Moix pointed out at the time of the singer's death that Jackson seemed to live life in reverse, in the direction of his famous moonwalk.

Born in 1958 in the industrial city of Gary, Indiana, Michael was the seventh of nine children in a strict family of Jehovah's Witnesses. By age five, he was performing with brothers Marlon, Jackie, Tito, and Jermaine as the charismatic centerpiece of the Jackson 5. With his authoritarian father, Joseph—a onetime steel-worker—setting the rules at home and backstage, the group was signed by Motown in 1968 and quickly launched to stardom. Within two years, the Jackson 5—with Michael as lead vocalist and principal showman—had four number-one singles: "I Want You Back," "ABC," "The Love You Save" and "I'll Be There."

By Joseph's own admission, he regularly beat the children. He'd tell Oprah Winfrey that he didn't regret the rigorous discipline, explaining, "It kept them out of jail and kept them right."

As the most visible member of the family business, Michael could have been indulged by his father. Instead, he became a chief target of Joseph's wrath. He also felt the pressure to keep generating income for the Jacksons. In 1972, he launched a solo career, churning out three hit albums in two years: *Got to Be There*, *Ben*, and *Music & Me*. In 1978, he starred as the Scarecrow in *The Wiz*, an African American version of *The Wizard of Oz*, opposite Diana Ross as Dorothy.

The next year, at the age of twenty-one, he released what would be regarded as his first "adult" album, *Off the Wall*, which produced two number-one hits, "Don't Stop 'Til You Get Enough" and "Rock with You." On the album cover, Michael sports a tuxedo and smiles at the camera, a handsome black man with copper skin and a proud Afro.

As the era of the video pop star boomed, Michael placed himself at the forefront, appearing in a John Landis–directed, fourteen-minute horror-themed video in 1983 for the title track of *Thriller*. With seven of the album's songs—including "Billie Jean" and "Beat It"—reaching the Top 10, *Thriller* became the best-selling LP in the United States, and would earn 33x platinum—meaning that thirty-three million album-equivalent units were shipped.

The video is best remembered for Michael claiming the moon-walk—previously used by entertainers like Cab Calloway and James Brown—as his own. Director and choreographer Vincent Paterson, who portrayed a zombie in the "Thriller" video and was one of the two dancing gang members Michael separated in "Beat It," recalled watching the singer rehearse a dance sequence in front of the mirror for hours. "That's how he developed the moonwalk," Paterson told the *New York Times*, "working on it for days, if not weeks, until it was organic."

But after his hair was set afire during the 1984 Pepsi commercial, Jackson was forced to endure painful skin grafts, and his appearance changed drastically. A cleft was implanted in his chin, and cosmetic surgeries whittled down his nose. Unbeknownst to the public, he also suffered from vitiligo, a skin disease that can wipe away color. He began a regimen of applying facial creams that seemed to transform him into a white man. "He wanted porcelain, flawless skin," Dr. Murray said in the *Mail*. "Those were his words."

Whether the treatments helped him is a matter of conjecture. "One never really knew if he was sick," friend Tarak Ben Ammar told the newspaper, "because he had become surrounded by charlatan doctors who were billing him thousands of dollars' worth of drugs and vitamins."

Gone was the cute little boy who'd charmed audiences on *The Ed Sullivan Show* and *Soul Train*. Michael was an odd adult who seemed terribly lonely, awkward, and sad. As much as fans revered Jackson's music and dance skills, many accepted the tabloid characterization of the star as "Wacko Jacko."

While Michael was making the album *Bad*, his favorite pet, Bubbles the Chimp, was present for recording sessions, and shared the singer's two-bedroom hotel suite. At home, Bubbles slept in a crib in Jackson's bedroom and used the toilets. Even after Bubbles aged, became aggressive, and had to be moved out, Michael continued to visit the chimpanzee at the animal sanctuary, sometimes throwing parties with other "celebrity" animals like movie-star dogs Lassie and Benji.

Aware that any public action would generate publicity, Michael invited a photographer to snap the singer sleeping in a clear hyperbaric oxygen chamber that he allegedly utilized to decelerate the aging process. His high voice was attributed to hormone treatments that were supposed to help him maintain the vocal range of his youth.

"People underestimate Michael all the time," Quincy Jones, producer of the *Off the Wall*, *Thriller*, and *Bad* albums, told the New York *Daily News*. "He knows exactly what he wants and exactly what he's doing. And if he really wants something, he will get it."

During a series of collaborations with Paul McCartney, Michael took in the former Beatles' wisdom about acquiring copyrights. Jackson then purchased more than two hundred Lennon/McCartney compositions, outbidding a combined effort by McCartney and Yoko Ono, for a reported $47.5 million.

Michael paid another $17 million to buy a 2,600-acre ranch, 125 miles northwest of Los Angeles, branding the property Neverland—after the fictional sanctuary of Peter Pan, the boy who refused to grow up—spending an additional $35 million to construct a zoo, amusement park rides, and other attractions.

According to Michael's sister La Toya, when the star arrived at Neverland, his employees would form two rows leading up to the front door. As Jackson paraded between them, each would blurt out, "Welcome, Mr. Jackson," "Good morning, Mr. Jackson," or "Hello, Mr. Jackson."

Occasionally Michael was accompanied by an underage child: this would cause him great distress later on. In 1993, a man named Evan Chandler accused the singer of molesting his thirteen-year-old son Jordan during several overnight visits. Although Michael insisted that nothing sexual had occurred, he did admit to a fondness for sleepovers with children, emphasizing that his intentions were always motivated by friendship, not lust. Not willing to endure a taxing trial, Jackson settled for $20 million.

In 1994, Michael suddenly married Elvis Presley's daughter, Lisa Marie. Although some viewed the union as the fusing of two musical monarchies, others believed that Jackson needed a wife to "appear normal." The pair divorced less than two years later.

Almost immediately, he married again, this time to Debbie Rowe. It was an unusual pairing. Unlike Lisa Marie, Debbie was not a show-business person. Rather, she was a nurse for Michael's dermatologist, Dr. Arnold Klein. Michael wanted to have children at this point, and Debbie was willing to bear him two—Prince Michael and Paris Michael Katherine—in rapid succession before the couple separated in 1999.

Michael agreed to take sole responsibility for the children. Paris claimed that when she was young, she was unaware that she had a mother at all. As the years passed, observers noted that neither child appeared to have any black ancestry, leading to rumors that Dr. Klein was the actual father.

In 2002, Jackson became the father of another son, Blanket. Although the identity of the mother was never disclosed, Blanket had darker skin than his half-siblings, and looked as if he might have been mixed race.

But if fatherhood was supposed to distance the King of Pop from innuendo regarding his appetite for underage children, he was mistaken. In 2003, he was charged with seven counts of child abuse for allegedly getting a young cancer patient drunk at Neverland and repeatedly groping him. Facing twenty years behind bars, Jackson tried to downplay the severity of the circumstances, dancing for fans on the roof of his SUV after the arraignment and wearing a different outfit to court each day, while his legal team depicted the boy's family as "dishonest gold diggers." The strategy apparently worked. On June 13, 2005—after fourteen weeks of testimony and seven days of deliberations—the jury acquitted the singer on all fourteen counts.

Yet Jackson never really recovered from the trial. Michael never returned to Neverland, and spent much of the next several years in transit, living for extended periods in Ireland, Japan, and Dubai, and as a guest of Sheikh Abdullah—the son of King Hamad bin Isa al-Khalifa—in Bahrain. Despite his substantial net worth, Jackson had acquired enormous debt. Although the Sheikh subsidized Jackson's opulent lifestyle for a while, he eventually sued the singer for repayment. Unwilling to have any more secrets made public, Michael privately settled.

Bankruptcy for the King of Pop was a very real possibility. To avoid it, Michael reportedly relied on his partner in the Beatles catalog, Sony, for hundreds of millions of dollars in loans. But it appeared that Michael would never be able to repay the money, and there was the prevailing fear that, in the not-too-distant future, the music company would claim the entire catalog for itself.

It was under these circumstances that Jackson agreed to perform fifty comeback concerts at London's O2 Arena in 2009 and 2010.

The shows immediately sold out, and Jackson was said to be in position to earn up to $50 million.

The problem was that Michael was not physically or emotionally ready for such a grueling undertaking. However, he had few true friends who would tell him this in person. Instead, he spent much of his time with enablers who worshipped the singer so much that they were willing to accommodate every destructive demand.

According to Michael's sister Janet, several family members had attempted to stage a drug intervention in 2007, but were blocked by security. During this same period, Michael also reportedly refused to accept phone calls from his mother. The people he would talk to, however, were doctors—particularly those receptive to satisfying his vices.

Since December 2008, his dermatologist Arnold Klein had regularly administered doses of the highly addictive painkiller Demerol while Jackson was getting cosmetic fillers Botox and Restylane. "You have to understand," Dr. Klein—who passed away in 2015—told the *Daily Beast*, "Michael Jackson was incredibly needle phobic. I had to sedate him."

Yet some wondered whether the Botox and Restylane injections listed on invoices were simply camouflage for additional doses of Demerol. Dr. Murray told the *Washington Times* that Jackson was using "unheard-of high" quantities of Demerol "not for pain, but for a habit."

After Jackson's death, investigators would focus on his capacity for propofol, a powerful anesthetic intended primarily for surgical settings. Michael called the drug his "milk," based on its nickname "milk of amnesia," apparently indifferent to propofol's notorious association with cardiac arrest.

Murray told police he gave Jackson nightly doses of propofol to help him sleep, as the singer prepared for his upcoming concert series. Michael was training with Lou Ferrigno, the title character of the *Incredible Hulk* TV series, in order to give his fans the type of physical performance they expected. "He might have been a little thin because he was under a lot of stress, training for the tour," Ferrigno told ABC's *Good Morning America*. "But when I put him through the routine and everything, I mean, it was just fine. I mean, very energetic . . . I think he was going to give the greatest tour in his entire life."

According to an aide, though, Michael could no longer sing, and would have to lip-synch onstage: this task was made easier by the O2 Arena's advanced lip-synching technology. "Nobody will care, as long as he shows up and moonwalks," a source told Ian Halperin, author of *Unmasked: The Final Years of Michael Jackson*.

Early rehearsals were difficult, Halperin wrote, quoting an aide who maintained that Michael needed medical attention during one session and had to stop for the day. In her memoir *Starting Over*, La Toya recalled Paris Jackson describing her father as sad, tired, and perpetually cold.

At Jackson's request, promoters AEG Live hired Dr. Murray as the star's personal physician—in May, 2009, at a cost of $150,000 a month—for the duration of the This Is It residency. "I agreed," Murray told the *Daily Mail*, "because Michael told me I'd meet kings and queens and all sorts of people I'd never get a chance to meet."

The two had known each other since late 2006, when Murray treated Jackson and one of his children for the flu in Las Vegas. As he administered a "banana bag," a combination of saline solution and vitamins, Murray said that he learned a surprising fact about the entertainer: "Michael Jackson wanted to be a doctor, not a singer. He was intrigued with medical science."

The doctor also emphasized that Jackson "liked me because I wasn't starstruck."

Murray told detectives that Jackson was already dependent on propofol, and the physician was trying to wean him off, giving the singer a nightly intravenous drip that started at 50 milligrams, but had been reduced to 25 milligrams combined with other drugs. Allegedly, Michael turned to the physician for the most private matters. "You want to know how close we were?" Murray questioned. "I held his penis every night to fit a catheter because he was incontinent at night."

Ultimately, Murray said, his plan was to return to private practice. "But Michael didn't want me to do that," he told the *Washington Times*. "Michael wanted me to be around him forever."

Despite the chemical sustenance, there were doubts as to whether Jackson could make it through the fifty scheduled shows. Murray said that the once flawless showman complained that he didn't feel capable of performing above a level of 60 percent. As the press speculated about Jackson's health, a series of concerts was postponed. AEG emphasized that Michael was fit, and that the delays were simply based on technical adjustments to the complicated production.

Three days before his death, Jackson appeared at his dermatologist's office. In Dr. Klein's version of events, the King of Pop was in buoyant spirits, dancing for fellow patients.

On Wednesday, June 24, 2009, Michael arrived at Los Angeles's Staples Center at 6:30 p.m. He joked about having laryngitis, and finally took the stage at 9 p.m. Once the music started, Jackson came alive, awing observers with both style and energy.

When he returned to his rented mansion at 1 a.m., though, Murray said Jackson was "hysterical. He was begging me, 'Please, Dr. Conrad, I need some milk so I can sleep.' This went on for hours." Murray contended that Dr. Klein had shut off the singer's Demerol pipeline some forty-eight hours earlier, and Jackson was experiencing withdrawal. "And with withdrawal," the doctor told the *Washington Times*, "certainly it creates a state of mind and state of potential risk where you can die. You're not going to be rational, and you take matters into your own hands."

At 11:07 a.m., Murray said, after Michael had finally fallen asleep, the doctor received a phone call. Apparently, the performer had a normal heartbeat and his vital signs were good when Murray said he walked out of the bedroom thirteen minutes later. "I left the room because I didn't want to disturb him," Murray told the *Mail*. "I believe he woke up, got hold of his own stash of propofol, and injected himself. He did it too quickly and went into cardiac arrest."

When Murray returned and found Jackson unconscious, Murray said, he checked Michael's groin and carotid artery, but could not find a pulse. Later, specialists would criticize him for administering CPR on a bed, as opposed to the recommended hard surface. "I am a trained cardiac specialist," he argued. "This is what I do. The bed was hard and Michael was slim. I have big hands. I placed a hand behind him, and immediately started chest compressions."

When Michael did not respond, Murray said he tried phoning the singer's head of security. But no one answered, so the doctor ran downstairs and shouted for a bodyguard. It was only then—some thirty minutes after Jackson was discovered—that 911 was finally called.

However, Murray maintained that he was following procedure as best he could. There was no landline in the house, he said, and he could not use his cell phone to call 911 since he didn't know the precise address.

Prosecutors would allege that Murray needed time to hide drugs before emergency medical technicians arrived. When they did, authorities said, the doctor failed to acknowledge that he'd administered propofol. The anesthetic was later discovered, among other medications, in the house. Some were prescribed to Jackson, others to pseudonyms, while still others contained no labels at all.

In the bedroom, paramedics worked on Michael for forty-two minutes without success. Murray climbed into the ambulance with the singer as it sped toward Ronald Reagan UCLA Medical Center. According to Murray, he worked on Jackson the entire time. The emergency room doctor who pronounced Jackson dead would testify that the singer arrived at the hospital with no sign of a pulse. Murray said otherwise, contending that the Michael still exhibited "signs of life."

Either way, the superstar was officially declared dead at 2:26 p.m.

Eighteen minutes later, *TMZ* informed the world in a terse, one-sentence statement that Michael Jackson had died. Within one hour, nearly a million visitors had visited Michael's Wikipedia page, the largest flow of traffic in the website's history. Wikipedia, Twitter—where 15 percent of all posts mentioned Jackson—and AOL Messenger all crashed from user overloads. The *Los Angeles Times* website suffered outages, and Google executives—believing their site was under attack—blocked all searches related to Michael.

Fans started to gather outside of Jackson's home; his parents' house; the hospital; Harlem's Apollo Theater; the singer's childhood home in Gary, Indiana; and the Motown Museum, built on the site of the Jacksons' recording studio in Detroit. In Portland, Oregon, devotees donned Jackson's signature sequin glove and went on a bike run around the City of Roses. Russian fans converged outside the US embassy in Moscow, while a *Salat al-Janazah* (Islamic funeral prayer) was performed in Midyat, Turkey. The House of Representatives held a moment of silence.

AEG Live organized a memorial service at the Staples Center, seen by 2.5 billion people. As Paris Jackson burst into tears, recalling Michael as "the best father you could ever imagine," and his brothers stood around the solid bronze casket in sparkling gloves, stars like Stevie Wonder, Mariah Carey, and Lionel Richie sang Jackson songs.

By this point, the investigation into Michael's death had already begun. Because of its authority to investigate cases otherwise protected by doctor-patient confidentiality, the DEA was brought in to help the LAPD. Murray's clinic and homes and the pharmacy that supplied some of the drugs found in the mansion were also raided.

On August 29, the Los Angeles coroner declared the death a homicide due to "acute propofol intoxication." Other drugs like the painkiller lidocaine, the stimulant ephedrine, and the sedatives midazolam and diazepam were also said to be in Jackson's system.

Court documents would confirm that Murray purchased five bottles of propofol in May, 2009, the period when he became Michael's traveling physician.

He'd enter a plea of not guilty to the charge of involuntary manslaughter. "I am an innocent man," the doctor said at the start of his 2011 trial.

Jury selection was a long, arduous process. Approximately five hundred citizens were considered, with each having to fill out a thirty-page questionnaire. Among the questions: "Have you ever considered yourself a fan of Michael Jackson?"

Murray's defense team was hoping to establish that he hadn't become an integral part of Michael's life until after other doctors had gotten the singer addicted to drugs. But the strategy didn't work. Six doctors—including Dr. Arnold Klein—were barred from testifying so jurors could solely focus on what Conrad Murray might or might not have done. Although Jackson's bodyguard, Alberto Alvarez, said that Murray "had the best intentions for" the singer, paramedics told the court that the doctor neglected to tell them that he'd given the star propofol. Despite Murray's contention that Michael had taken a fatal dose of the drug while the physician was out of the room, the medic who carried out the postmortem said that it appeared that the doctor had mistakenly given Jackson too much. Furthermore, propofol expert Dr. Steven Shafer testified, the drug should have never been used to treat insomnia.

It took jurors ten hours and seven minutes to find Murray guilty. According to Judge Michael Pastor, the doctor had exhibited a "continuous pattern of lies and deceit." Although sentenced to four years in a county jail, Murray would be released after slightly less than two, due to good behavior and to overcrowding in the California penal system.

But several members of the Jackson family were convinced not only that justice hadn't been served, but that the public was unaware of the true story behind Michael's death. In her book, La

Toya described Murray as "the fall guy" in a conspiracy to murder her brother for his music catalogue and estate. In 2017, Paris Jackson—by now a model—told *Rolling Stone* that her father had specifically told her, "They're going to kill me one day."

Given the value of Michael's assets and his weakened, vulnerable state, the murder plot was "obvious," Paris said. "All arrows point to that. . . . It sounds like bullshit, but all real fans and everybody in the family knows it. It was a setup."

9

HERE COME THE COPS
FANG'S LEAD SINGER GOES ON THE LAM

Twenty-two years after his release from prison, Sam "Sammy-town" McBride harbored no illusions about the type of person he was when his San Francisco Bay Area punk band, Fang, was cranking out songs like "Everybody Makes Me Barf," "Fun with Acid," "Suck and Fuck," and "Skinheads Smoke Dope."

"My twenty-year-old self would stab my fifty-year-old self," he told me, between customers at the tattoo parlor he was running along with a "sober living house" for men recently released from rehab or incarceration.

More than likely, those occupying the six beds in the three-bedroom house were oblivious or indifferent to the fact that Fang's songs have been covered by Nirvana, Green Day, and Metallica. "These guys are coming from prison," Sammytown pointed out. "They don't care. All they know is that I was a hard-core junkie and I killed my girlfriend."

Although the incident occurred in 1989, it continued following McBride around long after he purged his life of the drugs and alcohol that had helped him forget the repugnant details of his crime. "More than twenty-five years later, there are people who feel I shouldn't play music," he said. "They think I don't have a problem with what I did. I have a huge problem with what I did. I have more of a problem with what I did than anybody else.

"I hate my past."

The son of a forestry professor at Cal Berkeley, McBride was raised in an environment where ideas about parenting were fluid, and kids were largely left to make their own mistakes. By eleven, he was drinking and smoking pot, and getting into trouble with the police. He was thirteen in 1977 when his father took a nine-month assignment in the United Kingdom, and a misfit classmate turned the boy on to the Sex Pistols. From that point forward, Sammy was a punk rocker, subscribing to the genre's angry, pessimistic message. Upon his return to Northern California, he widened his record collection to include the Ramones, and began playing in bands—one was called Reign of Terror, another Shut Up. In ninth grade, he was the only boy in high school with an earring, tattoos, and purple hair. After enduring four separate beatings from the school's jocks, he dropped out.

Sam's mentors in the punk scene dropped acid and shot speed. A hippie he knew supplied him with quaaludes, a hypnotic sedative that would be discontinued in 1985. At a certain stage, he added heroin to his menu of vices—sometimes drawing the scorn of punkers who had little tolerance for junkies.

But his sense of daring was attractive to others. At fifteen, he had a thirty-year-old girlfriend and a growing reputation as a drug dealer for a well-organized conglomerate. "Very quickly, I became part of the Northern California drug family," he said. "Their values became my values. You don't snitch. You don't jump customers. They had a hit man, at one point, on the payroll. If you didn't follow the rules, there were definite consequences."

In 1982, drummer Joel Fox auditioned for the Berkeley band Fang and brought Sam along. When the session ended, both Mc-Bride and Fox were in the band. Sammytown quickly became the most visible member. After Berkeley introduced a policy of building ramps for the disabled—a progressive first in the United States—Sammytown stood at the foot of the stage, warbling the words to the tune "Destroy the Handicapped" while Fox, bassist Chris Wilson, and guitarist and cofounder Tom Flynn backed him up.

"Berkeley's full of heathen scum," went another song. *"I should know, I am one. I'm a drunken junkie bum."*

Around the East Bay, Fang was developing a buzz. After clashing with columnist Aaron Cometbus over some erroneous information that Cometbus had printed in the fanzine *Maximum Rocknroll*, Sam gave him license to invent any story he liked. "From then on, the scene reports were a lot more interesting," Cometbus recounted in Jack Boulware and Silke Tudor's *Gimme Something Better*. "'Fang drummer gets a sex change,' 'Sammy teaching preschool,' 'Fang bassist run over by ice cream truck.'"

Before the murder, Fang would produce four albums, drawing much of its fan base from Southern California, despite the L.A. punks' open disdain for most bands from the northern reaches of the state.

While touring with Fang, Sammy was able to expand his more nefarious activities. "In every town, I'd get introduced to the local pot dealer," he said, "and I'd offer to send him a hundred hits of acid—for free—if he'd consider working with me." Because he made his own blotter, McBride could grind out in excess of fifty thousand hits at a time. "From every tour, I got at least one or two regular customers, and was dealing to people all over the country."

But Sammy was more than a tradesman. As an addict with a $1,000-a-day heroin habit, he was subsidizing his own drug dealer—until the supplier lost his house and moved in with the vocalist. Now, Sammy could pocket more cash from his acid operation, since the dealer was often furnishing him with free dope.

When the band embarked on an extensive US tour to support the release of its 1984 album, *Where the Wild Things Are*, Sammy's girlfriend and her three kids camped out at Tom Flynn's house. After coping with McBride's heroin misadventures on the road, Flynn was looking forward to some time to himself. Instead, upon returning to the Bay Area, he discovered that Sam and his girlfriend liked the house so much, they'd decided to stay there, shooting up while the children romped, largely unsupervised, through the various rooms. Exhausted by the vista he witnessed each day, Flynn quit the group.

He thought that Fang would fold. Instead, it replaced Flynn with Bill Collins, whose guitar playing effortlessly mimicked that of his predecessor. For all intents and purposes, Fang now seemed to be guided by Sammytown's impulses and vices.

In 1985, Sammy was arrested in Texas for a small amount of marijuana and ended up spending three days in jail. After his release, he announced that he wanted a change of scenery and moved the band to England. He instantly regretted the decision.

"I was paranoid," he said. "Everyone I knew was poor, and a lot of venues were not allowing punk rock in anymore."

West Germany seemed more receptive both to the genre—Fang recorded their third and fourth albums there—and to the type of commerce Sammytown hoped to conduct. Once the band established itself, McBride found a German girlfriend, who was willing to act as his chief sales representative. During the group's regular forays back to California, the singer would ship over his homemade acid and his girlfriend would distribute it around the country.

Despite what would transpire later, "the guys who were playing with me benefited from me being a drug dealer," he said. "When I moved us to Europe, I paid for the instruments and I took care of the bills. But *they* weren't drug dealers, they didn't live the lifestyle, or invite that element of danger into their day-to-day lives, so when shit started to get real, they were scared."

For instance, while in Germany, McBride joined an anti-fascist gang called the Outsiders, battling neo-Nazis with chains and gas guns. "The other guys didn't particularly like this," Sammytown said. "They weren't criminals. They didn't like violence. And there were repercussions for their association with me."

Then, three days before the band was about to fly back to West Germany to tour and record its fifth LP, McBride received a phone call informing him that his girlfriend had been busted near Bremen, and that there was a warrant for his arrest. "Don't go to Germany," he was told. "The cops know you're coming. You're fucked."

Since Sam was the foundation of Fang, the band had no choice but to cancel and record the album in the States. "The clock was ticking," he said. "I felt Interpol was going to find me if I went anywhere near Europe."

So Sammytown stayed away, not returning to Germany for more than twenty years—after he was released from prison for murdering Dixie Lee Carney.

Sam and Dixie were not supposed to meet—at least, not on the specific day they did. Fang was scheduled to play a gig in Chapel Hill, North Carolina, but the roadie was confused about the schedule and drove to Roanoke, Virginia, instead. At a party that night, the roadie met Dixie and discovered that she was a Fang fan. At her request, he introduced her to Sammy, and the two clicked. She followed the band to Chapel Hill and returned with them to Roanoke for their scheduled show there. "First, we just slept together," McBride said. "Then, she came to California and we decided to be boyfriend and girlfriend."

She knew that in Sammytown's world, that designation meant that she'd also deal acid with him. Already she was part of his network of sales representatives receiving hundreds of hits of LSD a month. By the time she relocated, he'd been shipping her ten thousand hits every two weeks. "She was a very capable drug dealer," he recalled. "She started selling acid all over Virginia and then in North Carolina."

Like others in fringe trades, Dixie clung to the fantasy that she was going to funnel the funds from her acid enterprise into some legitimate business. McBride had no such intentions. He hadn't expected to live long and, as his heroin fixation increased, was starting to lose his focus on music. At times, Fang played without a singer. On one occasion, a substitute was conscripted to read off a song sheet. In 1989, the group broke up.

Despite her ardor for the money her LSD transactions generated, Dixie "was not a junkie," McBride said. In fact, she believed that the only way that the two could remain a couple was if

Sammytown got clean. "After hearing me say I was going to kick too many times, she got sick of me."

Dixie had met one of Sam's biggest customers while her boyfriend was away in L.A.—a Texas resident who'd purchase a hundred thousand hits at a time. With McBride's attention elsewhere, Dixie and the client became a surreptitious item, and began plotting to steal Sam's business. The singer only learned about the scheme when another customer called his apartment in Oakland and asked to speak to Dixie.

"I asked, 'Why do you need to talk to her?' and he started acting real cagey. This is a guy I'd helped out in the past and I reminded him of that. I said, 'If something's going on, you better tell me.'"

And so the customer confessed: "She says you're ripping everybody off, and you're super fucked-up all the time, and she's going to move to Texas with that guy from there."

As Sam probed further, he learned that Dixie also had a secret bank account.

According to the codes of the drug-dealing fraternity, Dixie's treachery was a capital offense, and needed to be dealt with accordingly.

Driving to his dealer's house, Sam purchased enough heroin to overdose. He shot up, but his tolerance was too high. At around 5 a.m., he returned home in time to look through the picture window and see his top customer leaving the bedroom, pulling up his boxer shorts. When the man stepped outside, he spotted McBride and ran away.

When Sam entered the bedroom, Dixie was sitting on the bed. "She wasn't sure I saw him leave," he said of his girlfriend's paramour and coconspirator. Eyeing Dixie queerly, Sam approached the bed. "I don't think I even said anything."

That's as much as McBride was willing to tell me about the murder. In court, he'd admit to smothering his twenty-four-year-old lover with a pillow, crushing her neck.

On August 6, 1989, three friends visiting from out of state discovered Dixie in the apartment. Despite their trepidation about informing, they knew that they had no option but to contact the police.

By that point, Sammytown was just beginning his six-month odyssey as a fugitive.

"I was in shock after the event," he recounted. "I went into autopilot. I knew I just had to get out of there."

There was money all over the apartment, but Sam knew where most of it was stashed. He gathered it up with a minimal amount of belongings, drove thirty or so miles to Richmond, dumped the car, and walked several miles to a gas station, where he called a cab. "There was a concert I knew about in Sacramento," he remembered. "For some reason, I think it was the Grateful Dead. I had the cab drop me off at the concert; then I switched to another cab and asked to go downtown."

Knocking on a friend's door, Sam said that he was in some type of trouble and needed to leave the West Coast quickly. "I gave the guy some money and told him to buy me a ticket to Baltimore," McBride said. "Back then, they didn't really examine your ID in the airport. I flew out that night."

From his travels with Fang, Sam knew where the junkies hung out and copped dope in Baltimore. He also was familiar with a diner where the local punkers gathered. When Sammytown from Fang walked through the door, he received the type of reaction he expected. A waitress invited him to crash at her place.

With the door shut and the window blinds down in the waitress's apartment, McBride began to believe that he'd put enough distance between himself and the crime scene, and that he might have time to formulate a plan. Then the phone rang. An on-again, off-again boyfriend of the waitress was calling from San Francisco to tell her that Sammytown from Fang had killed his girlfriend and was now on the run.

"Really?" the waitress replied. "He's here right now."

Although Sam's host hadn't reported him to authorities, she'd divulged enough information for the Bay Area punk rockers to know where McBride was hiding. And that meant that he had to keep moving.

Through a junkie friend, Sam found a ride to New York City. There, he avoided the punk hangouts, where he'd likely be recognized and betrayed. As his money began to run low, he envisioned himself doing time behind bars and concluded that he needed to take his own life.

"I ate thirty Valiums, shot up two bundles of dope, and cut my wrists in the bathtub. Four or five hours later, I woke up. I guess I wasn't very good at cutting my wrists."

Resolving to remain a fugitive, Sam remembered a rumor he'd heard, that if he traveled to Brazil and impregnated a local, the country would refuse to extradite him to United States. Unfortunately, his passport was back in California. "I did a few deals," he said, "flew back west, and went to my parents' place. But I could not get my passport."

Needing to exit the Bay Area quickly—and clean up, in order to remain alert—Sam had a phone conversation with a prostitute friend who'd moved to Alaska and kicked heroin. "If I can kick here," she stressed, "*you* can kick here."

It was as good a strategy as any. "I went to Alaska and I actually *did* kick. There was just no heroin there. They didn't have methadone. And it's not like now, where you can find OxyContin and other opiates. I was clean."

For several months, it appeared that Sam had gotten away with murder. To most Bay Area punkers, he appeared to have fallen off the face of the earth. As in the past, he had a new girlfriend who could help facilitate his needs. And he had a job—a straight job—in a screen-printing shop.

Meanwhile, a friend in Oakland would communicate with him periodically, letting McBride know which punk rockers were talking to the police—as well as to federal authorities, who'd joined the hunt, since Sammy had clearly been crossing state lines. One day, the friend called with a warning: "They know you're in Anchorage. Get out of there now."

McBride instructed his girlfriend to buy him a ticket to Seattle and drive him to the airport in the middle of a blizzard. The facility was snowed in, so the pair returned the next day. With all the snow on the ground, the flight was delayed, and McBride didn't want to spend too much time in a public setting. "We decided to go to a friend's house and wait," he said, "but the car broke down in the parking lot." With trepidation, he went back inside the building and proceeded to the gate.

After so much time on the run, he believed that he could detect a member of law enforcement anywhere. But, on this day, he was oblivious to the fact that a contingent of US Marshals were staking out the terminal.

"There was a man and a woman who looked like a middle-aged couple. There was someone else pretending to work at the newspaper kiosk. And there was another marshal who looked like a businessman with a briefcase, reading a newspaper."

What McBride didn't know was that there was a photo of him taped inside the publication. The moment that the agent confirmed the fugitive's identity, he signaled his partners. Before Sam could make sense of the situation, he was being tackled from all sides.

He never discovered who divulged his whereabouts to the feds, but suspected a peripheral member of the Anchorage punk rock scene. "I think he was in the witness protection program," Sam said. "I once talked to him, and his backstory was really sketchy. Or maybe my girlfriend told them. I'll never know."

Rather than stand trial for a murder he'd obviously committed, he agreed to plead guilty to voluntary manslaughter in exchange for an eleven-year sentence. He'd end up serving just six years—outraging those who believed that the punishment did not reflect the severity of the crime. But that was the deal he was offered.

He spent time in San Quentin, then was transferred to Soledad. Whatever fame Fang had enjoyed appeared to be over. But the band's music was still circulating, and acquiring new followers. Kurt Cobain listed the group's *Landshark!* LP as among his favorite albums, and Nirvana would produce their own version of Fang's song "The Money Will Roll Right In." So did Mudhoney, the Butthole Surfers, and Metallica. Green Day covered Fang's "I Wanna Be on TV."

Behind bars, McBride learned about the group's renewed popularity. "It was too hard to even wrap my head around," he told the *LA Weekly.* The misery and isolation of prison life inspired Sammytown to write several songs: "Electric Chair," "City of Pain," and "Burn It Down," the last about a paroled pyromaniac who dies in one of his fires.

During a concert on the yard at Soledad, a rumor started among the black inmates that the garbled punk rock lyrics were racist. Corrections officers ended the show after one song, as black and white inmates faced off with knives. The incident spurred another tune, "30 Days in the Hole," after Sammytown was placed in solitary confinement for the allegation that he'd tried to spark a prison riot.

"Soledad was not ready for punk rock, to be sure," he noted.

Drugs were not only accessible in prison, but plentiful, and Sammy fell back into both heroin consumption and dealing while incarcerated. Surrounded by other criminals, "I didn't have any remorse for what I'd done," he admitted. "I justified it because of the culture I was in."

Then, in 1993, during a conjugal visit—McBride had married an old friend while in prison—he experienced what he called "a moment of clarity. I had to get clean. I had to stop dealing. And now, I had to let my conscience return, and face what I did to [Dixie's] family, my family."

Once again, McBride kicked drugs. Yet he had to hide his revised lifestyle from his drug-dealing associates. "Prison is a violent place and I still had to survive. It's not like I could walk out onto the yard and say, 'You know what, guys? I just had this epiphany, and I don't want to do the same thing anymore.'"

A transfer to California State Prison, Solano, in Vacaville helped relieve the pressure. "There was a different set of prison politics. Of course, there were guys who challenged me on not moving dope anymore. And I told them, 'If you have a problem with it, we'll handle it.'"

As it turned out, Vacaville was the last stop on McBride's run through the California prison system. Within eighteen months of his transfer, he was discharged.

Because of all that had transpired in the Bay Area, he'd hoped to be paroled into another part of the state. But prison authorities refused. "They made me come right back to where I got into trouble," McBride said in *Gimme Something Better*.

Fang still had a following who clamored to see the parolee lead the band. So Sammytown reformed the group, albeit with a new lineup of musicians.

The first show took place at the familiar Trocadero Transfer in San Francisco. Shortly after McBride arrived at the club, the promoter called him aside and said that no fewer than ten death threats had been phoned into the venue. "If I'd had a shirt with a target on it, I would have worn it," Sam said. "But we played the show, and no one tried to kill me."

Explained punk-rock booker Eddie Lopez to the *LA Weekly*, "The band and the songs are bigger than one man's crime. Sammy will have to live with what he did for the rest of his life. He's served his time and has a right to sing those classic songs to a new generation of fans. . . . I have nothing against Sammy. From my brief encounters with him, it looks like he's trying to better himself."

But it took a liberated McBride some time to get to that place. "At one point, I did start using again and started committing crime again," he said. "I was touring, and in San Diego one night, someone handed me a beer, and it all started."

At Sam's request, two friends locked him in a basement room for a month in order for him to detox. But he continued to crush pharmaceuticals and shoot them up for another year before he made the decision to become completely sober.

For the first time in his professional life, Sammy could put the music first. Fang continued to play their old songs, as well as new material, releasing the album *Here Come the Cops*—featuring former bandmate Tom Flynn—in 2012, and *Rise Up*, a political album decrying the racism and sexism of the time, in 2017.

Having perfected his tattooing skills in prison, McBride also opened a tattoo parlor, the Tiger's Blood Social Club, in Alameda, California. "I've done more Fang tattoos than anything else," he told the *Phoenix New Times*. "It's kind of bizarre . . . that anyone would want to carry that on their skin. It's certainly not what I thought I would be doing in the twenty-first century. . . . Honestly, I didn't even think I'd be living this long."

For some indeterminable reason, though, Sam *was* alive. And because of that, he made the decision to manage a sober-living house so paroled addicts could "get their feet under them" before transitioning back into society. "I try to balance the scales," he said. "I should be doing life in prison. But I'm not. So I'm committed to helping other people not make the mistakes I made."

As of 2017, he was living upstairs with his girlfriend and daughter, both of whom were in recovery. "Some people can drink or smoke pot without having the disease of addiction," he said. "But my daughter, as soon as she started smoking pot at fourteen, she was cutting school, shoplifting, stealing from us. It was apparent right away that she was a drug addict. And I knew where that was going. I didn't want to be alarmist. But me, when I started smoking pot, I ended up killing my girlfriend and going to prison."

The episode would color the rest of his life, possessing the thoughts of even those acquaintances who didn't dare bring up the murder directly with the singer. "There's nothing I can say, nothing important enough, nothing meaningful enough, to explain the crime," he'd reflect. "Nothing I can say or do will ever make what I did right. But that's not an excuse to keep doing shitty things, either."

10

TUPAC AND BIGGIE

Nas was just achieving mainstream recognition when the bullets were fired. First, Tupac Shakur was gunned down after attending a boxing match in Las Vegas. Six months later, Biggie Smalls—aka the Notorious B.I.G.—was struck down following an industry event in L.A. The two had been friends who, according to the gossip at the time, turned into enemies, and their deaths were seen as interconnected, a manifestation of rap's bitter East Coast vs. West Coast feud. The murders inspired sadness, innuendo and, perversely, a boom in album sales. Yet Nas worried that the violence would symbolically close the curtain on the music he loved.

"What they meant to the art form can never be redone, can never be replaced," the Queens-bred entertainer—whose 1999 song "We Will Survive" honored both men—told MTV. "And when those two guys passed away, I thought [it] was the end of rap."

Oddly, the dual killings only increased rap's visibility. Imagery of Tupac and Biggie—the pair were depicted together—took on a religiosity, the liturgy consisting of songs like Shakur's "California Love" and B.I.G.'s "Mo Money Mo Problems." As the years passed without an arrest in either case, the pair were seen more as symbols—inevitable sacrifices to the cult of gangsta rap—than as the sensitive, intelligent kids they'd been at one time.

"The Chris I knew was a good guy," saxophonist and neighbor Donald Harrison told NPR about the real-life Biggie Smalls, Christopher Wallace. As a teenager in Brooklyn, Chris—who worked as a summer camp counselor at the Jewish preschool where his mother was a much-venerated teacher—sought out the older Harrison to teach him about jazz and the ability to scat to a

Cannonball Adderley solo. "He wasn't the guy who did all these things [the crimes portrayed in his songs]. He was really looking for love and acceptance at the end of the day. That's what he was looking for. And he paid a price for looking for love."

Likewise, Tupac was a natural poet raised to consider both personal and political issues in a wider societal context. Using his mother as his barometer, he praised the strength of women. Yet both his lyrics and lifestyle bore the stench of misogyny, while the words *Thug Life* were tattooed across his abdominals.

Each artist probably knew how his fame would end. In the video for his song "I Ain't Mad at Cha"—produced weeks before his slaying—Tupac is gunned down and seen rapping in the afterlife. Biggie's first album was titled *Ready to Die*. In one song, he intones, "I swear to God, I feel like death is fucking calling me."

Both were convenient foils in a business that had long been run by reprobates and felons. At first, the African American criminals in the music industry were brought in to serve masters of southern Italian and Eastern European Jewish ancestry. While those forces never abdicated, the advent of rap music created unforeseen opportunities for ravagers with roots in Alabama's "Black Belt" and the Mississippi Delta.

When rappers returned to their neighborhoods, driving ostentatious cars and flashing jewelry, drug dealers and other criminal types wanted to join the game. Some insinuated themselves into the performers' universes, finding jobs as security guards or road managers. As did certain entertainers, a number of these gangsters viewed hip-hop as a way to go legit, purchasing studio time for potential stars and signing them to management contracts. In underworld circles, there was a widely held perception that any crack slinger could rap. As a result, hundreds, if not thousands, of roughnecks and hoods embarked on the process of trying—through any means necessary—to transform themselves into celebrities.

The emergence of hip-hop coincided with the rise of two major criminal gangs. The Crips had started in South Central L.A. A few miles away, the Bloods had formed around Piru Street in Compton. While Crips wore blue bandanas—a tribute to a founding member named Buddha, who was partial to the color and was gunned down in 1973—Bloods adorned themselves in red, a shade associated with Compton's Centennial High. With the arrival of crack in the inner city, both gangs established distribution networks and chapters throughout the United States—not to mention a number of offshoots. In parks and recreation centers, MCs began to rap about the newly rich ghetto monarchs, idealizing the gangsta lifestyle. There was an exhilarating defiance in the way that the kingpins were able to flaunt excess and muscle without asking permission from white society. As hip-hop crossed racial boundaries, fans of other ethnicities adopted the clothing, terminology, and swagger of hoodlums who had nothing to lose.

So did African American rappers who were endowed with other options but chose to go gangsta and widen their street cred. Among them: Tupac Shakur and the Notorious B.I.G.

Tupac Shakur's name came from two divine sources: Chief Túpac Amaru—the last indigenous Inca monarch, whose story would inspire revolutions against the Spanish colonizers in the eighteenth century and the right-wing Peruvian government in the 1980s—and the Arabic word *Shakur*, meaning "thankful to God." His parents, Billy Garland and Afeni Shakur, were members of the Black Panther Party. Born in East Harlem, Tupac quickly became familiar with the ways of the New York streets. But he was an actor, as well, first appearing in a production of *A Raisin in the Sun* at age thirteen at a benefit for 1984 Democratic presidential candidate Jesse Jackson at Harlem's famed Apollo Theater, and later in movies like *Juice*, *Above the Rim*, and *Poetic Justice*. While writing the material that would launch him to stardom, Shakur worked as a dancer and roadie for the rap group Digital Underground.

Christopher Wallace was one year younger, the son of Jamaican transplants to Brooklyn, where the boy attended Catholic schools and won several awards for his English language skills. While his mother, Voletta, was busy working, though, a teenage Christopher—nicknamed "Big" because of his more than three-hundred-pound heft and six-foot-three-inch height—was secretly dealing crack, leading to a number of arrests. Still, his skill at turning a phrase was earning him distinction. The rapper's clever "flow," or spontaneous wordplay, would be compared to work of the jazz greats who once occupied the same African American precincts where the kid called "Biggie Smalls" was flourishing. As his mixtape circulated, Biggie was signed to Sean "Puffy" Combs's new imprint, Bad Boy Records, in 1992.

Despite the message of the music—Big brazenly sang about drugs, guns, and dirty money—Combs ordered his charge to quit the crack trade.

Big acquiesced, while still remaining close to other New York drug dealers, one of whom introduced the fledgling rapper to Tupac in 1993. At a meeting in Los Angeles, Shakur, whose recent album *Strictly 4 My N.I.G.G.A.Z.* had yielded the hits "Keep Ya Head Up" and "I Get Around," was in a gregarious mood, cooking for his guest and showing off a collection of weapons that included several machine guns. The two quickly formed a friendship, freestyling on the same stage, with Tupac hanging out and playing dice with the Brooklynite's buddies in New York, and B.I.G. sleeping on Shakur's couch during treks to L.A.

Biggie was still on the way up, and Tupac was happy to impart advice, telling his friend that if he concentrated on drawing females to his concerts, the males would be close behind. Concerned that Bad Boy was not yet established, B.I.G. asked Shakur to manage him at one point. But Tupac was certain that Combs could turn the young man into a star.

His instincts were proven correct when, fueled by such hits as "Big Poppa," "One More Chance," and "Juicy," *Ready to Die* sold four million copies.

His sage advice notwithstanding, Tupac exhibited a reckless streak that threatened to eclipse his entertainment acumen. Not only did he sing about "Thug Life," he had begun to behave like a common criminal. He was arrested in 1992 when he became embroiled in a scuffle and a stray bullet killed a six-year-old boy. The next year, he was charged with shooting two off-duty police officers. In both cases, the charges were dismissed. However, after attacking director Allen Hughes, Tupac served fifteen days in jail.

In 1993, Tupac grew close to a Biggie associate named Jacques "Haitian Jack" Agnant, a rap promoter and reputed gangster. One night, Shakur brought a nineteen-year-old woman to his suite at New York's Le Parker Meridien hotel. They were joined by Haitian Jack and two other men. Tupac claimed that he left the bedroom and fell asleep when the trio entered. The woman told police that the four gang-raped her and forced her to perform oral sex. When authorities searched the room, they found guns that Shakur maintained belonged to Biggie.

Before the case went to trial, Haitian Jack pleaded guilty to two misdemeanor charges in exchange for six months in jail. Jack claimed that his case was severed from that of the other defendants because he could not be linked to the guns in the room. Shakur was incredulous. He was sure that the felon—who'd later be deported back to Haiti after serving time on an unrelated conviction—had cut a deal to rat on the star.

In an interview with *Daily News* gossip reporter A. J. Benza, Tupac implied that Jack was a snitch and dismissed him as a "hanger-on." Shakur was aware of the repercussions of such a public diss; everyone knew that Jack was a dangerous man. Still, the rapper continued to conduct himself as if his aura of celebrity could shield him from harm.

On November 30, 1994, Tupac agreed to do a cameo on a song for a Brooklyn rapper named Little Shawn. Shawn was not in the same category as Shakur or B.I.G., but he knew Puffy and Biggie, and his manager was Jimmy "Henchman" Rosemond, whom Tupac had met through Haitian Jack. A night session was scheduled at

Quad Recording Studios in Times Square—while B.I.G. and Combs were also in the building, working on a separate project.

As Shakur and his entourage stepped through the entrance, he noticed three men in combat fatigues, a standard hip-hop fashion on the Brooklyn streets where Biggie roamed. Just as the rapper was about to enter the elevator, the strangers pulled .9mm weapons and demanded that Tupac and his posse hit the ground and hand over their jewelry. When Shakur refused, he was pistol-whipped. Even so, he would not accommodate his attackers. Reaching for his own gun, the rapper pressed the trigger and accidentally shot himself in the groin. The three opened fire as well, hitting Tupac four more times in the head and neck. The assailants also beat the star, relieving him of a $40,000 medallion. He played dead until the muggers fled, then stumbled onto the elevator. He ascended to the tenth floor, where the doors opened and the injured singer spotted Biggie, Combs, and Henchman, listening to playback tracks. Puffy—later known as Diddy—contended that he was upset by the sight and immediately tended to the rapper.

Yet by Shakur's estimation, the whole thing felt like a setup. Someone had told the shooters Tupac's schedule. Despite his injuries, Shakur claimed to have the presence of mind to read the faces of B.I.G. and his associates. According to Tupac, they looked guilty.

Whether Biggie had planned the violence or not, Shakur believed that he had known about it beforehand.

The next day, Tupac arrived in court in a wheelchair, swathed in bandages, for the rape case verdict. Although acquitted of the sodomy and weapons charges, he was found guilty of sexual assault. He'd be sentenced to one and a half to four years behind bars. A short time later, his appropriately titled album *Me Against the World* would be released, enabling Shakur to become the first performer to have a record hit number one on the *Billboard* charts while its maker was in prison.

"It was a trip," he told MTV. "Every time [people] used to say something bad to me, I'd go, 'That's all right. I got the number-one record in the country.'"

Still, there was much that Shakur was reticent to admit. Trapped within the Clinton Correctional Facility, a maximum-security prison more than 250 miles north of New York City, he contemplated Biggie's success. When B.I.G had just been getting started, it was Shakur who'd advised and encouraged his friend. Now, what were Biggie and Puffy going to do for him? Feeling embittered, he contacted Marion "Suge" Knight, a powerfully built former football player with a menacing past. In 1987, he was arrested in Las Vegas and charged with shooting a man three times while stealing his car. After pleading guilty to a misdemeanor, Knight received probation. Regardless, those in the hip-hop community believed that Suge was capable of this and far worse. According to one rumor, the hulking cofounder of L.A.-based Death Row Records once hung Vanilla Ice from a hotel balcony, demanding that the white rapper sign over his publishing rights to an associate.

Despite the success of *Me Against the World*, Tupac needed money; his mother was on the verge of losing her house. Suge provided cash, as well as the use of a Death Row lawyer to pursue an appeal. After feeling betrayed by B.I.G and Combs, a grateful Shakur was willing not only to sign with Death Row but to assist in Suge's scheme to obliterate Bad Boy Records.

At the 1995 awards ceremony sponsored by the magazine the *Source*, Knight spoke for himself and Tupac when he took the stage and angrily mocked Puffy's penchant for including himself in his performers' videos: "Any artist out there want to be an artist, and want to stay a star, and don't have to worry about the executive producer trying to be in all the videos, all on the records, dancing—come to Death Row."

Many in the audience at Paramount Theater at Madison Square Garden pelted Suge with boos. Yet the derision seemed to make him taller onstage, as he glared back at his detractors.

The East Coast–West Coast hip-hop war had begun. To emphasize this point, Suge declared, "We got no love for the East Coast."

At hip-hop events around the United States, there were violent altercations between loyalists of the two camps. While traveling in California, Combs reportedly hired Crips to work security at several stops. Puffy vehemently denied working with gang members. But since Knight was associated with the Mob Piru faction of the Bloods, there was the perception that Combs was deliberately instigating his rival—as well as Tupac.

To many fans, B.I.G.'s 1995 song "Who Shot Ya?" directly referenced the Quad Recording Studios attack, particularly when the rapper intoned, *"You rewind this. Bad Boy's behind this."* As always, the track's producer, Puffy Combs, proclaimed his innocence, insisting that the song had been recorded before the shooting even occurred. But fans weren't sure, and it was exciting to imagine that Biggie was boasting about an incident that had nearly claimed Tupac's life.

With Death Row's assistance—most notably, a $1.4 million bond paid by Knight—Shakur was paroled from prison after serving eight months. His subsequent music lashed back at Bad Boy. On the 1996 single "Hit 'Em Up," he went after the core of the East Coast establishment, attacking Biggie and Puffy by name. *"Die slow, motherfuckers,"* he sang. If that weren't enough, he also rapped about allegedly having sex with the Notorious B.I.G.'s singer wife, Faith Evans.

"That's why I fucked your bitch," he practically spat, *"you fat motherfucker."*

Behind the bluster, though, Tupac was clearly concerned about being shot again. At the 1996 MTV Video Music Awards, he was surrounded by bodyguards and seen speaking into a walkie-talkie. Yet he also appeared to be titillated by the threat, and continued to place himself in situations that were destined to end badly.

In July 1996, a Death Row associate named Trevon "Tray" Lane had been mugged by at least eight Southside Crips at Lakewood Center mall, a shopping complex between Compton and Long Beach popular with the gangsta element. In the course of the beating, Tray's cherished Death Row medallion was stolen, a slight he wouldn't forget.

Two months later, on September 7, Tray accompanied Tupac and Suge to see Mike Tyson defeat the overmatched Bruce Seldon in the World Boxing Association championship in Las Vegas. Afterward, the three were in the lobby of the MGM Grand hotel when Tray spotted one of the offenders, Orlando "Baby Lane" Anderson, crossing the room.

"That's the dude," Tray told his companions.

It was Shakur who opted to get revenge, literally walking up to Baby Lane, asking a quick question about where the Crip lived, then flooring him with a punch. Suge and the others in the rapper's posse joined in, kicking and punching the accused thief.

It was the way Tupac rolled. Security broke up the altercation, but no one was in the mood to detain the celebrity, and Shakur and his group went on their way, joining a cavalcade of vehicles cruising down Las Vegas Boulevard. Seated in the passenger seat of Suge's new black BMW 750 sedan, Tupac was instantly recognized, and he basked in the adulation of pedestrians and other motorists. Knight steered the car toward the night spot he owned, Club 662—the numerical equivalent of the word *MOB* on a telephone— where, ironically, the hip-hop artist was supposed to perform at a benefit to guide young people away from violence. Among the luminaries expected to be stopping by: Tyson, the subject of Shakur's song "Let's Get It On (Ready to Rumble)," who'd flattened his opponent in a stunning 109 seconds.

The music was booming out of Suge's car, attracting the attention of the police. At around 11 p.m., the BMW was pulled over by an officer from the Las Vegas PD's bicycle corps, who also noticed that the car was devoid of license plates. Suge found the missing tags in the trunk, and the officer waved the pair on without writing a ticket.

Tupac was standing now, his upper body through the sunroof, drawing everyone's attention. While stopped at a red light in front of the Maxim Hotel, he engaged four attractive women in a convertible in a quick exchange, and invited them to the event at Club 662.

The night was just getting started, as far as Shakur was concerned. But just before the rapper arrived at the location, a white Cadillac pulled up next to the BMW as a stoplight. A .40-caliber Glock was pushed through the rear window, then fired. The vehicle's tinted windows shattered. Four bullets hit Tupac in the chest, hip, arm, and hand. Although he'd tried to duck, his seat belt held him in place. "Get down," Suge yelled, leaning over to try to pull Shakur's body out of danger. In the process, the impresario was hit in the head and neck with shrapnel and pieces of glass.

It happened so quickly that the Cadillac was able to slip past the rapper's security contingent, following in other cars. Suge grabbed the wheel and pulled a U-turn, taking off after the Cadillac with two busted tires. But the assailants quickly escaped.

The BMW skidded into a concrete median.

"You hit?" Knight asked the rapper.

"I'm hit."

When police arrived, they treated everyone in Tupac's convoy as a potential suspect, laying them down on the sidewalk in handcuffs. The only exception was Shakur, who was in no condition to leave the BMW. Eventually, the rapper was placed in an ambulance and taken to University Medical Center. A bloody Suge climbed in beside him.

At the hospital, Tupac was worried that his attackers were going to return and finish the job. While connected to life-support machines, and surrounded by his security team, he continuously tried to rise from his bed, prompting medical staff to place him in a barbiturate-induced coma.

Six days after the shooting, twenty-five-year-old Tupac Shakur went into cardiac arrest after an operation to remove his right lung. Despite doctors' efforts to revive the singer, they were unable to stop the hemorrhaging. Eventually, his mother made the decision to stop treatment and allow her son to die.

A prolific recording artist, Tupac left behind enough material to fill three successful albums—*The Don Killuminati: The 7 Day Theory,* released under the pseudonym Makaveli; *R U Still Down? (Remember Me)*; and *Still I Rise*—which would be released over the next three years. Meanwhile, fans speculated wildly over the circumstances of his death: Suge Knight ordered the hit after hearing a rumor that Tupac was going to leave Death Row, Suge Knight was the actual target, the CIA orchestrated the murder to prevent Shakur's words from radicalizing African American youth. The most popular theory involved the East Coast–West Coast rivalry, particularly a scenario that had Biggie holed up in a suite at the MGM Grand, ready to dole out $1 million to the Crips if his rap rival perished.

"It was so ridiculous," Voletta Wallace told *Rolling Stone.* "My son is Notorious B.I.G. If my son is going to go to Las Vegas, don't tell me nobody didn't see him."

The stories had an impact on Biggie. "I think it's fair to say he was probably afraid," Faith Evans—who always denied an affair with Tupac—told MTV, "given everything that was going on at that time and all the so-called hype that was put on this so-called beef that [B.I.G.] really didn't have in his heart."

At the 1997 *Soul Train* Music Awards in Los Angeles, Biggie was booed by a large portion of the audience. Although he was seen leaving with a large security presence, he insisted that the precaution had nothing to do with the East Coast–West Coast feud and everything to do with his growing celebrity. The next night, March 8, he was invited to attend a party at the Petersen Automotive Museum, hosted by Qwest Records and *Vibe* magazine. Tired from the various obligations he'd had to meet during this latest jaunt to L.A., B.I.G considered staying away. But Puffy convinced him to attend, arguing that the rapper needed to show the hip-hop community that he was standing strong, despite the reaction he'd received at the *Soul Train* Music Awards.

Indeed, B.I.G arrived at the museum's Mullin Family Grand Salon to a warm reception. As cameras flashed and fans shouted his name, Biggie strolled over to a booth beside the dance floor and made himself comfortable with Puffy, sipping Cristal champagne and taking drags on the blunts passed in their direction. In the rapper's honor, the DJ played the single "Hypnotize" nine consecutive times. Both Crips and Bloods were in attendance, creating an undertone of potential peril. Apparently aroused by both the tension in the air and the presence of a hip-hop superstar, a number of women left their partners behind on the dance floor to dance provocatively in front of Biggie.

The number of people crammed into the building far exceeded the guest list. At around 12:30 a.m., the fire marshal concluded that the event would have to be shut down. A firefighter appeared with a bullhorn, beseeching the attendees to leave. Accustomed to a system that treated any large group of African Americans as a threat to the public order, a number of celebrants responded with angry shouts. As they moved toward the exit, they were met by a crush of fans attempting to enter the museum.

Biggie and Puffy had made their point. The jeers at the *Soul Train* Music Awards were yesterday's story. Now, everyone wanted to take a photo, receive an autograph, or share a complimentary word with the Notorious B.I.G. For forty minutes, Biggie and Puffy tried meeting every fan request on the way to the exit.

Although they'd been invited to an after-party, the pair decided to return to their hotel. Biggie had a studio session the next morning, and wanted to rest. When the posse's cars pulled up, Puffy swung open the passenger door and entered the first SUV in the procession. Biggie sauntered past the car and stepped into a matching vehicle.

At the corner of Wilshire and Fairfax Boulevards, the cars stopped at a red light. When a black Chevy Impala SS pulled up on the right, no one seemed particularly concerned; fans had been trailing Biggie practically since he'd woken up that day. In a flash, the driver pulled an automatic weapon and fired at the rapper. The shooter was so precise that no one else was hurt. One bullet hit Biggie's left forearm and continued to his wrist. Another smashed into his back, missed all vital organs and exited through his left shoulder. A third passed through his left thigh, damaging his scrotum. The fourth pierced his colon, liver, and heart, as well as the upper lobe of his left lung before becoming lodged in his left shoulder.

The Chevy then sped away, leaving Biggie with a torn chest and stomach. Looking through the rear view mirror, Puffy's driver made a U-turn and stopped in front of the rapper's SUV. Puffy jumped out and pulled open B.I.G.'s door. Biggie had a stunned look on his face and did not respond to Combs's questions. With the help of several fans who'd witnessed the incident, Puffy tried removing Biggie from the car, but the 360-pound singer could not be budged. Without bothering to wait for an ambulance, the entourage sped to nearby Cedars-Sinai Medical Center.

It took six men to move B.I.G.'s large body out of the car and onto a gurney. Biggie was hemorrhaging internally; his layers of fat closed up on his wounds, blocking the blood flow. There was nothing that doctors could do. At 1:15 a.m., twenty-four-year-old Christopher Wallace was pronounced dead.

As Tupac's had for his own, Biggie's violent end resulted in a windfall for his record company. Sixteen days after the shooting, his second album—justly titled *Life after Death*—was released. It quickly reached number one on the *Billboard* 200 charts.

The storied East Coast–West Coast war, along with the fact that both Biggie and Tupac died in drive-by shootings, led many observers to deduce that the killings were related. On the surface, revenge appeared to be the motive. But that was just one of many theories. Some speculated that the people who shot Shakur were mad at B.I.G for stiffing them on the fee for the Las Vegas hit. Others said that Biggie had antagonized the Crips by reneging on a payment for protection. Suge Knight's possible involvement was mentioned often, as was the FBI, rogue elements of the LAPD, and the Nation of Islam. According to one hypothesis, Puffy Combs was the actual target. According to another, he engineered the murder to drive up *Life after Death* sales There was also a story that, back in Brooklyn, the Notorious B.I.G had done something to piss off the Genovese crime family.

As with Tupac's death, the theories never evolved past the conjecture stage. According to the credo of the streets, gangstas didn't snitch.

But they talked just enough that investigators involved in both cases said that they kind of knew what occurred.

Greg Kading, a former LAPD detective, who wrote the book *Murder Rap*, was among a group of investigators who contended that the death of Tupac could be traced back to the incident in the MGM Grand, when he sucker punched gang member Orlando "Baby Lane" Anderson. When Knight and Shakur left the hotel, the story went, Anderson followed, in a car driven by his uncle, Duane Keith "Keffe D" Davis, a veteran Crip who didn't appreciate his nephew being humiliated.

If detectives hoped to get Baby Lane's version of events, they wouldn't have long. Two years after Tupac's death, Anderson was killed outside a Compton car wash in a gunfight over a debt.

As much as the hotel lobby fight likely hastened Tupac's demise, Keffe D claimed that a plan had been in the works for a while. In a police interview with Kading, Keffe D said that Puffy—fearing violence from Death Row and its allies—had offered him $1 million to kill Tupac and Suge. When the pair was shot, Knight "knew who was responsible," Kading told Complex.com in 2012. "He looked directly into the eyes of Keffe D, who was in the shooter's car. Keffe D was a member of the Southside Crips, and a person well-known to Suge."

In retaliation, Kading said, Knight ordered a girlfriend to sub-contract a hard-core Mob Piru Bloods member named Wardell "Poochie" Fouse to murder Biggie. "He received two payments," Kading maintained, "one for $9,000 and one for $4,000. Poochie lay in wait outside the Petersen Automotive Museum. As soon as he became aware of where Biggie was sitting in his car, he drove up and he shot him."

Poochie's life span would turn out to be longer than that of Baby Lane. In 2003, though, he was shot in the back while riding his motorcycle through Compton—allegedly because of a battle between the Mob Pirus and a competing Bloods faction called the Fruit Town Pirus.

With both supposed shooters dead, Kading said, law enforcement viewed the Tupac Shakur and Biggie Smalls cases as closed. "That's all the justice that these cases will see," the retired lawman maintained in his 2012 interview. "The coconspirators are never going to be prosecuted. Unfortunately, the cases are so complicated and convoluted. These will never see criminal prosecution."

In death, the friendship that Biggie Smalls and Tupac Shakur once enjoyed was rekindled. Fans who were too young to remember the killings, or weren't born at all, listened to both singers with identical ardor and displayed their pictures side by side. While the Crips, the Bloods, and their numerous offshoots continued to kill each other over beefs as senseless as the ones that consumed the two artists, in white America, Tupac and Biggie were perceived as martyrs—and partners—for some romanticized reason that's difficult to define. Forgotten in this idolization were the names Voletta Wallace and Afeni Shakur, women who grieved not for music never produced, disses never uttered, or scandals never started, but for two lyrical sons who loved their mothers and—like the characters in their songs—never made it past age twenty-five.

"His death is not something I want to celebrate," Voletta told the New York *Daily News* as the twentieth anniversary of Biggie's murder approached. "But I am grateful to everyone who remembers him. . . . Whatever the world sees him as, I just see him as my son. He may not be here, but his memory is etched in me for life."

11

J'ACCUSE

THE TRIALS OF THE FRENCH JIM MORRISON

By the time the elegant French starlet arrived at Vilnius University Hospital, in Lithuania's capital city, she'd been in a coma for two hours. Although her celebrity parents hoped to move her back to France, the possibility was out of the question. Doctors suspected that forty-one-year-old Marie Trintignant—a woman known for playing provocative but deeply flawed characters—had a brain hemorrhage, and rushed her into neurosurgery. She had no noticeable brain activity and was being kept alive through artificial respiration. "Mortality rates in this type of case are between 90 and 95 percent," neurosurgeon Robertas Kvascevicius told the press.

Earlier in the night, an Italian tourist had heard Marie and her boyfriend, singer Bertrand Cantat, arguing loudly in their room at the Domina Plaza hotel, after others saw them drinking at a party. Police wanted to question Bertrand but couldn't. He, too, was in the hospital in a semicomatose state, the result of an excessive intake of alcohol and various medications. Authorities suspected that he'd tried to commit suicide.

Almost immediately, the French media was reporting every snippet it could uncover. Cantat, thirty-nine, was the lead singer of the cult rock group Noir Désir—or "Dark Desire"—arguably the country's most influential band of the 1980s and '90s. With his acerbic lyrics and propensity for borrowing from poets like Arthur Rimbaud and Charles Baudelaire—the fathers of surrealism and modernism, respectively—the charismatic Cantat was frequently

referred to as the French Jim Morrison. There were also compari-
sons to Kurt Cobain. But Bertrand was slightly different from his
ill-fated American counterparts. He was idealistic and immersed
in the issues of the French streets, using the energy of his music
to lash out against capitalism, racism, and the mistreatment of
asylum seekers from Africa and the Middle East.

When Bertrand finally awoke, with his bandmates seated
alongside Lithuanian detectives at the foot of the hospital bed, he
provided an explanation for Marie's unfortunate condition. The
actress, he said, had fallen and hit her head.

After two surgeries, Marie's family was given permission to
airlift her by private jet to Paris, where she died on August 1,
2003, five days after the altercation. An autopsy revealed that
she'd suffered a series of blows to her face and head. At that point,
Bertrand had been transferred from his hospital room, as well—to
one in a Vilnius prison.

For the remainder of the summer of 2003, the death of Marie
Trintignant and the pending trial of Bertrand Cantat was a favorite
topic of conversation for vacationers on French beaches. More
than two hundred reporters, most of them from France, would
come to Vilnius for the legal proceedings, trailing after Marie and
Bertrand's family and friends, particularly the actress's black-clad
mother, director Nadine Trintignant. Prior to the incident, both
Bertrand and Marie had been vocal opponents of America's decision to invade Iraq, inspiring the media to dwell on the irony of
two self-professed pacifists ending their romance so violently.
One French publication likened the couple to Romeo and Juliet.
But the Trintignant family lawyer, Georges Klejman, argued that
the stories bore little resemblance.

Cantat was still alive—and Romeo hadn't killed Juliet.

Even after his name was associated with domestic abuse, Bertrand maintained a loyal following in Bordeaux, the southwestern
French city known for a UNESCO World Heritage designation
for its architectural magnificence and a wine industry that dates

to the eighth century. It was there that Bertrand, the son of a naval officer, moved on the cusp of his teen years, attending the Saint-Genes secondary school, where he met future bandmates Frédéric Vidalenc, Serge Teyssot-Gay, and Denis Barthe. The quartet became famous quickly, and were labeled one of the most important French bands of their generation.

He sang of "weapons buried deep in our souls" and "the river of warm blood." Only later would people examine his lyrics and wonder if they betrayed a cruelty that the public hadn't seen.

In 1997, he married arts director Krisztina Rady after meeting her at a music festival. Her Hungarian-born mother, Csilla, remembered the singer as being slight in appearance, reserved and courteous. Despite his fame, he seemed to have a kind of innocence. Krisztina gave birth to a son, Milo, in 1998. By the time she was pregnant with their second child, Alice, Bertrand's interests had begun to shift.

"We knew that Bertrand had fallen in love with Marie Trintignant," Csilla told *Paris Match*. "That's not a crime. But we didn't think he would leave Krisztina five days after she gave birth." Even Csilla had no objection to the popular singer enjoying "parallel relationships." "With Bertrand, [Krisztina] made a promise. If a great love comes along, let the other go." Yet Krisztina was shattered that her husband would move out when she felt most vulnerable. "She still loved him."

While breastfeeding, Krisztina would anxiously wait for Bertrand to check in, sometimes before he went onstage. But according to Csilla, she harbored little animosity toward Marie. When Bertrand and the actress were together, Marie often took care of Alice. It came naturally to her, since she already had four children of her own.

Interestingly, Marie's mother's initial reaction toward the rock star had been no different than that of Csilla. "I thought he was a gentle man," Nadine Trintignant would testify in court.

For some forty years, Nadine had been known not just as a director, but as an author and activist. Her 1967 film *Mon Amour,*

Mon Amour dealt with a young woman's internal struggle about whether to have an abortion, and was nominated for the Palme d'Or at the Cannes Film Festival. In 1971, she included her name among those of 343 women who admitted to having had abortions in a "manifesto"—published in the magazine *Le Nouvel Observateur*—raising awareness about reproductive rights. The sister of actors Christian and Serge Marquand, Nadine was married to Jean-Louis Trintignant, who'd starred in several of her early films, and was best known by international audiences for appearing opposite Brigitte Bardot in *And God Created Woman* in 1956, and for receiving a Best Actor award at Cannes for his role in Costa-Gavras's political thriller *Z* in 1969.

Marie had been on movie sets practically from birth, appearing in *Mon Amour, Mon Amour* at age four. In 1971, after her infant sister Pauline died, Marie took part in an unusual project directed by her mother. In the semiautobiographical *Ca N'Arrive Qu'Aux Autres* (It Will Not Happen), Marie played the daughter of Catherine Deneuve and Marcello Mastroianni, a couple racked with torment following the death of their younger child. Nadine cast her own sibling Christian as Deneuve's brother.

By the time of her death, Marie had appeared in some forty movies and plays. Nominated for France's prestigious César Award on five separate occasions, she preferred characters "with problems," scorned by proper society. "I like to understand and defend such women," she was quoted as saying in the *Telegraph*. "It's that 'elsewhere' that interests me."

In the 1992 movie *Betty*, for instance, she played an alcoholic cast out by her bourgeois ex-husband and isolated from her children. Befriended by a compassionate older woman with similar drinking issues, Marie's character sabotages herself, obliterating all good faith by scheming to seduce her new companion's lover.

Before her relationship with Bertrand began, Marie had given birth to four sons, each from a different father. Yet she insisted that her life was "normal and balanced." As an artist, she found love to be an overpowering emotion, and sometimes saw mother-hood as the manifestation of that.

Despite her domestic demands, Marie seemed to always find the time to work. When she died, French audiences were awaiting the release of *Janis and John*, starring Marie as singer Janis Joplin, directed by her estranged husband Samuel Benchetrit. She'd gone to Lithuania to shoot a television miniseries based on the life of Colette, the French novelist who'd written *Gigi* in 1944 and had been nominated for the Nobel Prize in literature four years later. Like prior projects, it was a family production. Marie cowrote the series with her mother, who also directed. Her brother Vincent was the first assistant director.

Marie was buried in good company at Paris' Père Lachaise cemetery, not far from the graves of Edith Piaf, Frédéric Chopin, and Jim Morrison. Among the attendees at her funeral were De-neuve and former prime minister Lionel Jospin. Although Noir Désir's albums were experiencing an upsurge of sales, the curiosity factor brought Bertrand little public amity. A month after Marie's interment, the singer's house was burned down. While his wife and children were not home at the time, investigators believed that the arsonist had hoped they would be.

The incident started at the *Colette* wrap party. Drink in hand, Bertrand circulated among the cast and crew, interacting nicely with both Nadine and Vincent Trintignant. The group then re-turned to the Domina Plaza, where Marie is said to have received an affectionate text message from Benchetrit. That was how the argument started, Bertrand said. Feeling both drunk and jeal-ous, he said that he questioned the nature of the relationship with her husband, prompting Marie to "explode." She was so irate, he'd say in court, "I didn't recognize her anymore. She was very nasty, her words were incredibly cold, insulting to me, Krisztina, my children." Later on, he wished he would have simply stormed out of the room. "Marie was out of control. I was out of control."

He claimed that Marie struck him first. "After she hit me, I was furious," he said. "Even then, Marie did not stop screaming. I had never seen her like that." Bertrand confessed to slapping her four times. "They were really hard slaps." It was a response that he said that he quickly regretted. "Everything happened so fast. Never, never did I want things to happen that way. This hand never should have risen. And I do not accept myself having raised this hand."

Lithuanian authorities offered a different version of the encounter, estimating that Bertrand hit Marie nineteen times, fracturing bones and causing brain damage. She never awoke from her coma, and died of brain swelling.

Cantat characterized the death as a tragic accident, rather than a murder. He spoke of accompanying Marie to the hospital, then of returning to the hotel so distraught that he began plotting his suicide. After arranging a number of razor blades, he maintained, he took a large dose of medication to desensitize himself. Before he got around to cutting his wrists, he said, he passed out.

When Marie finally died, Bertrand claimed that his lawyer waited three days before delivering the news to the singer, fearful that the information might incite the star to try suicide again.

Because the most important scenes had already been shot, Nadine Trintignant was able to complete her series about the novelist who examined, among other topics, the role of female sexuality in a male-dominated world. She dedicated *Colette* to her daughter.

She also wrote a book about Marie, describing Bertrand as a man too insecure to handle his girlfriend's friendships with the fathers of her children. "The two children of this man," she said in the neoclassical Vilnius courtroom, "apparently such a good father, have become the children of a murderer."

Before court each day, members of the press began gathering three hours early. When they entered the small chamber, a handcuffed Cantat—dressed in the informal attire he might wear to a press junket—stared out at photographers, as camera strobes bounced off the glassed-in dock.

To Lithuanians, it seemed unusual to see so many Western Europeans converging in Vilnius. Although the trial received a great deal of local media attention, the average citizen of the Baltic republic appeared more concerned with indigenous news, specifically the impeachment of the country's president, Rolandas Paksas.

Interestingly, one of Bertrand's staunchest defenders was the wife he'd left for Marie. Krisztina Rady told the court that her husband was "an honest man, very good and very gentle." Indeed, no one was "as incorruptible and honest as him." Despite the challenges in their relationship, the singer had "taught me to be strong," and never once came close to raising a hand to her. "I could never have lived with a liar, a macho, and a beater," she emphasized.

In her interview with *Paris Match*, Krisztina's mother, Csilla, said that the entire family was stunned by Marie's death, and forgave Bertrand for the circumstances that led to it. "We immediately thought it was an accident, that Bertrand did not intend to kill her."

However, Samuel Benchetrit claimed the family was attempting to sanitize the traits of a dangerous man. Indeed, the director testified that he'd spoken with Krisztina after the incident and learned that Cantat had been violent at home, and had even chased his wife with a knife. The day after Marie was rushed to the hospital, Benchetrit said, "Krisztina told me that the same thing had happened to her."

Each night after the trial, Bertrand was returned to the Lukiskes Isolation Unit, a prison dating back to the Tsarist era. His attorneys' legal strategy centered on describing the incident as a crime of passion, far out of character for the conscientious performer. In the witness box, Bertrand appeared contrite, and made an effort to address Marie's family directly. "I know that all I can do is ask for forgiveness, just as I have done from the outset," he said. "I loved Marie with all my heart, and I will always love her. And I am thinking at all times of her family, of her children . . . and I know the misery I have put them through."

At times, he attempted to make direct eye contact with Marie's mother, but the director always looked away. "I've heard too many lies," she explained, "and if I had to speak [to him], I would express myself poorly."

More than anything, Bertrand said that he wanted the victim's loved ones to understand "that Marie did not die of hate. And I also want to say that there are other people in this story . . . my wife, my children. . . ."

Before he could complete the sentence, Bertrand dissolved into tears.

Prosecutor Kazimieras Modeka countered that, despite his outward signs of grief, Bertrand "did absolutely nothing to help Ms. Trintignant after he hit her. He said he thought she was sleeping on the floor, and simply left the room. It's difficult to believe that such an educated person could think this."

On March 29, 2004, the three-judge panel found Bertrand guilty of murder with indirect intent. Judge Vilmantas Gaidelis acknowledged that the singer had never intended to kill his girl-friend. "He did not want the consequences," said the magistrate, "but they occurred. The guilt is unquestionable."

Under Lithuanian law, he was facing anywhere from five to fifteen years' imprisonment. When the panel imposed a sentence of eight years, Bertrand solemnly nodded when asked if he under-stood what had just transpired. Later, he'd attempt to appeal, asking a higher court to downgrade his crime to manslaughter. By contrast, Nadine petitioned authorities to impose a harsher sentence. Eventually, both parties withdrew their requests, and grudgingly accepted their predicaments.

Confined to a cell, illuminated by a fluorescent light from 6 a.m. to 10 p.m., Bertrand was forbidden to speak to other inmates and could barely sleep. When he did, he said, nightmares quickly invaded his mind. "I always hoped to wake up, pinch myself," he told the French cultural magazine *Les Inrockuptibles.* "And the day was worse than the night. There was no limit to this nightmare."

He claimed that he screamed at the walls, shouted for Marie, and wished he could join her in death. "I was overwhelmed by pain, thinking of her." He also agonized over the way the public viewed him. "My remorse, my suffering . . . did not work in this story. I became a caricature. The fact that I loved Marie so much has been erased. . . . All that was beautiful was hidden. . . . I had to be condemned as heavily as possible."

Although yoga provided temporary relief, his creative energy appeared to be gone. "There was no miracle by writing. It takes a minimum of self-confidence to write. There, I had nothing left."

At one point, he was invited to perform a concert in the prison chapel. But when he strummed the guitar, he said, he felt as if he no longer possessed the skill. "I finished with bloody fingers. I was utterly dazed. I have no recollection of this concert."

In September, 2004, Lithuanian authorities agreed to a request from Cantat's lawyers to allow him to be transferred to a prison near Muret, France. It was there that he started to write poems, lyrics, and songs, preparing for the career that he hoped to resume after his incarceration ended.

In total, Bertrand served four years behind bars, attaining his freedom via a French law that allows an inmate to be paroled on good behavior after half a sentence is served. Marie's family appealed directly to President Nicolas Sarkozy to block the release, but to no avail. In October 2007, Cantat left prison and returned home to his wife, Krisztina, and children.

That wasn't the only relationship that he tried to revive. He also rejoined Noir Désir.

He later said that he'd been severely depressed at this time, and unprepared for the repercussions that the band would suffer after welcoming him back. In *Les Inrockuptibles*, he described Noir Désir as "another prison, where you had to ask permission to sing. It hurt me a lot."

In October 2010, Cantat and the group performed in Bordeaux, but the concert was marred by protests from women's activists. The next month, Noir Désir announced that it was permanently disbanding.

By then, Bertrand was being reviled for the role he might have played in another premature death.

On January 10, 2010, Cantat's twelve-year-old son, Milo, came home in the middle of the day to make a horrifying discovery. Sometime during the previous night, his mother, Krisztina, had hung herself. Nearby was a message in a notebook apologizing for the impact of her actions.

Reportedly, Bertrand was home when Krisztina made the decision to take her own life. But he was allegedly in another part of the house and unaware of what had transpired.

Initially, Krisztina's parents were supportive of Cantat. Police investigated, interviewing Bertrand's ex-girlfriends to determine if he'd physically abused them. Each woman insisted that she'd never witnessed the singer's violent streak. The death of Marie appeared to be an aberration. Unable to prove that Bertrand had been snuffing out his lovers, authorities closed the case.

Only later would Krisztina's parents tell the press that six months prior to the suicide, their daughter had warned them that Bertrand was subjecting her to both physical and psychological harm, ranting and throwing objects around the house. In a telephone message, they said, she urged them to inform the authorities if anything happened to her. After Bertrand's release from prison and reunion with his family, she purportedly said, "a series of events worse than those of 2003" had taken place.

According to Csilla Rady, Bertrand resented Krisztina for working outside the house, and was jealous of other men who came into her life. "Everyone thinks he's an icon and wants what's best for him," Krisztina said in the voice mail, "but then he comes home and does these terrible things to me in front of the family."

Yet Krisztina had willfully testified for her husband, her mother said, in order to keep that family intact. "At first we did not understand why she was not telling the truth," Csilla told *Paris Match*. "But, for her children, she could not do otherwise. She did not want their father to spend his life in prison as a murderer."

Despite the investigation that absolved Bertrand of any crime, Csilla continued to wonder if her daughter had really died by her own hand. "When Bertrand was at his lowest in prison, Krisztina had only one fear—that his children would find themselves without a father. She'd never consider leaving her children behind as orphans. I cannot believe that she committed suicide."

When interviewed by *Les Inrockuptibles*, Bertrand refused to discuss his late wife's mental state. "Her act belongs to her, and all I can say is that there was a great deal of complexity behind it." He claimed that he wondered about the signs that he missed, and agonized over what more he could have done to save Krisztina. "The delirious accusations against me are unacceptable. It's appalling, disgraceful to have become the symbol of violence against women."

That reputation tarnished every subsequent musical project Bertrand attempted. When he was invited to Montreal to sing in a show written by playwright Wajdi Mouawad, politicians attempted to ban the musician from entering the country. Although Mouawad reasoned that Bertrand's appearance would help him reintegrate into society, the invitation was eventually rescinded. In 2013, Cantat released an album with bass player Pascal Humbert, and was warmly welcomed back onstage. Yet even this triumph was viewed through the prism of Marie Trintignant's death, with coverage of the performances focusing on the justifications fans made to forgive their idol.

In Bordeaux, where his fan base was strongest, Bertrand was able to open a restaurant with two friends. Nonetheless, a sizable number of his followers had abandoned him forever, viewing each high-profile undertaking as a desecration of the memories of Marie Trintignant and Krisztina Rady. "This is not a tale of forgiveness and redemption," *Le Point* magazine editor in chief Franz-Olivier Giesbert editorialized. "It's the story of a narcissistic killer, a master of self-pity.

"Most murderers, after they're released, just want to be forgotten. Not Bertrand Cantat. He needs to show his wounds to the people. He's made a career of it."

12

ONE LAST COLD KISS
THE SHOOTING OF FELIX PAPPALARDI

It was just after 6 a.m. when a New York City emergency operator received a call from Manhattan's moneyed Upper East Side. "I killed my husband," reported the woman on the other end of the telephone. "I didn't mean to?"

"How did you do it?" the operator asked.

Rather than explain the details, Gail Collins Pappalardi instinctively focused on motive. "Anger," she responded. "But . . ." She paused. ". . . not intentional. Never, never, never."

When officers from the Thirteenth Precinct arrived at 30 Waterside Plaza, a high-rise overlooking the East River, Gail exhibited a similar disconnect. "I just shot my husband," she stated.

"Where?"

"In the neck."

The officer calmly rephrased the question. "No, I mean, where is he?"

Gail led her visitors into the bedroom, where her spouse, forty-one-year-old Felix Pappalardi, lay dead in his underwear. As Gail specified, a single bullet had passed through his neck and entered the carotid artery. While Pappalardi's music was recognizable—he was the bassist and vocalist on the hard rock band Mountain's hit "Mississippi Queen"—he was not so famous that a New York City police officer would instantly recognize him. Nor would police have realized that the frazzled woman next to them had made her own contributions to rock 'n' roll, cowriting the lyrics to the song "Strange Brew" on Cream's 1967 *Disraeli Gears* album with her husband and Eric Clapton. How she'd become the sole survivor at a crime scene was something that she was anxious to explain.

According to her supporters, Gail hated guns, including the .38-caliber Derringer that killed Felix. "Gail didn't like them at all," entertainment attorney James Mosher would later testify. "She was extremely unhappy that [Felix] kept guns in the apartment."

But Felix insisted that Gail overcome her fear, she said. Since she didn't know how to shoot, Gail told authorities, her husband had decided that the time had come to administer early-morning firearms training. In the course of the lesson, she continued, the weapon unexpectedly discharged.

It would be several hours before Pappalardi's former Mountain bandmates Leslie West and Corky Laing learned that Gail—a woman with whom they'd both worked and feuded—had been arrested for murdering her husband. West was dismissive of the news at first. After all, rumors about Felix's demise—usually via OD—were common. But Corky had listened to the radio reports, and knew that this was more than idle gossip.

As the pair stood in their hotel lobby, before a show in South Bend, Indiana, Corky repeated the particulars he'd been able to glean. "I was not surprised," West told TeamRock.com, "because I knew Felix had guns. When you have guns and drugs around, and you have jealousy, frustration and depression and all the things that are in that negative, gray area, you're going to have a disaster."

Felix Pappalardi Jr. had always shown promise as a musician. Unlike those rock 'n' rollers whose inspirations came from the experience of personal struggle, Felix was raised in relative privilege. The son of a Bronx physician, Felix qualified for the exclusive High School of Music and Art in Manhattan, where he studied the piano and the viola. After graduation, he moved on to the University of Michigan, Ann Arbor, to train as a classical conductor.

Fellow students remembered him exhibiting star quality. But there wasn't enough action or opportunity in Ann Arbor to maintain Felix's interest. Returning to New York, he joined Max Morath's

Original Rag Quartet—a unit reviving Scott Joplin's ragtime music—on the Greenwich Village folk scene, as well as the college circuit. He also found work as a session musician who could play virtually anything, including the trumpet, the bass, the ukulele, and the *guitarrón*, the large bass guitar associated with mariachi bands. Among the artists whom he accompanied: Joan Baez, John Sebastian, and Mama Cass Elliot. Despite possessing a personality that could sometimes be caustic, he ingratiated himself to the right people and was regularly called upon to write arrangements and produce at such labels as Atlantic, Vanguard, and Elektra.

In 1966, Clapton, along with drummer Ginger Baker and bassist Jack Bruce, formed the band Cream in London, an effort to merge rock with its blues roots. In contrast to other popular bands consisting of longtime associates—Mick Jagger and Keith Richards, for instance, had attended the same class in primary school—this was an effort to create a "supergroup," based on musicianship. Although the band's debut album, *Fresh Cream*, charted respectfully, something appeared to be missing.

Because Atlantic's Atco subdivision was slated to be the US label for the band, Cream's manager Robert Stigwood sent the members to New York to record at Atlantic's studio with engineer Tom Dowd. At the time, Dowd, a future Rock and Roll Hall of Famer, was accustomed to working with jazz and folk combos. However, Felix was already a Cream fan, and had positioned himself in the Atlantic building in anticipation of meeting the band. Once he did, he asked Atlantic boss Ahmet Ertegun about participating in Cream's next project.

The request was granted. Felix produced the group's next two albums, *Disraeli Gears* and *Wheels of Fire*, and he and Dowd would come to be regarded as the fourth and fifth members of Cream. Pappalardi—sometimes called "Boom Boom" for his style of bass playing—played viola, keyboards, and trumpet during the *Disraeli Gears* sessions, reworking lyrics and transforming some of the bluesy melodies into something more commercially appealing. The album, which combined psychedelic rock with pop, traditional English song, and African rhythms, would chart in the Top 10 in both the United States and Great Britain, and would become the model for what is now defined as "classic rock."

■ ■ ■

Leslie Weinstein was an overweight, raspy-voiced kid from Queens, working in Manhattan's Diamond District, selling jewelry. Every afternoon, during his lunch break, he'd walk a few blocks over to the music stores on West Forty-Eighth Street and look at the various guitars. When he lost track of time one day and returned to work late, his boss apparently said, "Don't bother coming back."

That was fine with Leslie. He'd been playing guitar since he'd received a Fender Stratocaster for his bar mitzvah. With the possible exception of baseball, there was nothing that Leslie could do better. Turning his outsize back on the rudimentary working life, Leslie devoted himself to music. By 1969, he was Leslie West, the star of Mountain—named both for the group's deep, electrified blues sound and the girth of the lead singer. Jeff Beck would later call Leslie the world's greatest living guitarist. But he needed good people to help him attain that status, and asked Felix to back him on bass. All Leslie knew about Felix was that he was a killer musician who sure seemed to get a lot of studio work. It would take a while for West to realize that this was also the same guy who he'd cheered, while tripping on acid, at a Cream show at the old Village Theater.

Felix, in turn, brought in Corky Laing on drums. "I'll never forget them telling me I was going to be joining their band," Corky told *Classic Rock*'s Dave Ling. "Felix was sitting next to a big pile of cocaine—I didn't know what it was at the time—which he pointed to and told me, 'See this stuff here. I don't want you ever touching it.'"

The investment paid off quickly. The band's fourth gig was in front of 400,000 fans at Woodstock.

When the group went into the studio to record its debut album, Felix was the producer, as well as bassist, vocalist, pianist, and rhythm guitarist. He also received songwriting credits on six of the nine songs. Under his stewardship, *Climbing!*—released in March 1970—reached number seventeen on the American music charts.

The album's most outstanding offering was "Mississippi Queen," which happened to become a hit during a period when the American airlines were on strike. While other bands canceled their bookings, Mountain traversed the country by Greyhound bus. "We toured our asses off to get behind that song," Laing said.

Pappalardi's impact would be felt for decades. Performers like Jack White and the Black Keys would cite him as an influence. Jay Z, Nas, De La Soul, Lana Del Rey, and A Tribe Called Quest were among the artists to sample the Mountain song "Long Red."

Besides profiting from his natural talents, Felix also benefited from his partnership with his wife, Gail—whom he'd met in 1964 on the New York folk scene. A natural rhythmist, Gail not only cowrote many of the tunes on *Climbing!* and Mountain's 1971 LP, *Nantucket Sleighride*, she painted the psychedelic art on both album covers.

After Jimi Hendrix died, Gail memorialized him in the song "Tired Angels." Her impressions of Woodstock were included in "For Yasgur's Farm." Much of the couple's creative collaboration took place at their retreat on the small island of Nantucket, off Cape Cod. It was there that they co-wrote the song "One Last Cold Kiss," which included a lyric that fans would revisit after Felix's death:

"Husband, come to my side, let your feathers warm my pain
For I feel I will not share another day with you again."

According to Felix, the pair were generally in sync about music. "Me and my old lady fight," he told *Sounds* magazine, "but never about that."

The partnership was not necessarily healthy for the band. Laing later compared Gail to Jeanine, the interfering girlfriend in *This Is Spinal Tap*. "But at least *Spinal Tap* was funny."

West told Ling, "As Mountain became more famous, she seemed to hate the fact that I was becoming better known than Felix. That was when the shit really started. There were a lot of drugs, and things got nasty."

The friction was exacerbated by a taxing schedule. "We were constantly playing," Laing told *Goldmine* magazine. "We did every gig that they called in. When we had a number-one hit, we were playing high schools that were booked basically a year in advance. They started booking Mountain in '69 and there we were, in 1970 and '71, playing previously booked gigs that we had to make. . . . As a result, I think the pressure and the familiarity with each person— because we were on top of each other the whole time—caused contempt between the old ladies. . . . It was all really congested, so that contributed a great deal to the unhappiness."

Laing acknowledged that Gail was a woman of significant capacity. Yet he'd developed an extreme distaste for her. "She was very talented, very smart, but evil," he told TeamRock.com. "Gail claimed she loved Felix, but they were always fighting. Felix was not a big guy, and Gail would beat the shit out of him. Other times, they'd get high and shoot at the walls in their house."

West claimed that there was a reason for the gunplay. When Gail refused to pay a contractor, West said, the workmen stuffed hornets' nests between the walls of the couple's home—prompting Felix to fire at the places where he imagined that the insects were buzzing.

As time passed, scoring drugs appeared almost as important as the music. West said that his more-than-three-hundred-pound frame allowed him to consume substances in far greater amounts than average-size people. As for Felix, West told *Classic Rock*, the bassist "was more interested in waiting for his drugs to show up than [in] coming to rehearsals." The result was a lackluster third album, *Flowers of Evil*, in 1971, consisting partially of live songs.

What followed were a series of breakups and reconciliations. During one encounter, Felix slugged Corky for suggesting that the group bring in a new producer. In 1974, the band released *Twin Peaks*, recorded live in Japan—featuring a Pappalardi bass solo that went so long, it was split between side one and side two. In 1975, the group disbanded.

Officially, the split occurred because Felix's hearing had been damaged from performing next to large, Sunn bass amplifiers on stage. In reality, both West and Laing later maintained, Pappalardi's drug dependence had rendered him incapable of contributing to the band.

He had no intention of retiring. The Japanese band Creation collaborated with Felix and Gail, writing songs with them: together, Pappalardi and the band recorded the 1976 album *Felix Pappalardi & Creation*. Three years later, Pappalardi released a solo project that concentrated more on funk and reggae than on his usual jazz and blues. But even without the day-to-day grind of performing with Mountain, Felix didn't turn the corner. There were sightings of Felix, high on Percodan, driving around Nantucket in his Rolls-Royce, firing out the window at glass resistors on telephone poles. When he and Gail approached Corky about reforming Mountain in 1982, the drummer demurred.

At home, Felix and Gail tried testing the boundaries of traditional monogamy. "We sometimes shared a woman lover," Gail would testify. "He liked that best. We had what I've called an open marriage."

The experiment didn't always work. Gail claimed that both parties were capable of jealousy. Nonetheless, they'd gone too far to roll things back. For a period, Felix had a relationship with the couple's housekeeper. There was also Valerie Merians, an aspiring singer and the daughter of a friend who owned a club in Woodstock. "[Felix and I] were very much in love, and talked of marrying," she told the *New York Post*. "We talked of getting an apartment together, even of going to Australia together."

The connection seemed deeper than with other lovers, causing distress for Gail. She phoned her in-laws and tearfully fretted that the end of the marriage was inevitable. "She knew she was going to lose her world," Laing told TeamRock.com. "It was a matter of that time coming when she was going to explode."

■   ■   ■

By all accounts, Felix returned home on the morning of April 17, 1983, after spending the night with Valerie. Gail was reportedly high on Percodan. After Felix's shooting, she opted to call her lawyer before dialing 911. The attorney recommended seeking medical help immediately.

Police found the couple's wedding certificate—normally framed and hanging over the bed—torn and on top of the same desk where the .38 Derringer was located. Gail explained that this was Felix's doing. He'd unintentionally ripped the document, she said, in the course of removing it from its old casing so that it could be reframed.

"He had a habit of tearing up papers he was about to throw away," she stated.

Likewise, she emphasized, the shooting had been an accident. "He was trying to get me familiar with [the gun]," Gail testified. "Something happened that I have no recollection of, a noise, something . . . and I moved or something, and the gun went off. Time froze for a second when I realized Felix had been hit. I could not remember my own name at that point."

She claimed that she and Felix had been getting along fine that day. Their neighbors, though, maintained that they'd overheard a loud argument. Investigators deduced that Gail was lying about the chain of events. She was arrested at the scene and charged with second-degree homicide—the most serious murder charge one could receive in New York, unless one was accused of killing a member of law enforcement.

The motive, authorities said, was sexual jealousy.

"You don't go home when your wife is waiting for you with a gun and tell her you're going to leave her," Corky told reporter David J. Krajicek on Goodreads.com. "You know she's going to Sam Cooke your ass."

From jail, Gail phoned her husband's business partner and made him an offer. She was short of cash, she said, and was willing to sell a share of the song publishing for the Cream tunes "Strange Brew" and "World of Pain" in exchange for bail money. The partner agreed. An incredulous West later said that he asked the man how he could possibly have assisted the woman who murdered his friend. The partner allegedly replied, "Felix probably would have wanted me to help her."

At the trial, the defense disputed the prosecution's contention that Gail murdered her husband in a possessive rage. "From time to time, they each had sex with other people, but it was no big deal," said entertainment lawyer James Mosher. "They even made jokes about it."

Regardless of what the prosecution stated, Mosher insisted that Valerie Merians was no threat to the marriage. When defense attorney Neal Comer asked about Felix's opinion about the younger woman, the attorney replied, "He thought she was a flake."

Furthermore, Gail said that she encouraged Felix to date another woman because "she had a calming effect on him."

"Did the affair hurt you?" assistant district attorney Maureen Barden queried.

"Not at all. We were very close friends."

An actor named Frank DeLuca was called to the stand to regale jurors with tales about his sexual exploits with Gail. Pappalardi not only approved of the trysts, DeLuca said, but invited the thespian to spend time at the couple's Nantucket home. He slept downstairs during the visit, he testified, since the Pappalardis were sharing their bedroom with another woman.

"Did you ever see the three of them in bed together?" defense lawyer Neal Comer asked.

"Yes," DeLuca responded shyly.

The entire episode was an unfortunate fluke, Comer's defense partner, Hal Meyerson, told the jury. "No one felt worse than Mrs. Pappalardi. But let's not punish Mrs. Pappalardi for what was an accident."

In the months since the shooting, Gail had been able to add texture to the story about the gun inadvertently firing. She'd found the silver Derringer while poking through a drawer, she maintained, and showed it to Felix. As the musician was explaining the proper way to shoot, Comer said, the couple's pet cat leaped forward, prompting Gail to pull the trigger.

Yet prosecutors were emphatic in their position that Gail was not only familiar with the weapon—apparently carrying it around in her purse—but had wielded it previously in a bout of jealousy. When Corky Laing's wife, Frances, was summoned as a witness, she recounted an incident in which she and Felix had attempted to have a private conversation in her car to escape the loud noise in Mountain's rehearsal space. "All of a sudden, Gail showed up . . . obviously very irate," Frances said. "She was standing at my window. She pulled a gun and pointed it at me. She was upset about Felix and I [sic] sitting and talking in the car."

The most dramatic moment of the trial occurred when a court officer placed the .38 in front of the suspect. Shrinking back in her seat, Gail burst into sobs. "I can't touch that gun," she cried. "I can't, I can't touch that."

Prosecutors were confident as jurors began deliberating. Gail's story about the bedside firearms training appeared to be false. Plus, on the 911 call, she admitted to having shot in anger. Yet, in the jury room, the six men and six women expressed sympathy for Gail, attributing the inconsistency and confusion to her drug use. Felix was hardly a good guy, they surmised, making the perverse demand on his spouse to have sex with other people. If anyone was a victim in this case, it was Gail. And her revulsion at the sight of the .38 seemed to suggest that she truly felt regret.

Before they reentered the courtroom, four of the jurors outright insisted that Gail be acquitted on all counts.

Instead, she was convicted of criminally negligent homicide—an act generally seen as devoid of premeditation—rather than murder, collapsing into her attorney's arms as the verdict was read.

"We don't believe Felix was planning to leave or that jealousy on Gail's part was a motive," juror Richard Ozores told United Press International.

"We were very impressed with her," fellow panelist Grace Walters told the *New York Post.* "We did believe her story. We felt there was no intent. She did not want him to die."

Judge James Leff remained skeptical. "She called her attorney instead of calling for help," he reproached the jury. "She was concerned with her own well-being."

But the twelve citizens had made their decision. Sentenced to the maximum penalty of four years, Gail served just two behind bars before receiving parole.

Following her release, Gail kept a low profile. In New York, she organized dinner cruises around Manhattan, but was careful not to publicize her roles in Cream, Mountain, or Felix's death. She then moved west, living for a time in a waterfront apartment on the opposite side of the Golden Gate Bridge from San Francisco, and then in Vancouver, Washington. In 2005, she relocated to Mexico, settling among the community of expat Americans and Canadians in the mile-high town of Ajijic, on Lake Chapala, near Guadalajara. Some of the songs she cowrote had been rereleased or included in movies and TV shows, and Gail lived off the royalties and Social Security. She picked up extra money using her artistic talent to design beaded jewelry and develop a clothing line. For a period, she had her own boutique. Visitors could tell that she'd had an eventful life, but she was cagey about details, preferring to use her middle name, Delta.

She described herself as a cancer survivor who'd been part of a control group of two dozen patients receiving experimental treatments. The type of cancer she had seemed to change but, invariably, she claimed to have been miraculously cured.

She was special, after all.

The traits that had alienated her from Felix's bandmates were still there. When a neighbor put up a fence to prevent Gail's cats from splaying about on the adjoining property, the woman's children were reportedly warned that their mother might turn up dead. "She was one of the most brilliant people I have ever known," a friend, Diane Pearl, told Krajicek, "but she was an opinionated jackass. . . . She just needed to be the star. And if someone else was going to be the star, she rebelled against it."

In late 2013, Gail's landlord discovered the seventy-two-year-old woman's body on the floor of her apartment. Having isolated herself from a significant amount of the human population, she'd grown so close to her cats that she'd mandated that the animals be euthanized and their ashes mixed with her own. In keeping with her wishes, a veterinarian was dispatched to her home. Neighbors reportedly saw him leave the residence with three dead cats.

It had been thirty years since Felix had been killed. And although both the songs and the beats he helped create were well-known, his name recognition had diminished over the past generation. But Leslie West and Corky Laing were still around, convinced that there was still much to be learned from Boom Boom's tale of woe.

West advised husbands to purchase their spouses jewelry, roses, or sexy lingerie. But under no circumstances, he emphasized, should a man buy his wife a gun.

13

ANOTHER THING COMING
JUDAS PRIEST ON TRIAL

The six hours spent listening to Judas Priest probably wasn't the best thing for their inner health. But eighteen-year-old Raymond Belknap and his twenty-year-old best friend, James "Jay" Vance, didn't have a lot going on in the first place.

The pair talked about suicide a lot, and guns and drugs—particularly crank, a powdered form of methamphetamine. But, above everything else, the two metalheads loved Priest. The friends had seen the band once, in Reno, in 1982, while the group was supporting its *Screaming for Vengeance* album. Ray managed to steal a poster from the World Vengeance tour to hang over his bed. Jay fantasized about meeting the group. He later said that he would have gladly "done anything those guys asked me to do."

When the pair tried suicide in late 1985—Ray succeeded and Jay didn't—the members of Judas Priest were nowhere near the dreary churchyard where the young men took turns firing a sawed-off shotgun at their respective faces. Yet the boys' parents, as well as supporters from coalitions looking to restrict the content in heavy metal music, came to believe that the two were following orders, issued directly by Judas Priest. It had to do with those six hours repeatedly playing the band's 1978 album, *Stained Class*, and the messages lawyers claimed were woven throughout the record.

Jay seemed to say as much in a letter he wrote to his friend's mother four months after the incident: "I believe that alcohol and heavy metal music, such as Judas Priest, led us or even mesmerized us into believing that the answer to life was death."

His assessment would lead to a $6.2 million lawsuit against the band and its label at the time, CBS. For close to three weeks, four members of Judas Priest—lead singer Rob Halford, guitarists Glenn Tipton and K. K. Downing, and bassist Ian Hill—traded their leather and spikes for blazers and collared shirts, appearing daily in Nevada's Washoe County Courthouse to defend heavy metal in general, and the band in particular, against charges that the album had sent the boys subliminal messages like "try suicide," "do it," and "let's be dead" in their version of the song "Better by You, Better Than Me."

"It tore us up emotionally, hearing someone say to the judge and the cameras that this is a band that creates music that kills young people," Halford told *Billboard*. "We accept that some people don't like heavy metal, but we can't let them convince us that it's negative and destructive. Heavy metal is a friend that gives people great pleasure and enjoyment, and helps them through hard times."

But the families' advocates contended that the purpose of the music was far more sinister, since production of *Stained Class* had included a technique called "backward masking." Its purpose: controlling listeners' minds via destructive messages deliberately recorded in reverse.

It was the first time Halford, who joined the group in his native Birmingham, England, in 1974, had ever heard of the concept. "It's very, very intriguing subject matter built in psychology," he told *Rolling Stone*. "But I haven't got a clue. I'm just a fuckin' singer in a heavy metal band."

Although Judas Priest—named for the 1967 Bob Dylan song "The Ballad of Frankie Lee and Judas Priest"—had been around since 1969, it took the band a while to develop its look and sound. Characterized by Halford's operatic vocals and Tipton and Downing's twin guitars, Priest became the consummate metal combo, incorporating pyrotechnics, onstage monsters and robots, and medieval and Armageddon themes. Fans nicknamed Halford the "Metal God." He liked the moniker so much that he had it trademarked.

Over time, he developed back problems from performing in "literally thirty pounds of leather and steel spikes," along with choke collars and other S&M paraphernalia. If you were into that type of thing, Halford's costumes might have led you to believe that he was homosexual. At least that's what people in the gay community said. But Halford—who'd later joke that he'd become the "Stately Homo of Metal"—didn't officially come out until 1998. Although some fans may have had homophobic leanings, his announcement, he told the *Guardian*, "didn't affect Priest one iota. The record sales didn't plunge. The show attendance didn't plunge. Unconditional love will accept you for who you are, and I think that was the blessing I had from the fans."

It was a feeling that was consistently reciprocated. When members looked out into the audience, they saw some version of themselves pumping their fists and bobbing their heads. "Metal has . . . that controversial attribute, and that's what makes it appealing to a lot of people," Halford told the Canadian publication the *Georgia Straight*. "You can either be in the mainstream . . . or you can go in a more rebellious form with something that's got some meat and substance and, to some extent, a little bit of stimulation and aggression."

The band has always "flown the flag for metal," Tipton told the *Rock Is Life* website. "Judas Priest is proud to be part of heavy metal. We never disowned the tag of heavy metal when many other bands did because it wasn't fashionable. We love every minute onstage playing heavy metal."

Ideally, fans would use that inspiration to propel themselves toward their dreams. Which was why the trial was so heartbreaking to the bandmates. "I've got strange feelings about those kids," Downing told the *Village Voice*. "It's not guilt, you know, but I do feel haunted when I hear about their lives. Because they were the same as mine. . . . I think our music was the best thing they had."

The tale of Ray Belknap and Jay Vance is just one of many tragedies connected to Reno, a three-square-mile, former gold rush destination in the Sierra Nevadas. Once known for quickie divorces, along with its tawdry casinos, it's a place where people traditionally came to seek out a fortune or satisfy an impulse. But after these travelers moved on, families like the Belknaps and Vances remained, short-changed at the roulette table.

In his youth, Jay saw beyond the neon signs, savoring nature in the mountains and desert outside the city, backpacking and gardening, and pondering a future as a hunting or fishing guide. Nonetheless, there were obstacles at every turn. Although innately intelligent, Jay was diagnosed with attention deficit disorder and left back twice, acting out as frustrations mounted. In second grade, he tied a belt around his head and began pulling out his hair. The next year, he attempted to choke his mother in the car one day after getting into trouble at school. In the years to come, he'd attack her with both a hammer and a pistol. After a junior high flirtation with born-again Christianity, he briefly dabbled in white supremacy, supplementing his meth usage with barbiturates, LSD, cocaine, PCP, and heroin.

Judas Priest was among the few pure pleasures he had, and he rotated their albums on the stereo to suit his temperament. "It doesn't matter if you're a beggar or a king," Halford would later preach. "Metal will find its way into your heart if you accept it."

Jay's mother, Phyllis, agreed with the religious analogy. Her son, she told the *Voice*, recited Priest lyrics "like Scripture."

Ray was a kindred spirit. The two had been best friends since sixth grade, listening to music, shooting targets in the hills and bats in nearby caves, and playing "knuckles"—punching each other's fists until one drew blood. At six foot two and just 141 pounds at the time of his death, Ray tended to be withdrawn and, according to a stepbrother who testified at the trial, the victim of their stepfather's angry lashings. In high school, he only passed two classes: Shop I and Shop II.

After two years at Edward C. Reed High in Sparks, he left to start working. Yet there was always some kind of problem. He lost a job at a used-furniture store after stealing $454 from his boss's desk. Shortly before he died, he was fired from a print shop for refusing to work overtime.

Still, when everything else was going badly, Ray and Jay always had Priest.

"Those boys who shot themselves, they weren't driven mad by music," Halford told *Guitar World* magazine. "Music was their only escape. It was the only thing they loved."

■ ■ ■

On December 23, 1985, Ray accompanied his four-year-old sister, Christie Lynn, to the hair salon, took photos of the little girl getting groomed, then asked for a buzz cut that matched a haircut Jay had recently acquired. He was planning to give Jay a copy of *Stained Class* for Christmas two days later, but, upon arriving home, decided to open the gift and listen to the album himself. It wasn't that big of a deal, because soon Jay—who had missed a ride to his job—was in the house as well, smoking pot, drinking beer, and playing air guitar.

At some stage, Jay's parents turned up to take him to work. Only now, he wasn't in the mood to leave. His mother tried to reason with him, emphasizing that he couldn't buy cigarettes if he didn't have any money. But he shouted that he wanted his folks to get lost. He was blowing off work, and staying with his best friend.

As *Stained Class* spun around the turntable, Jay later said in a deposition, two lines jumped out at him: "*Keep your world of all its sin/ It's not fit for living in.*" Suddenly, it all made sense. "The answer to this life is death," he told Ray.

Smitten by the wisdom of his friend's observation, Ray danced around the room. The two smashed knuckles until their hands hurt, then began destroying everything in sight. This greatly upset Christie Lynn, as well as an older half-sister who phoned their mother, who was playing cards at a nearby casino. She came home and tried entering the bedroom, but the boys barricaded the door, then leapt out the window with a twelve-gauge shotgun. Hopping the wall to the Community First Church of God, the pair headed to the playground area. Jay would testify that he saw Ray spinning around on a small, shaky carousel, repeatedly imploring his buddy to "do it."

At that point, Jay told police, Ray stopped the carousel and positioned the gun beneath his chin. "I sure fucked up my life," he said before firing a bullet into his skull.

Later, Jay contended that he hadn't really wanted to kill himself, but had believed that he had no choice. If law enforcement arrived and saw him standing above the corpse of his best friend, he'd surely be charged with homicide. When he slid the gore-stained barrel of the weapon into his mouth, though, he started to retch. So, following Ray's example, he stood with the gun below his chin, remaining in the same pose for approximately five minutes. "I didn't know what to do," he said. "I thought somebody was going to stop me."

Spurred on by the sound of an approaching police car, he attempted to stabilize the weapon in his hand. But, unlike Ray, he couldn't center the rifle in the proper place. "There was just tons of blood," he said. "It was like the gun had grease on it. There was so much blood, I could barely handle it." When he finally pulled the trigger, the bullet missed his brain, blasting off his chin, nose and mouth.

Remarkably, officers arrived in time to help save his life. When detectives questioned him at the hospital, he was unable to speak. But he was still able to make his point when asked about why he and Ray opted to kill themselves. Using a finger, Jay drew out the words LIFE SUCKS.

Despite massive doses of morphine, Jay had a difficult time sleeping. He claimed to hear the album Stained Class over and over in his mind before a friend brought him a tape. After returning home from the hospital, Jay would ride his bicycle around town, freaking out neighbors with his mutated features. In court one day, an attorney's six-year-old daughter is said to have fainted when she saw Jay on the elevator.

In a television interview from that time, Jay sat on the church-yard carousel where he attempted to end his life, his eyes lopsided on his face, a bandana covering a gap in his forehead. His pro-boscis—crafted with skin pulled down from his forehead—was disproportionately large in comparison to the rest of his face, and resembled a misshapen potato. Overall, his skin seemed bumpy, like the shell of a haphazardly stuffed sock puppet. His mouth—containing one tooth and a crude pair of lips fashioned from the flesh behind his knee—moved awkwardly above a chin made of bone from his shoulder blade. Because it sounded like he was mumbling and swallowing his words, producers were forced to include subtitles as he commentated on the wretched circum-stances that had preceded the shooting.

He and Ray were listening to Priest, he said, when "all of the sudden, we got a suicide message, and we got tired of life."

When Jay expressed this in his letter to Ray's mother, three local lawyers became involved. In 1986, they filed a product liability lawsuit against the band and CBS, holding both accountable for Ray's "wrongful death" and Jay's grievous personal injury.

"We were just about to go onstage one night," Tipton told VH1's *Behind the Music*, "and the sheriff walked in and gave us a subpoena."

The plantiffs' attorneys argued that the hypnotic beat and de-structive content in two songs, "Heroes End" and "Beyond the Realms of Death," along with the suggestive artwork on the *Stained Class* album cover, rendered the boys defenseless before the group's commands. But the lawyers apparently misread the lyrics in "Heroes End," and failed to realize that it was a song with an anti-suicide theme. At that point, the complaint was amended to include the tune "Better by You, Better Than Me" and the contention that the friends were compelled not by the literal lyrics, but by subliminal messages and backward masking.

"How do you prove to somebody that there are not subliminal messages on your record when you can't hear them in the first place?" Halford would ask when confronted with the charges.

If there had been subliminals on the album, the band's manager Bill Curbishley added, he'd have encouraged band members to coerce their devotees to buy more albums.

Meanwhile, Jay became addicted to Percodan and Xanax to deal with his pain, as well as cocaine. Unable to snort the drug through his nostrils, he began mainlining. On November 29, 1988, as the third anniversary of Ray's death approached, Jay was on suicide watch in the psychiatric unit at Washoe Medical Center when he died of a methadone overdose.

Only Glenn Tipton seemed to see the parallel between Jay's death and the upcoming trial, wondering if—after enduring so much mental and physical agony—the thought of testifying against his favorite band may have erased what still existed of the young man's will to live.

While the lyrics of Judas Priest songs were protected by the First Amendment, Judge Jerry Carr Whitehead determined that "non-decipherable sounds below the conscious threshold of awareness" were not, and allowed the case to go to trial in 1990.

Among the experts called by the plaintiffs was Dr. Wilson Key, an author of books about hidden messages who claimed to see the word sex and depictions of skulls and penises on everything from Ritz crackers to Rembrandt paintings to the etching of Abraham Lincoln's beard on five-dollar bills. At least two of the witnesses— Robert S. Demski, who'd banned Judas Priest music from the Texas facility he ran for troubled adolescents, and Fullerton, California, probation officer Darlyne Pettinicchio, who argued that the band's songs glorified Satan and compelled young people to hurt themselves—were recommended by the Parents Music Resource

Center (PMRC), a watchdog committee cofounded in 1985 by Tipper Gore, wife of future vice president Al Gore. After compiling a list that they called the "Filthy 15"—a collection of songs that included offerings by Priest, along with Prince, Mötley Crüe, Twisted Sister, AC/DC, Def Leppard, and Madonna—the PMRC mandated the removal of rock records and magazines from Wal-Mart and other chain stores, and the placement of warning labels on albums containing "explicit" lyrics.

"A lot of people didn't think we'd show up, except to testify, but we feel this is a very serious issue," Halford told the *Los Angeles Times*, recalling his stations-of-the-cross-type journey each day past both adoring metalheads and chanting moralists. Were the band found culpable, members said, the entire art community would be imperiled, with authors, artists, and fellow musicians all taken to court for the notion that they might have planted injurious subliminal messages into their work.

"I think the fallout would have been horrific," Halford told the *Georgia Straight*. "I mean, you would have needed to be told each time before you heard a radio broadcast that you weren't going to be submitted to subconscious messages."

What made the case even more surreal was that Vance family attorney Vivian Lynch described two of her own kids as "extreme metalheads." "The prosecuting attorneys have children," Halford noted in an interview with *Rockline*, "and we were giving them autographs and albums and all of those nice things during recesses, and it was quite strange to have to stand there and sign autographs for a person that's trying to destroy you."

The defense—subsidized by CBS—argued that the victims came from dysfunctional backgrounds and saw minimal prospects in their future. If it hadn't been Priest, the logic went, Ray and Jay would have found another inducement toward suicide. But Ray's family attorney Ken McKenna maintained that these were exactly the type of young people that heavy metal targeted. "Judas Priest and CBS pander this stuff to alienated teenagers," he told the court. "The members of the chess club, the math and science majors don't listen to this stuff. It's the dropouts, the drug and alcohol abusers. So our argument to you is you have a duty to be more cautious when you're dealing with a population susceptible to this stuff."

Sitting in the courtroom, Halford understood why the boys' families felt the need to lash out at somebody. "It's obviously a highly charged, emotional circumstance when you've lost your children," he told *Rolling Stone*. "You're bound to be angry. You're bound to be upset. You're bound to be looking for some explanation."

The only answer that the band could offer was that "subliminals" was a fabricated syndrome. Were the opposite true, Halford said, dozens, if not hundreds, of fans would have taken their lives in the seven-year span between the release of *Stained Class* and the double suicide attempt in the northern Nevada churchyard.

In fact, the defense claimed that, when you listened closely, no instruction to "do it, do it" was ever delivered on "Better by Me, Better Than You." Instead, there was the sound of a guitar played through a Leslie speaker effect, combined with the sound of Halford exhaling.

During a break from the proceedings, Tipton had gone into a local record store and purchased a copy of *Stained Class*. Then, he and his bandmates booked time in a Reno studio, played the music backward, and detected a number of what he termed "innocent phonetic flukes."

"On any forward lyric by anybody, whether it's Frank Sinatra or Judas Priest, you will hear some message if it's turned around," Halford explained to the *New York Times*. "That's the way humans hear."

Despite some hesitance from the band's attorneys, the revelation led the group to push for a strategy that incorporated the lead singer's penchant for showmanship. Halford would demonstrate the futility of the backward-masking argument by performing in court.

What followed was the kind of spectacle for which the Metal God was renowned. Sauntering into the courtroom one afternoon, Halford took the stand, wielding a tape recorder and explaining that he'd spent the earlier part of the day at the studio, spooling *Stained Class* backward. If it was all right with the judge, the singer offered to play the tape forward, sing the proper lyric, then play the song in reverse and sing that.

Judge Whitehead seemed amused by the proposal. There was really no need to sing the second lyric, he said with an uncharacteristic grin. "I want to hear this, though."

In a demonstration that was pure theater, Halford played an excerpt from the song "Invader," singing the verse a cappella, then playing the purportedly backward-masked version. "It's so fishy, personally, I owe it," went one section. Another sounded like the vocalist was trying to say, "Hey look, Ma, my chair's broken."

Halford apologized for any grammatical errors.

As the plantiffs' attorneys looked on angrily, Halford served up a third excerpt, this time from the song "Exciter." Played backward, the lines, *"Stand by for Exciter/ Salvation is his task"* came out as *"I asked her for a peppermint/ I asked her to get one."*

"That was when the judge thought, 'What am I doing here?'" Halford told the *Telegraph*. "'No band goes out of its way to kill its fans.'"

After seventeen days and more than forty witnesses, Judge Whitehead rendered his decision. Although there were subliminal "do its" on the album, the term—as well as others that could be construed as calls to suicide—was placed there unintentionally. Even if the opposite had been true, the plantiffs were unable to prove that this and other such stimuli were capable of provoking "conduct of this magnitude." In addition, the judge accepted the defense argument that there were other factors in the victims' lives that compelled them to hop the fence in Ray's backyard and take turns shooting themselves on the carousel.

Judas Priest had been vindicated. While the band members never forgot the two fans who ended their *Stained Class* listening binge with gunfire, there was a sense of poetic justice and even exultation. "People in court said that heavy metal is bad, is Satanic, and everybody that listens to Judas Priest is mad, is crazy, is full of drugs, hates the world," Halford told Radio MCB. "If somebody said that to you, you'd be pissed off. I was pissed off. So we stood up in court and said, 'Fuck you. Heavy metal is great.'"

14

Amor Prohibido
The Death of Selena

The loud bang startled the maid working at the Days Inn in Corpus Christi, Texas. When she turned around, Norma Martinez spotted Selena Quintanilla-Pérez—the queen of Tejano music—running from room 158, bleeding and begging for mercy.

"She was in a green suit," Martinez would tell a jury, "like a jumpsuit, and she was yelling, 'Help! Help!' I didn't know she was Selena."

Trailing the raven-haired singer—known for her bustiers and midriff-baring outfits, as well as for singles like "No Me Queda Más" ("I Have Nothing Left"), "Bidi Bidi Bom Bom," "Como La Flor" ("Like the Flower"), and "Amor Prohibido" ("Forbidden Love")—was another woman, shorter and considerably dowdier, wielding a snub-nosed .38. Martinez would describe it as a "cowboy gun." "It was real big," she noted. "But I've never been around guns."

In the parking lot, the second woman—later identified as Yolanda Saldívar, the president of Selena's fan club—raised the gun, then lowered it without shooting. The maid heard Yolanda shout a single word—"bitch"—before calmly returning to the hotel room.

When Tejano music station KEDA-AM reported the March 31, 1995, shooting, many listeners assumed that the disc jockey was joking, given the proximity to April Fool's Day. Selena was just seventeen days shy of her twenty-third birthday, and on the verge of crossing over to an Anglo audience. On the surface, the motive for the attack was bewildering; Yolanda's responsibilities for Selena had recently increased, and she'd described the singer as her "best friend." Over the next several months, Selena's fans would hear stories about embezzlement, problems within Selena's show-business family, and an alleged secret life. But most saw the slaying for what it was: the tale of an unremarkable fan who managed to worm her way into a glamorous starlet's orbit, only to snap when the entrée to celebrity was about to be removed.

Selena's success—and even the tragic way her life ended—can be tied to the yearnings of her father, Abraham, the son of migrant workers who'd embraced the Jehovah's Witness faith as they circulated through the towns along the Rio Grande, picking cotton, fruit, and vegetables. Anxious to elevate himself from his humble beginnings, Abraham defied his parents by dropping out of high school to pursue a singing career. His band Los Dinos (or "The Guys") achieved a modicum of fame in south Texas when their songs "So Hard to Tell" and "Give Me One Chance" received generous airplay in the early '60s. After a stint in the military, Abraham—now married to Selena's half-Chicano, half-Cherokee mother, Marcella—and Los Dinos picked up where they'd left off, receiving local adulation of their single "Con Esta Copa" ("With This Cup") in 1964. By the end of the decade, though, Abraham—frustrated with the band's inability to capitalize on their early renown—had quit and moved his young family to the Houston suburb of Lake Jackson.

While working at Dow Chemical, Abraham tried putting his musical aspirations in the past. But he never could. As the story goes, he was teaching his older son, Abraham "A. B." Quintanilla III, the guitar when Selena entered the room and began singing. Struck by the power of her voice, Abraham knew that he had a star on his hands. In 1982, he appropriated his band's old name to create Selena y Los Dinos. At the Tex-Mex restaurant he'd opened in Lake Jackson, customers could watch A. B. on bass, sister Suzette on drums, and eleven-year-old Selena on lead vocals. When the

Texas oil bust resulted in the loss of both the restaurant and family home, the Quintanillas relocated to Corpus Christi, and the band became the clan's primary source of income. Selena and her siblings performed at weddings, *quinceañeras*—the Hispanic version of Sweet 16 parties, celebrated when girls turn fifteen—fairs, and store openings.

By Abraham's design, the band played Tejano, a distinctly Texan style of music dominated by Mexican sounds, but incorporating influences from country, jazz and even the polka music once favored by the state's German immigrants. It was a challenge for Selena, since most Tejano stars were male and her Spanish was so poor that her father had to phonetically coach her through recording sessions. By eighth grade, Selena was showing up exhausted to school after gigs, and Abraham withdrew her from classes, prompting some teachers to threaten to report the family to authorities. While the Quintanillas toured the region in a renovated bus they called "Big Bertha," Selena earned her equivalency degree.

Year after year, Selena piled up honors at the Tejano Music Awards, but her reach remained limited. Then, in 1989, she signed with a major label, EMI Latin, and released her self-titled debut album. Always conscious of his daughter's image, and of her growing audience of underage fans, Abraham rejected beer sponsorships but approved an endorsement deal with Coca-Cola. The jingles she sang on two commercials aimed at the Hispanic market were composed by her brother A. B.—now the singer's primary producer and songwriter—and bandmate and future husband, Chris Perez.

After expressing their love for one another at a Pizza Hut, Chris and Selena had tried to keep their relationship a secret, correctly fearing an explosive response from Abraham. When the patriarch of the Quintanilla family discovered the romance—after Selena's sister, Suzette, spotted the couple behaving in a less than platonic fashion—he kicked Perez off Big Bertha and fired him from the band. While she had pledged fealty to her father, Selena continued to sneak off to see Chris, and in 1992 they eloped. The news forced Abraham to do something that was generally not part of his character: he apologized to his new son-in-law and welcomed him back into the group.

With order restored, the family could shift their focus to expanding Selena's popularity. She and Tejano musician David Lee Garza drew a then-record audience of 57,894 to the Houston Livestock Show and Rodeo at the Astrodome in February 1993. The next year, Selena was the headline act, and attracted a crowd of 60,948—including 8,000 who'd purchased standing-room-only tickets. A month later, her live album won a Grammy for best Mexican American LP. By the summer, "Amor Prohibido" was number one on *Billboard*'s Latin chart.

To those unfamiliar with the machinations within the Quintanilla clan, Selena remained the humble Jehovah's Witness girl who sewed many of her own outfits backstage, lived among her relatives in a fenced-in complex of three brick houses, and recorded her songs at a studio operated by her father and uncles. But life was changing quickly. News reports described her as "bigger than Tejano," and plans were in place to repackage her as an English-language star once her next album came out.

With each triumph, Selena was beginning to transition away from the control Abraham exerted. "More and more decisions were being made by Selena," Rudy Treviño, executive director of the Texas Talent Musicians Association—producers of the Tejano Music Awards—told *People*. "There was a growing independence with commercial endorsements."

To María Celeste Arrarás—former anchor of Univision's tabloid news show *Primer Impacto* and author of the 1997 book, *Selena's Secret: The Revealing Story Behind Her Tragic Death*—fame was also creating the types of conflicts that the sheltered pop singer hadn't anticipated. "The official story out there was she was at the height of her career . . . and that everything in her entire life was perfect,"

Arrarás told the *Huffington Post*. "But the story is much more rich than that and much more elaborate than that, and the fact is that Selena's life at the time of her death was far from perfect.

"She was a victim of a lot of people who were trying to manipulate her and that loved her, just like she loved them, but when you're in a situation of power, you get a lot of people around you that want you to do things the way they want them."

Chief among these manipulators was her seemingly devoted fan club president, Yolanda Saldívar .

In Yolanda's apartment, the shadows from votive candles flickered against posters of the Queen of Tejano. When people visited, Yolanda was quick to show off her array of videos of Selena in concert. According to a relative, Yolanda had said that she willing to "die" for the performer.

"She was like a cuddly bear, [a] teddy bear that would allow you to love her," Yolanda would tell the ABC television show *20/20*. "I told her that I loved her like a daughter. . . . She would call me Mom."

But some observers suspected that Yolanda's fixation with Selena was something other than maternal. "If people think that Selena and I had a lesbian relationship," Yolanda scolded when confronted with this rumor, "you're not a fan of Selena."

Like Selena, Yolanda had grown up around the restaurant business; her father was headwaiter at Jacala—or "Little Hut"—a popular Mexican eatery in San Antonio since 1949. But while Selena was encouraged to go into show business, Yolanda—the youngest of seven children—became a registered nurse in 1991, primarily attending to patients with terminal cancer and respiratory diseases. By several accounts, she was compassionate to her patients and their families—so altruistic, in fact, that she became a single mother to three adopted children, including a niece.

When she could, Yolanda amused herself by attending Tejano concerts. But she wasn't content being confined to the audience. After a Shelly Lares concert in San Antonio one night, Yolanda appeared backstage, offering to start a fan club. There were a number of parallels between Shelly and Selena. Chris Perez had played in Shelly's band before switching to Selena y Los Dinos. And Shelly also depended on her father, Fred, to make most management decisions. Upon meeting Yolanda, Fred demurred, explaining that, if someone were going to run a fan club for his daughter, he preferred a member of the family.

With Selena, Yolanda was less willing to accept rejection. Abraham would say that she left him fifteen messages about her concept of a Selena fan club; Yolanda said that she left only three. Either way, once they met, Abraham was receptive to her proposal, believing that a fan club could enhance his daughter's growing popularity. In 1991, Yolanda began collecting fees from fan club members, promising them, in return, a Selena T-shirt, factoids about the band, and updated concert listings. Extra proceeds were supposed to be donated to charities.

In three years, Yolanda managed to sign up eight thousand fans. Although she claimed that she'd earned more as a nurse, she was willing to sacrifice her career to dedicate herself to Selena.

As Selena's endeavors expanded, so did Yolanda's list of tasks. In 1994, Selena began designing and manufacturing her own clothing line, and opened two boutiques called Selena Etc. Each shop—there was one in Corpus Christi and another in San Antonio—contained a beauty parlor. Given her success at generating interest in the fan club, Yolanda was chosen to manage both businesses. She was such an insider by now that she also had the keys to Selena's house, and occasionally accompanied the singer on tours.

To observers, no one seemed more loyal to the star. Indeed, she reportedly told boutique employees that her goal was to "be like Selena." If people had an issue with the way the shops were being run, they were instructed to take their concerns directly to Yolanda. Selena was too busy, the fan club president said, and couldn't be bothered with such trivia.

What Selena may not have realized is that Yolanda had a history of difficulties which would come back to haunt her at her current job. A San Antonio dermatologist, Dr. Faustino Gomez, suspected Yolanda of stealing from him when she was his receptionist, starting in 1983. She was terminated and sued, and later settled with Gomez's insurance company. She was also involved in a lawsuit with a lending institution for failing to repay more than $7,300 in student loans.

Despite the general aversion to Mexican American performers in Mexico, Selena had developed a significant following below the Rio Grande, and was planning on opening a boutique and clothing factory in Monterrey. The effort was aided by a cosmetic surgeon she'd befriended there named Ricardo Martínez. When the pair were together, Selena is said to have complained to the doctor that neither her father nor husband were supportive enough of her outside ventures.

Abraham admitted as much in an interview with *People*: "I did not want to get directly involved in the business because I did not know anything about it. Chris is the same. His world is music, not fashion."

As Selena grew into her own person, she apparently began to feel a greater connection to Martinez than to the men at home. "Everything that happened between us was because there was a love that you can't put into words," Martínez told *Primer Impacto* in 2012. "Even though it was short, we gave ourselves to each other completely. . . . I was willing at that moment to change my life for her."

During her trips to Monterrey, Selena often arrived in disguise, according to the doctor's assistant, wearing wigs and using her husband's surname. While Chris may not have been aware of the clandestine liaisons, Yolanda was, and reportedly despaired about seeing Selena turn to someone else for help, protesting that the surgeon was not conducting himself as a professional.

But it wasn't Martinez whose professionalism was being questioned. In 1995, Abraham began hearing complaints that fans hadn't received anything in return for their membership payments. The same year, designer Martin Gomez quit Selena's clothing line, claiming that Yolanda regularly berated the seamstresses. He also accused Yolanda of deliberately damaging some of the clothing he'd created. By then, staff had been reduced at both boutiques because Yolanda had purged the businesses of people she disliked.

While Yolanda used her company credit card to rent Lincoln Town Cars and entertain associates at expensive restaurants, the boutiques sometimes lacked the funds to pay the bills. Clients maintained that they never received payments for hair-care supplies, nail files, radio advertising, and other services. Selena's cousin Debra Ramirez was brought in to assist, and discovered missing receipts and other paperwork, as well as incomplete sales reports. When Yolanda was alerted, Ramirez told the *Houston Post*, "she said that was her business and she would deal with that."

Abraham was convinced that Yolanda had forged checks to embezzle more than $60,000 from the fan club and boutiques. On March 9, 1995, he and his daughter Suzette confronted Yolanda at the family's Q Productions studio. While Yolanda stared back at Abraham without answering, he said, he threatened to report her to the police unless she could produce documents to disprove his fears.

The next day, Yolanda returned to the studio as if the conversation hadn't occurred. Abraham swiftly banned her from the premises. Although Selena had been hesitant to end her relationship with the fan club president—both for personal reasons, as well as out of the singer's belief that Yolanda could play a useful role in promoting the clothing line—she had seemingly lost patience. After arguing with Yolanda by phone, Selena removed the devotee's name from the boutique's bank account and replaced her as head of the fan club.

On March 11, Yolanda entered a San Antonio gun range, describing herself as a home care nurse and claiming that she was worried after a patient's relative had threatened her. She left with a

Taurus Model 85 snub-nosed .38 and hollow-point ammunition—bullets that expand after entering a victim's body.

Two days later, she went to attorney Richard Garza, who composed the following letter to Selena: "It is with great regret and reservation that Ms. Yolanda Saldívar submits her employment resignation from your company, Selena Etc., Inc. The day to day dealings with certain members of your family [have] made it impossible for Ms. Saldívar to work for you or Selena Etc., Inc."

Selena was still interested in retrieving bank statements, financial records, and other documents from Yolanda that the singer needed for tax reasons. On March 14, the two met in a parking lot twenty-five miles from Corpus Christi. Although Selena told Yolanda she could continue handling business affairs for the clothing line in Mexico, she was apparently stalling until she could find a replacement. At a certain point, Yolanda displayed the .38, expressing her fear of Abraham, but the singer managed to calm her fan. Had she not, Abraham is convinced that Yolanda would have killed Selena right there.

Regardless, Yolanda returned the gun the next day. But Selena raised the anxiety level by continuously asking for the financial records. On March 27, Yolanda repurchased the .38.

The pair arranged to meet at the Days Inn on March 31. The night before, Yolanda used a corporate American Express card from Selena Etc. to check into the hotel—just off Interstate 37 on Corpus Christi's north side—while Selena went to one of her boutiques to get a manicure. But the singer was clearly troubled, and told nail technician Celia Soliz that she intended to pick up her documents and fire Yolanda the next day.

Selena rose at 7:30 a.m., changed into green workout clothes, and drove over to the Days Inn, hoping to dispense of the uncomfortable task of terminating her employee before the day really started. But when Selena knocked on the door of room 158, she found a distraught Yolanda weaving a harrowing tale about a trip to Mexico the day before. There, Yolanda said, something terrible had occurred. She'd been beaten with a bat, she claimed, and raped. Under these circumstances, Selena could not rally the energy to ask for the necessary paperwork or relieve Yolanda of her job. Instead, the singer drove Yolanda to Doctors Regional Hospital for an examination.

Selena appeared concerned about her employee, stroking Yolanda's hair as the older woman repeated her story to emergency room director Patricia Biggs in a gloomy monotone. Under Texas case law, hospital staff could not perform a gynecological exam because the alleged crime had occurred outside the country. Still, Yolanda insisted that her neck ached and that she was experiencing vaginal bleeding.

"I didn't see any evidence to indicate she had been assaulted," registered nurse Karla Anthony would testify. Although Yolanda claimed to have been hit on the back and abdomen, Anthony could not find the type of bruises she normally associated with a baseball bat attack. From time to time, while Yolanda was looking away, Selena would make eye contact with the nurse and shake her head.

As Yolanda sat in the examining room, Selena and Anthony stepped outside. "The story that she's telling us," the nurse began, "isn't the same as the one she told you, is it?"

Selena wagged her head, but held her finger to her lips, gesturing at the examining room.

When the pair drove back to the Days Inn, Selena suggested that she and Yolanda stay apart for a while, at least until Abraham's anger at the recently deposed fan club president subsided.

It was 10 a.m. when Abraham called Chris Perez, asking him about Selena's whereabouts. A recording session about been scheduled at Q Productions and Selena wasn't there yet. Chris hung up with his father-in-law and called his wife.

"I forgot about the session," the singer admitted. "But I'll be there soon. I just have to take care of one last thing."

At the hotel, it became obvious to Selena that Yolanda was never going to be able to explain the company's missing assets. Other guests reported hearing two women arguing loudly about business issues. At one point, Yolanda and the other Selena Etc. employees had given the Grammy winner a 14-karat gold and diamond ring, topped with a white-gold egg. Now, Yolanda insisted that the trinket was hers. But that was the least of Selena's concerns. Frustrated over Yolanda's reticence about handing over the financial documents, the singer grabbed a bag containing bank statements and emptied it on the bed. As the papers fell out, so did the .38.

Frightened, Selena reached for the door. Yolanda fired, striking the performer in the back, near the shoulder blades. The bullet passed through Selena's chest cavity, shattering her collarbone, damaging her lung, and severing an artery before exiting the right upper chest area. Bleeding, Selena ran toward the lobby, clutching her chest. At first, she tried to push the door open, but it wouldn't budge. Despite her injured state, she gathered her thoughts and pulled the knob toward her, cracking open the door and stumbling inside.

"Help me!" she yelled, collapsing on the ground. "Help me! Call the police!"

Desk clerk Shawna Vela did not understand the gravity of the situation. "She was saying, 'Help me,' and I looked at her and I said, 'Help you what?' She said, 'I've been shot,' and she turned toward me and I saw enormous amounts of blood."

The trail stretched 392 feet back to Yolanda's room.

Selena's panicked eyes fixed on the lobby door. "Lock the doors," she demanded. "She'll shoot me again."

"Who shot you?" asked the motel's sales director Ruben DeLeon.

"Yolanda Saldívar. Room 158."

DeLeon watched the singer's eyes roll back in her head. She tapped her fingers a few times until they stopped.

When EMTs arrived at the hotel, paramedic Richard Fredrickson observed that the blood was "thick from [Selena's] neck to her knees and all around on both sides. I felt some twitching. I never felt a pulse." Selena's green sweatshirt was torn away, and gauze applied to the bullet wound to stop the surface bleeding.

In the ambulance, an attempt was made to hook the singer to an intravenous drip, but—because of the heavy blood loss—her veins had collapsed. "When you lose a lot of blood," Fredrickson said, "the body sucks up all the blood from the legs and arms, and keeps it in the upper part of the body to keep the brain and heart and kidneys alive."

In a final effort to rescue Selena, he inserted the needle into her neck. "It did not work." When Fredrickson looked at the heart monitor, the line was flat. "It means she was dead."

Yet doctors at Memorial Medical Center did detect an erratic heartbeat, and attempted to start to reestablish circulation with blood transfusions. It was a long-shot procedure. Selena's veins were empty of blood. The artery leading from the heart had been sliced in two by the bullet. As a result, all six units of blood from the transfusion spilled from her circulatory system.

At 1:05 p.m., Selena Quintanilla-Pérez was declared dead.

After the shooting, witnesses had seen Yolanda return to her room, then walk, emotionless, to her red 1994 GMC pickup in the parking lot. Corpus Christi police sergeant John Betz had been eating lunch two blocks away when he heard the reports, and ran out to his vehicle. Spotting a red pickup, he turned on the sirens and gave chase. When the driver pulled over, Betz realized that the motorist had nothing to do with the crime.

His lunch partner, plainclothes sergeant Bernardo Torres, drove to the hotel instead. In the lot, he saw Yolanda move her pickup to another spot and park there. Leaving his car, he took cover behind a nearby vehicle, drew his gun, and kicked the truck's tailgate to get the shooter's attention. "She looked at me," he'd testify. "I showed her my badge and told her to roll down the window. She rolled it halfway down. I asked her to present her hands, and she reached up and stuck one hand out the window. The other hand stayed down."

When Torres asked about the shooting, Yolanda calmly stated that she had nothing to do with it and needed to make a phone call.

Once again, he ordered her to display both hands. Instead, she reached down and placed the .38 against her temple. "That was the first time I saw the gun," he said. "I pointed my weapon at her and told her to drop the gun."

Yolanda shouted that she wanted to die.

The standoff continued for nine and a half hours. The pickup was blocked on one side on a squad car, and on the other by a large, open field. Yolanda's mood shifted, from conversational to hysterical. But the one constant was the threat of suicide. As Yolanda raised the gun to her head over and over, Sergeant Larry Young, a fifteen-year veteran, assumed the role of lead negotiator, communicating with the suspect via cell phone while gently trying to coax her out of the vehicle.

"Look at what I did to my best friend," Yolanda agonized. "I should kill myself. I did something wrong. I'll never be forgiven my entire life. . . . I should know better, and I did know better."

Aided by people familiar with the dynamics at Q Productions, Johnson spoke about the fond feelings Yolanda and Selena had had for one another, as well as the shooter's disdain for Abraham.

"He made me shoot," she said. "He made me shoot her." Abraham, she insisted, "tried to get between us. . . . We'd been together for so long."

According to Yolanda, Abraham had sexually assaulted her. "He raped me," she said. "He stuck a stick in my vagina. He said, 'If you tell anybody, I will kill your parents, I will kill your family.' . . . He pushed me to this, Larry."

It was his threats, she asserted, that prompted her to purchase a gun in the first place.

In that case, Johnson reasoned, if Yolanda committed suicide, Selena's fans would only know Abraham's side of the story.

For the moment, Yolanda seemed pacified. Selena was talking to her from the dead, Yolanda claimed, urging her to be strong.

"Don't commit suicide," the singer apparently said, "because I'll never see you in heaven."

But the effort to create an agreeable atmosphere was hampered by the negotiating team's knowledge that Yolanda was listening to radio reports about the shooting. In other standoffs, radio signals had been jammed, and electricity cut off from buildings. In this instance, negotiators had to simply convince Yolanda that Selena's public knew better than to believe what the media told them.

Around hour six, Yolanda seemed ready to surrender. But when she exited the truck and spotted an officer pointing a rifle at her, she ran back inside and, once again, held the pistol to her head.

As day turned to night, police turned floodlights on the pickup and drained the gasoline out of its tank. Just before 9:30 p.m., negotiator Isaac Valencia urged Yolanda to think of her family, leave the pickup, and move toward Larry Young.

With tears streaming down her face, Yolanda screamed, "I don't want to live anymore. No, Larry, I don't want to live. I am tired."

"Yolanda, you are tired," Valencia said. "We are tired. Yolanda, take three steps."

"I am scared.

"Yolanda, I am here on the phone with you, and Larry is out there. Yolanda, take three steps."

Slowly, she stepped out of the truck. Officers quickly handcuffed her, covered her head with a police jacket, and placed her in a squad car. As it sped away, a hundred or so spectators who'd been standing across the street applauded and ran after the cruiser. Hundreds of others lined the streets—some playing Tejano music on boom boxes—clapping and shouting as Yolanda was taken into custody.

Within hours, she'd signed a confession. It was a decision that she'd quickly regret. Detectives had tricked her, she said, neglecting to include her assertion that the shooting was an accident. She'd just announced her resignation, she told *20/20*, when Selena "grabbed my feet and told me not to leave her. . . . And I grabbed the gun, put it to my head . . , and I said, 'If you don't leave, I'm going to do it, Selena,' And she got up and she says, 'Mom, we need to talk about this. We need to talk about this.'"

As Selena attempted to exit, Yolanda claimed that she gestured with the pistol for the singer to close the door. "And at that instant, the gun went off."

Because of the fervor surrounding the killing—according to one story, Chicano gang members were trying to raise money for Yolanda's bail so they could whack her on the street—the trial was moved to Houston. As police and witnesses from the hotel testified about what they'd seen and heard that day, Yolanda's defense team repeatedly argued that she'd never intended to hurt Selena. "Time and again, consistently, unrehearsed . . . she said, 'This was an accident,'" attorney Fred Hagans said in his closing arguments.

Nueces County district attorney Carlos Valdez countered by waving the .38 in court. "How come in nine hours," he questioned, "when the defendant had the gun to her head, it did not go off accidentally?"

Yolanda never took the stand. But it probably wouldn't have mattered anyway. There was just too much evidence that the murder of the pop star had been premeditated. When the verdict was announced—on October 23, 1995—it was greeted with horn honking and cheers from fans who'd traveled from other parts of Texas to gather outside the Harris County Courthouse. Many chanted *"culpable,"* the Spanish word for "guilty," while Selena's music blasted.

Despite a tearful plea for leniency from her father, Yolanda was sentenced to life behind bars.

By then, Selena's crossover album, *Dreaming of You*, had been released, becoming the first LP by a Latin artist to debut at number one on the *Billboard* 200 chart. The upcoming Day of the Dead commemorations would feature an abundance of *ofrendas*— or altars—in the singer's honor. These would include heart-shaped candles colored purple—Selena's preferred hue—her favorite flowers, white roses, and marigolds—the Aztec symbol of death, since the conquistadors had come to the New World to loot its gold. The year would end with "Selena" ranked among the top one hundred names for newborn girls in the United States.

Selena's death would ignite an interest in Latin music, with such stars as Ricky Martin, Shakira, and Jennifer Lopez—who'd play the Queen of Tejano in her cinematic life story—attributing much of their success to the singer.

In prison, Yolanda Saldívar continued to assert that her infamy was unearned. "I just want to say, I did not kill Selena," she told *20/20*. "It was an accident and my conscience is clear."

Asked if she could change the events of March 31, 1995, she replied, "I would want her to kill me."

15

SIDE OF A BULLET
DIMEBAG DARRELL'S PUBLIC EXECUTION

The two round-faced Texans warmed up on the side of the stage. "Dimebag" Darrell Abbott gripped the whammy bar of his V-shaped guitar, knowing that—even through all the clamor and distortion—his real fans would be able to decipher each distinct chord. Older brother Vinnie Paul tapped his sticks together, ready to pound the cymbals and extra-large toms. In many ways, the two seemed indistinguishable from the working-class metalheads who attended their shows. Each was on the stocky side. Vinnie's long, dark hair was swathed in a bandanna, while Dime had added tint to the goatee that dangled below his chin.

The pair had stuck together since the beginning. When Megadeth had invited Darrell to join their group, he'd declined. If Vinnie couldn't come, Darrell said, he wouldn't either. As members of Pantera, they'd sold more than 7 million records, received four Grammy nominations, and cranked out genre-defining albums like *Cowboys from Hell*, *Vulgar Display of Power*, and *Far Beyond Driven*. Madonna would play Dime's riff from "A New Level" on her 2008 Sticky & Sweet tour, while the group's track "Walk" filled interludes during Major League Baseball and NFL games. Despite this, interactions within the group could be as unruly as the music. When Dime and Vinnie concluded that they could no longer mesh with lead vocalist Phil Anselmo, they left as a team and started a new group called Damageplan.

On this night in late 2004, Damageplan was scheduled to headline the Alrosa Villa, a small rock club in Columbus, Ohio.

The crowd would be in the hundreds, not the thousands—a sharp contrast from 1991, when Pantera had performed for 1.6 million at the Monsters of Rock festival in Moscow. Yet the brothers knew where they came from and what the alternatives could have been. At thirty-eight and forty years old, respectively, they were still excited to be in the game, and grateful to be playing a form of music that always gave them elation, purpose, and a link to the giants who'd come before.

Vinnie looked over at Dime and smiled. "Van Halen?" he queried.

Dime lit up and gave his brother a high five. "Van fuckin' Halen."

"Our code word to let it all hang out and have a good time was 'Van Halen,' man," Vinnie told TeamRock.com. "And that's the last two words we ever said to each other."

Outside the club, a food vendor named Medhat Mokhtar spotted Nathan Gale, twenty-five, a stern former US Marine with a shaved head and pronounced brow, loitering in the cold. Gale said little and paced a lot. As Damageplan's set began, Mokhtar watched Gale walk purposefully toward the Alrosa Villa. The vendor next remembered hearing shrieks as spectators fled the club. Bewildered, Mokhtar left his food cart and entered the building to investigate. He soon found himself at the edge of the stage, where a group of hysterical fans surrounded a fallen, bloody Darrell.

"I tried to push them away, but people loved him too much," Mokhtar told *MTV News*. "The people were kissing his hands and his feet and trying to give him CPR."

■   ■   ■

The first songs Darrell had learned on guitar had been infinitely more conventional than the groove metal sound he'd help develop: Deep Purple's "Smoke on the Water" and Boston's "More Than a Feeling." His father, Jerry Abbott, owned a studio outside Arlington, Texas, primarily recording blues and country artists. When Jerry noticed his son's fascination with guitars, he taught the boy scales and music theory. Despite the intricacy of each task, Darrell showed virtually no fear of failure. "When I tried to play something and screwed up, I'd hear some other note that would come into play," he told MTV. "And then I started moving it around and trying different things to find the beauty in it."

By his early teens, Darrell was eclipsing older musicians in a region that took pride in its guitarists. In one contest, he was awarded the burgundy Dean ML that became his favorite guitar. "I heard stories about this fuckin' kid who was so badass that he kept winning this contest every year for the best new guitar player," Alice in Chains guitarist and founder Jerry Cantrell—a part of the Dallas music scene in the mid-1980s—told *Billboard*. "He won it so many times in a row, they fuckin' kicked him out and made him a judge."

By then, his future was evident. He'd met his life partner, Rita Haney, in third grade after she pushed him off a bicycle. Once they discovered that they were Kiss fans, they became inseparable.

In Kiss guitarist Ace Frehley, Darrell found a musician who he truly wanted to emulate. Darrell would tattoo Frehley's likeness on his chest, inking in an autograph that Ace added to Abbott's flesh after the two eventually met. "If there were no Ace Frehley, there would have been no Dimebag Darrell," Dime told *Guitar World* magazine.

Other influences included Tony Iommi from Black Sabbath, Randy Rhoads from Ozzy Osbourne's group, Pete Willis from Def Leppard, and Billy Gibbons from ZZ Top, who shared the Abbott brothers' Texas roots and sensibility.

"He could take a riff that would take somebody a year to master and he could rip it off in seconds," Slipknot's Corey Taylor told *MTV News*. "He made everything look like he was playing 'Smoke on the Water' with one finger."

Van Halen always loomed large in Dime's thoughts. He learned the song "Eruption," note by note, and would play it in live shows.

He also liked the way guitar god Eddie formed the band with his drummer brother Alex. In 1981, the Abbott siblings decided to do the same, creating Pantera. Unlike the later version of the group, the early unit had a glam metal flavor. In tribute to Van Halen lead singer David Lee Roth's "Diamond Dave" persona, the teenage guitarist labeled himself "Diamond Darrell" Lance—his middle name."

The undertaking was a family project, with father Jerry engineering the band's first four albums and releasing them on an independent label. Later, Darrell would downplay this period of the band's history. He was a kid, he admitted, and was imitating his heroes rather than designing a separate identity for Pantera.

Everything changed in 1988 when Phil Anselmo became the lead singer, bringing along an electrifying exuberance that transformed Pantera into a thrash metal unit that observers compared to Megadeth and Slayer. Unlike Vinnie and James Abbott, Darrell had always wanted the band to move in a harder direction, and now he'd found a kindred spirit. In 1990—nine years after Pantera was formed—the band finally signed with a major label, Atlantic's Atco imprint. The first release under this deal, *Cowboys from Hell*, elevated the band to the upper reaches of the movement.

Despite his reputation as a partier, Darrell spent long hours in the studio, crafting the sound for 1992's *Vulgar Display of Power*. For those who viewed Pantera as a religion, this was the album that converted them. "The opening guitar riff to 'A New Level' was always my favorite Dimebag Darrell riff," Billy Talent's Ian D'Sa recalled for *Billboard*. "As a teenager, I imagined those ascending bare chords as the soundtrack to an army of demons marching out of hell, only to go into an incredible Latin rhythm that sounded like machine gun fire."

As grunge apparently overtook heavy metal, Pantera defied the trend. The band's heaviest album, 1994's *Far Beyond Driven*, debuted at number one on the *Billboard* 200 and went gold within six weeks. For the first time, the guitarist was listed on the LP's credits not as Diamond Darrell, but as Dimebag Darrell—a moniker earned from facilitating low-level marijuana sales for Anselmo.

Dime had transformed from a fan to a name the masters of metal wanted on their projects. Pantera supported Judas Priest lead vocalist Rob Halford on the song, "Light Comes Out of Black"—part of the *Buffy the Vampire Slayer* soundtrack. Darrell contributed tunes on two separate Ace Frehley tribute albums, and worked with Anthrax so often that members called him the sixth member of the band. In recognition of the family's Lone Star origins, Dime and Vinnie recorded with country headliner David Allan Coe, while Pantera created the theme for hockey's Dallas Stars.

When he was in town, Dime regularly turned up to encourage local bands on both the metal and country circuits. He opened a strip club for both the musicians and the women who loved them to mingle, and endorsed Dean's Razorback guitar, a variation of his beloved ML. He even had his own cocktail, called Black Tooth Grin—two shots of Seagram's 7, two shots of Crown Royal, and a splash of Coca-Cola.

The beverage was Pantera's "official drink." Nonetheless, the dynamics in the band were changing. The Abbott brothers were reportedly frustrated with Anselmo for taking too much time away from Pantera for side projects, and for attempting to soothe his ever-present back pain with painkillers and other addictive drugs. In 2003, the band officially split.

The brothers quickly started Damageplan with singer Patrick Lachman and bassist Bob Zilla. Without Anselmo, it would take time to build a following, but Dime was confident that he'd always attract a certain type of fan. "People that love this form of music have loved it from way back—Sabbath, Zeppelin, the early days," he'd once told MTV. "Once you're into it, you're into it for a lifetime."

From the moment that he'd first heard *Vulgar Display of Power*, Brooklyn-born Tim Martinez believed that he'd found an ally in Darrell. "You listen to the song 'Walk,' and it's really an anthem," he said. "I had a very unhappy childhood, but I knew that if I saw Dime play live, there'd be solidarity. I'd be part of a movement of outcasts."

Raised in a fundamentalist, ethnically Puerto Rican home, Tim was forbidden to listen to secular music until age ten. When the opportunity presented itself, he eased his way in. "As a gay boy, I started out as a fan of Madonna," he remembered. "At around twelve or thirteen, I began listening to Green Day. The guitar was heavier than I was used to. There was growling and emotion, not pretty singing." By fifteen, he'd discovered Nine Inch Nails, Metallica, and Pantera. "They were one of the angrier bands. I hadn't come out yet, and I'd always been told that I'd go to hell for feeling the things I did. So I was depressed. I was a cutter. I didn't know how to deal with my identity. I thought Pantera's music was dark, but it was a form of expression I liked."

At a telemarketing job, he befriended Ukrainian-born Juliya Chernetsky, who ended up hosting the metalcentric show *Uranium* on Fuse TV. When Juliya needed a correspondent, she invited Tim to appear on-air. Almost overnight, it seemed, he was a recognized name in metal circles.

Shortly after the breakup of Pantera, Damageplan was touring New York, and Juliya invited Tim to see the band at the Roseland Ballroom. "I'll never forget this," he said. "We got backstage and Dime introduces *himself* to *me*. That's how down-to-earth he was. I told him it was an honor to meet a legend—someone who'd made me happy for a long time. And he said, 'I'm just a hillbilly who rocks on guitar.'"

When the band went out after the show, Tim came as well. Once again, Darrell initiated conversation. As they walked around the city, the group passed a homeless man asking for money. Tim watched as Dime reached into his wallet and handed over a hundred-dollar bill. The panhandler held the bill and stared in disbelief.

"You've just been blessed by the pink-bearded angel." Darrell smiled.

Tim felt bonded. It was one thing to have a hero act courteous, quite another for him to astonish you with his humanity. "I'm going to tell you something," Tim confided to the musician, "something I've never told anybody on this scene, something I've never told my parents."

Darrell made eye contact.

"I'm gay."

The guitarist shrugged. "Who gives a fuck?" he replied. "It's all about the music and the passion you feel for it."

It would be several years before Tim would learn that when Dime returned to Texas, he repeated the conversation to his common-law wife, Rita. "You're the guy from New York," she'd tell Tim when they finally met.

"*Everyone* was [Darrell's] family," Anthrax rhythm guitarist Scott Ian told *MTV News*. "Once you came into contact with Dimebag and became friends with that guy . . . you became part of his extended family."

Generally, this philosophy aided him, breaking down the barrier between performer and spectator, conveying the feeling that he understood his fans' emotions and was endowed with a gift to express them through his music. When Darrell played, he seemed happiest with the audience close. After all, everyone was in this thing together.

It was a beautiful worldview—until it killed him.

In mid-2004, Nathan Gale attended a Damageplan concert in Cincinnati and attempted to climb up onto the stage. Security roughly escorted him out. Some equipment got knocked over the course of the altercation, causing approximately $5,000 in equipment damage.

Darrell never thought about the incident—or Nathan Gale—again. Shit like that happened all the time. That's what rock 'n' roll was all about.

Gale had grown up in Marysville, Ohio, about thirty minutes from Columbus, before enlisting in the Marines. Back at home, he did landscaping, worked in construction, and found a job at an oil change shop. More recently, he'd shown up unsolicited at a bar called Lee Dog's Locker Room and applied for a bouncer position. He wasn't hired.

Neighbors noted that Gale appeared to have a gentle side, getting down on the floor to play toy cars with children. It seemed unusual, since Gale was a six-foot-three-inch, 250-pound brooding, lumbering presence. Somewhere along the way, he'd earned a brown belt in judo. He also played offensive guard for a semipro football team called the Lima Thunder.

Teammates remembered him, sitting quietly on the bus after games, listening to Pantera on his headphones. He told a friend that the band had stolen songs he'd written and that he was planning a lawsuit.

Most days, he stopped by the Bear's Den tattoo parlor across the street from his home. He was particularly intrigued by Bo Toler, an artist who played guitar, engaging him in questions about music. Sometimes Gale was seen talking and laughing to himself. Other times, he stared down at the floor, straightening up with a jolt if someone mentioned his name. "I tried to keep him away from the clientele," manager Lucas Bender told *Rolling Stone*. "He kind of gave everyone a weird impression."

Early on the evening of December 8, 2004, Gale turned up at the shop at about 6 p.m. "He was asking about how he could buy a tattoo machine," Toler told the *Marysville Journal-Tribune*. "I told him it was illegal to own a tattoo machine without a license. He swore at me and started shouting, 'You're a liar.' Then he left with a lot of attitude. It was the first time I ever noticed his temper."

Damageplan was about to play its thirty-fourth gig of the Devastation across the Nation tour, supporting the band's album, *New Found Power*. The group had been to New Orleans; San Francisco; Boise, Idaho; and Milwaukee, among other locations, and with just two more shows to go, the Abbott brothers were looking forward to getting home, celebrating Christmas, doing their New

Year's Eve gig—the pair, along with some musical colleagues, always went incognito, billing themselves as Gasoline—then going back to the studio to record another album.

Although the Alrosa Villa was small, Dime was happy to be playing there. He'd first appeared onstage at the club during Pantera's early years, and he'd made it a point to thank the owner for bringing him back with his new group. After soundcheck, Dime and Vinnie hung out on the tour bus, then went back to the club to watch the opening groups, local bands 12 Gauge and Volume Dealer.

In the parking lot, a fan noticed Nathan Gale—bespectacled and in a Columbus Blue Jackets hockey jersey—hanging out near the door. The music inside was loud, but it was hard to make out specific lyrics or chords. "Why aren't you watching the show?" the man asked Gale.

Gale retorted that he had no interest in seeing local bands.

"You can at least go inside and stay warm."

Nathan wasn't interested. He intended to remain outside, he said, until Damageplan went on.

Whenever one of the musicians from 12 Gauge or Volume Dealer came outside, Gale approached, distracting the performer as he tried to clear his head or retrieve a piece of gear. "He was just a crazy fan trying to talk to members of the band," club manager Rick Cautela told *Rolling Stone*. "One of my guys who helps set up the bands eventually told him to leave."

But Gale only went far enough to placate the staff. As Damageplan was introduced and launched into their first song, Gale marched into the building, passing the pool table and sound booth.

"The dude was determined," noted Volume Dealer's Billy Payne. "He was on a mission. He looked angry. He was walking like he was going into battle."

Entering the stage on the left side, Nathan rumbled past a seven-and-a-half-foot wall of amplifiers. At first, he seemed like a fan who wanted to stage-dive. This perception changed the moment that he removed his .9mm Beretta 92FS handgun, his eyes locked on Darrell. Dime was headbanging, sweeping his hair back and forth, lost in the music. Volume Dealer bassist Joe Dameron saw Gale say something, but couldn't hear the words over the feedback.

Gale held up the gun and fired. Cautela, who was tending bar by this point, thought he heard firecrackers. Others assumed that the shooter was part of the act. Vinnie Paul knew better, standing up behind his kit and staring incredulously. One bullet struck Darrell in the hand. Another was a direct hit to his forehead.

In the audience, US military veteran Travis Burnett put down in his beer and ran toward the stage. Gale was now firing into the crowd.

Burnett managed to get up close to Gale, looking him straight in the eye and scolding, "Dude, what the fuck are you doing?"

"Get out of here. Get away."

Instead, Burnett reached forward and tried to disarm the shooter. A bullet passed through the fan's shirt, but, in the chaos of the moment, Burnett didn't feel it.

Security camera footage of the incident would capture fans screaming and a voice shouting to call 911. But emergency operators were already being besieged. One frantic voice pleaded, "We need to get out. We need to get out. I can't, I can't get out."

Shouted another, "There's been a shooting. Somebody's shooting. He's shooting the band. Oh, shit. He's still shooting."

In total, fifteen shots were discharged. Seven people were wounded. Jeff "Mayhem" Thompson, Damageplan's head of security, managed to tackle Gale, but was killed in the process, along with Alrosa Villa employee Erin Halk and Nathan Bray, a fan who tried administering CPR to the fallen guitarist.

Damageplan's drum tech, John "Kat" Brooks, grabbed at Gale's arms in an effort to grapple the gun away. Nathan shot him three times, then gripped him in a headlock, apparently hoping to escape by using a hostage as a shield.

Officer James Niggemeyer raced into the club without waiting for backup. As he raised his Remington 870 12-gauge shotgun, Niggemeyer accessed the situation. "I knew . . . I could shoot the suspect as long as I aimed high enough and wouldn't hurt the hostage," he told *MTV News*. "At that point, almost immediately, I fired."

Nathan Gale fell, mortally wounded, as Brooks scrambled to safety.

Impervious to the gunfire, registered nurse Mindy Reece did chest compressions on Darrell for twenty minutes. "Dimebag," she begged, "come on, come on. Please stay with me."

Niggemeyer was touched by the multiple displays of bravery. "When tragedy strikes, there are people in this world who will step up and try to stop it," he told *Billboard*. "There are people who will stand up in the face of death and give their life to try to save others. . . .Those are the true heroes to me."

By the time paramedics arrived, Darrell was dead. His brother, Vinnie, had fled onto the Damageplan tour bus, where he slid into Dimebag's bunk and wept. As fans, musicians, and reporters attempted to distill the attack in their minds, people realized that Darrell's shooting had occurred on the twenty-fourth anniversary of John Lennon's assassination.

Initial reports stated that Gale had stormed the Alrosa Villa because he blamed Darrell for Pantera's breakup. But this was a simplified explanation. The shooter was mentally ill, believed he'd written songs for the band, and was motivated by a head full of delusions.

Volume Dealer singer Billy Payne was traumatized. Darrell had wanted to meet with the opening band after the concert. "It was a local band's dream coming true," Payne told *Rolling Stone*, "turned into a nightmare."

Officer Niggemeyer suffered post-traumatic stress disorder and eventually left the police force. "I found out real quick that you don't have any control over your brain," he told the *Columbus*

Dispatch. "It's going to do what it's going to do. . . . Cops are regular human beings. Things affect us the same way they affect everyday citizens. We relive it and have to deal with the consequences."

Metalheads braced for an expected backlash. "Society was looking at this and saying, 'This is heavy metal,'" Megadeth's Dave Mustaine told *Rolling Stone*. "That's not heavy metal. That's a random act."

In recognition of Dime's alcoholic tastes, the band Slayer sent a floral arrangement shaped like a bottle of Crown Royal to the viewing. Ozzy and Sharon Osbourne expanded on the theme, ordering an arrangement made literally from Crown Royal bags. Dime had recently met Eddie Van Halen and offered to purchase one of his idol's guitars. Instead, Eddie ventured to the funeral parlor, carrying his original yellow and black guitar from 1979. It was gently placed in the coffin, in Darrell's arms.

"An original should have an original," Eddie said.

Alice in Chains, Anthrax, and Slipknot were among the fifteen heavy metal bands in attendance at the funeral. Each mourner, it seemed, added another bottle of booze to the casket. "I was worried the coffin stand was going to collapse," Rita told *Billboard*. "The pallbearers complained about how heavy the coffin was. . . . It was such a weird day, but the feeling of family was so wonderful. It was like Darrell was there, throwing one more party."

The invitees reciprocated. Machine Head guitarist/singer Robb Flynn wrote a song, "Aesthetics of Hate," in Darrell's memory. Frehley dedicated his album *Anomaly* to Dimebag, whose chest was adorned with a tattoo of the former Kiss guitarist. The Nickelback song "Side of a Bullet" featured one of Dimebag's actual guitar riffs.

Despite these acknowledgments, Rita believed that Darrell would have wanted to give something back. So, starting in 2005, she endorsed Ride for Dime, a national bike run that raised money for US military veterans, public school music education, and programs for runaway, homeless, and disenfranchised youth.

Yet the senselessness of the tragedy never diminished. Surrounded by artifacts from Dime's rock 'n' roll journey and consoled by the good deeds of his fans, Rita tried finding meaning in her pain. "The first three years were a blur," she told *Billboard* at the ten-year anniversary of the murders. "People would say things like, 'Oh, it gets better after a year.' But in many ways, it never really does."

16

It All Dies Anyway
The Slaying of Seattle Punk Siren Mia Zapata

Mia Zapata and her band, the Gits, were still unsigned when her body was wheeled into the Seattle Medical Examiner's Office in the summer of 1993. It had been a particularly violent year in the Emerald City and the tousle-haired woman with the odd, chicken tattoo on her leg was unfortunate enough to qualify as Seattle's thirty-third homicide victim.

Mia didn't drive, so there hadn't been a license in her possession when police found her. Yet no one had to be called to identify the corpse. On the Seattle music scene, the Gits were spoken of with the same awe as Nirvana and Pearl Jam—possibly more, since Mia's strong female voice seemed able to overpower the wails of the men who ruled the grunge movement. As soon as the coroner looked down at the casualty, there was instant recognition. He was a Gits fan who'd seen Mia perform live on several occasions.

It was strange to view the twenty-seven-year-old singer postmortem since, onstage, Mia was the embodiment of life. She was pretty and tough, the type of chick no one would want to anger. *"I don't like to be a violent woman,"* she warned in the song, "Here's to Your Fuck," *"but I know I have it in me."*

Lots of people saw Mia as she circulated around Seattle, and they remembered the sightings. Indeed, Mia's day on July 6 was fairly well-chronicled. People saw her eating Thai food and record shopping and drinking at one of her favorite dive bars. Yet there was an eighty-minute gap, post-midnight, in the early morning hours of July 7—a time in which the singer was raped, beaten, and left lying in the street, faceup, her arms spread apart like those of Jesus on the cross.

At the time, the Gits were on the verge of becoming actual stars. The group had recently returned home from a West Coast tour, proving that they were something more than a local phenomenon. There'd been business meetings, and a major label was poised to sign them. An indie album was already out and—regardless of how subsequent discussions went—the Gits were in the midst of recording their second LP.

In death, a legend would grow around Mia, with tales depicting her as a celebrity dedicated to raising people's consciousness about women's issues. But what Mia really liked to do was sing. And none of the stories about the force and authenticity of her voice were exaggerated. Her bass player, Matt Dresdner, remembered the first time he heard Mia sing, at a coffeehouse when all the members were in college. "Her voice literally made me cry," he told the *Seattle Times*.

In an interview with CBS, Gits drummer Steve Moriarty recalled "the urgency and honesty of her vocals. Her art and the music were the most important things to her, and everything else, who cares?"

After the murder, benefits were held and concerts arranged in her honor. A group of famous Seattle musicians even raised funds to hire a private investigator. But for ten years, no one knew why Mia lost her life. Nor was there any clue as to who had killed her.

Recounted her father, Dick Zapata, "I came to accept the fact that it was never going to be solved."

Despite her close association to Seattle, Mia was actually born in Louisville, Kentucky, a naturally inquisitive child who would sneak over to the fish tank in preschool simply to observe the way the small animals reacted to the rippling water. On family camping trips, Mia would sit beneath a tree and write poetry. At age nine, she began playing the guitar and piano, drawn particularly to songs about sadness and struggle. Among her favorite artists: Billie Holiday, Bessie Smith, and Hank Williams.

Double-jointed, Mia had an unusual way of walking, with her feet pointing inward. When other kids referred to her as "Chicken Legs," she embraced the name—hence the tattoo on her leg. When she died, the Gits' upcoming album was titled *Enter: The Conquering Chicken*.

Rarely did Mia discuss the part of her childhood that had involved private schools and tennis clubs. "Material things didn't mean anything to her," her father told the *Seattle Times*. Instead, she aspired to have "a complete and total social conscience. . . . She would see people on the street, homeless, and tell us it wasn't their fault."

Later, she would take in friends who were recovering from addictions. Whatever satisfaction eluded her in her charitable deeds would be compensated for by the enrichment derived from her music.

The Gits—featuring Mia, Moriarty, Dresdner, and guitarist Joe Spleen (Andy Kessler)—formed in 1986 while Mia was a student at Antioch College, a liberal arts school in Yellow Springs, Ohio. The original name, "Sniveling Little Rat Faced Gits," was based on a Monty Python skit; another band, California's Toad the Wet Sprocket, had used the same television troupe for the inspiration of its own moniker. After developing a following on campus and the surrounding area, band members made the decision to join the burgeoning music scene in Seattle in 1989, moving into an abandoned structure that would come to be known as "The Rathouse."

Despite their association with grunge, the Gits considered themselves progressive punkers, emitting the type of sound made by such riot grrrl bands of the era as L7 from Los Angeles, Babes in Toyland from Minneapolis, and Bikini Kill from Olympia, Washington. While Nirvana's Kurt Cobain and Pearl Jam's Eddie Vedder often used their music to brood, Mia bared her teeth and growled. When a friend was raped, Mia fantasized about catching the assailant and administering her own justice. *"I'll take a pan to your head,"* she sang in "Spear and Magic Helmet," *"'cause I'm full of rage."*

Although she'd later be characterized as a feminist musician, Mia, in many ways, saw herself as one of the boys, writing more songs about drinking than about gender.

In moments she kept from the band, Mia would sneak into the studio and practice her singing, instructing the engineer to erase material that didn't meet her benchmark. At the time of her death, she'd been working on a brawny cover of Sam Cooke's "A Change Is Gonna Come."

"'Making it' is such a relative term," Cristien Storm, a poet friend from Seattle, told ABC. "To Mia, doing her thing—performing her music, writing poetry—doing what she loved was 'making it.'"

In 1992, the band released its birth album, *Frenching the Bully*, on the independent C/Z label. In certain social circles, the album was well known, with copies sometimes passed from fan to fan. "The Gits . . . were just starting to break through," Dresdner told the *Stranger* website. "We weren't anywhere close to being the biggest band in Seattle. We had developed a very tight-knit, loyal following, and it was interesting because we got to know most of the people who came to our shows, and there was a real sense of community."

Friend Peter Sheehy described Mia as a unifier among people in divergent scenes. Because of her "magnetic personality," he told the *Seattle Post-Intelligencer*, she "drew all sorts of people together who otherwise might never have met."

In early July, 1993, Mia told her father that her recent West Coast tour had been a success. "I don't think I can ever remember my daughter looking so satisfied, so content, so at ease with herself," Dick Zapata told the television show *Unsolved Mysteries*.

But Mia apparently acted differently around her bandmates. "She said, for some reason, 'I don't want to be back in Seattle,'" Moriarty told CBS. "'I have a really bad feeling here.' She was a real intuitive person, extremely intuitive."

It was warm and clear in Seattle on Tuesday, July 6, when Mia left her home to meet her father, who'd made the long drive from Yakima, Washington, to spend the afternoon with his daughter. The two ate Thai food and walked the aisles of Tower Records, talking about music and life in the city. Then Dick drove them to the Seattle Art Museum, where the works of Pacific Northwest painters, sculptors, and photographers were among the items prominently displayed. When Dick left, Mia caught up on laundry before wandering over to the Winston Apartments, a three-story, wood-frame building in the Capitol Hill neighborhood, where a rehearsal space had been set up. For the next several hours, she jammed with Robert Jenkins, a Vietnam veteran whom she'd recently dated, and his band, Hells Smells.

To those who didn't know him, Robert could be a gruff, intimidating character. But his friends described him as warm and artistic. He did a routine in which he described a genre called "alien folk music," consisting of sounds that came from outer space that he claimed kept him up at night. In the studio, he and Mia had recorded a cover of the country song "Devil in the Bottle," with Jenkins using a silver dollar to pick at his guitar. Nonetheless, there was an undercurrent of tension in the rehearsal space. Because of the recentness of their breakup, Mia didn't know where they stood and seemed to be moody.

At around 8:30 p.m., she arrived alone at the Comet Tavern, a dive bar where musicians tended to congregate, clad in boots, rolled-up jeans, and a black sweatshirt with the word *Gits* written on the back. But she was clearly preoccupied, separating herself from friends and associates at one point to use the bar's pay phone. Although she hadn't been drinking much lately, observers noticed her constantly refilling her glass. With two friends, she excused herself to visit Piecora's Pizza, the restaurant where she had a part-time waitress job. There, they downed several shots before returning to the Comet, where she ordered more alcohol.

At 1 a.m., she left to Comet to go back to the Winston Apartments and see if Robert Jenkins was still in the rehearsal space. Her goal was to clarify the status of their relationship, and when she couldn't find him, she became angry. Hells Smells singer Tracy Victoria Kenly—known as "TV"—lived upstairs, and Mia knocked on the woman's door for a visit. Mia appeared frustrated, as well as drunk, and TV invited her guest to spend the night. Instead, Mia announced that she planned to take a taxi home.

She descended down the building's central staircase toward the exit doors, and wandered out onto the street. A neighbor later reported seeing a group of people smoking crack in the building's lot, but Mia allegedly avoided them—either deliberately or just because her mind was someplace else.

As she turned down the sidewalk, Mia was listening to music with a set of headphones connected to a Sony Walkman. Because of this, she may have never seen whoever came up behind her and attacked her.

A neighborhood resident remembered hearing a scream at around 3 a.m. At 3:20, a twenty-seven-year-old prostitute who used the name Charity spotted what she believed was a bag of trash on Twenty-Fourth Street South, between South Yesler and South Washington Streets, a dead-end road, near an overgrown and heavily littered field. As Charity inched closer, she realized that the object was a human being, a partially clothed woman whose face pointed up at the street lamp. Her ankles were crossed and arms spread apart.

Mia's sweatshirt was pulled up beneath her arms, with her hood knotted below her throat. Authorities would find her wallet, underwear and torn bra jammed into a pocket.

Charity rushed to a fire station a block and half away and reported her finding. Medics were immediately dispatched to the scene. The victim was dead, strangled with the drawstring of her sweatshirt. An autopsy would reveal vaginal and anal injuries, consistent with rape.

The medical examiner determined that if Mia hadn't died from asphyxiation, she would have succumbed to internal injuries—a lacerated liver and blunt impact to the abdomen—sustained after she fought back against her attacker. Although there was no semen detected in her body, a forensic scientist was able to take DNA swabs from the saliva found among the abrasions along the sides of the singer's nipples.

Mia's death shook the local music community. There was a dusk-to-dawn wake in Seattle, attended by a thousand of Mia's friends and fans. Dick Zapata was so taken by the outpouring of affection that he bought beer for the mourners. On the way to his daughter's funeral a few days later, he became lost. Suddenly, he noticed some of the same people—uncombed, tattooed, and pierced—holding flowers, along with admission tickets to the ceremony. They recognized him as well, and led him to the service.

"We were all angry, and there wasn't anyone to be angry at," TV told the *Seattle Times*, referring to the anonymity of the killer. "We were suspicious. We were frustrated. When we all hung out together, we were all sad. A lot of bands broke up."

The females seemed to take the homicide particularly hard. "[They were] all very tough people and, as a group of women . . . really strong, outspoken and hard-hitting," Cristien Storm told NPR. "And that perception of, "We're not victims at all in any way, and this can't happen to women who aren't victims, and [the murder] shattered that myth to us. . . . It happens to all types of women."

Hoping to restore some sense of control, a group of women on the scene formed a self-defense group in Mia's honor called Home Alive. Instructors offered advice on everything from pepper spray to martial arts techniques to fending off an attacker with a broken bottle or knife. Former members of the Black Panthers, as well as representatives of the NRA, volunteered to offer firearms training.

At first, police were convinced that Mia's death was related to prostitution or drugs. The assumption evaporated when investigators recognized the status that Mia held on the local music circuit. Both musicians and fans were pressuring detectives to solve the crime quickly. Hoping to accomplish this, they found Mia's estranged boyfriend, Robert Jenkins, and began questioning him.

He appeared to fit the profile of the killer. He was a veteran who'd witnessed wholesale murder in Vietnam, and wore the scars on his face. More than one person on the scene categorized him as "scary." And, of course, Mia had been angry at him on the night she died. But Jenkins was a cooperative witness. Unlike other associates who'd get distracted by one crisis or another on the way to the police station, he turned up for every appointment, allowed detectives to take hair and blood samples, and passed two lie detector tests. He appeared genuinely sad and asked police the types of queries that came from a concerned friend, as opposed to those of a sociopath attempting to hide his crime. Plus, he had an alibi. During the time when Mia was furiously searching for him, he'd been with another woman, who verified his story.

Still, police thought Mia might have known her killer, and began questioning virtually every guy on the scene, and requiring a DNA sample. Later, each would repair to a club or a bar to recount the ordeal. Acquaintances would listen, feeling a mixture of sympathy and suspicion. Said Dresdner in the *Seattle Times*, "I'd walk into the Comet and look at people I knew as potential murderers."

Reaching beyond the music circuit, police surveyed the neighborhood, questioning some two hundred onetime criminals with violent records. Not only didn't anyone emerge as a suspect, but nobody could remember hearing or seeing anything unusual after 2 a.m.

There were multiple theories. Both Ted Bundy and the Green River Killer had operated in Washington State, so it was not beyond comprehension that Mia might have been targeted by a serial murderer. Or perhaps someone had mistaken Mia for a streetwalker and propositioned her. She'd been in a bad mood that night and could be loud and cutting when offensive. Had she hurt someone's ego so badly that he became violent? Mia had told TV that she'd planned to take a taxi home. Did the driver assault her and then leave her in the street?

Some believed that more than one person was involved, possibly cult members who deliberately posed Mia on the asphalt like a crucified Christ.

The tragedy was turning Mia into a household name, at least in the punk world, and new fans were listening to her music. The singles "Seaweed" and "Precious" from the Gits' second album achieved moderate success. One San Francisco tattoo parlor included a likeness of Mia in its book of selections, along with images of Jim Morrison and Jerry Garcia. "She was sainted and that was very peculiar," Dresdner noted. "She became the icon for feminism and all kinds of things that she had very little to do with in her actual life."

As Mia sang on the Gits' single "It All Dies Anyway," "*Is death the only way to get attention?*"

Nonetheless, the leads dried up quickly. "Someday, somebody's going to say something about the murder that only [the police] know about," Seattle detective Tom Pike told the *Seattle Times*. "Somebody saying something might be the only hope for solving this case."

If police could not decipher the crime by themselves, Mia's friends and associates were determined to take action to move the case along. Shortly before his suicide in 1994, Kurt Cobain and his Nirvana bandmates enthusiastically took part in a benefit that raised $70,000 to hire a private investigator. Seattle giants Pearl Jam and Soundgarden also participated. Joan Jett—who'd never met Mia, but became enthralled by her legend after the murder— added to the fund by touring with the remaining members of the Gits. The combination was called "Evil Stig," backward for "Gits Live." Then-Warner Brothers heads Mo Ostin and Lenny Waronker arranged for the company to fund one of the shows and release an album.

Jett and Bikini Kill front woman Kathleen Hanna also cowrote a song for Joan's 1994 album, *Pure and Simple*, called "Go Home." The video included a scene of a woman being stalked and attacked, but overcoming her assailant.

But when fans attended Seattle-area concerts, something appeared to be different. "When Mia died, there was a sense that the scene was dying," Moriarty told CBS. "It took the wind out of many people here. Kurt Cobain's death was the nail in the coffin."

Three years after the killing, Dick Zapata purchased a condominium near the crime scene, enabling him to repeatedly retrace his daughter's final steps. "There are a hundred ways of getting to where her body was found," he said. "Sometimes, I'll take what I think was the route she took. Other times, I'll try a different route to see if it fits into the scheme of things. I want to understand. . . . Maybe I think by doing this, I'll figure out what happened."

But after five years, the investigation appeared to be at a standstill. "We're no closer to solving the case than we were right after the murder," Detective Dale Tallman told the *Seattle Times*.

In 2001, Seattle investigators began reviewing the city's three hundred cold case homicides and resubmitting DNA swabs to the Washington State Patrol Crime Laboratory for additional analysis. In the years since Mia's slaying, technological advances had been made, and cases could now be solved with smaller amounts of DNA material than ever before. Detectives Richard Gagnon and Greg Mixsell paid particular attention to sex-related murders, since the presence of bodily fluids increased the possibility of yielding results. In Mia's case, the concentrations of saliva found around her left and right nipples were removed from cold storage, and the profile of the unknown male attacker entered into a national DNA database.

In December 2002, forensic scientists found a match to a fisherman living in the Florida Keys. Despite the distant location, the lab concluded that the likelihood of error was one in 1.5 trillion.

Jesus Mezquia had arrived in the United States in 1980 as part of the Mariel boatlift, when President Jimmy Carter opened up the border to any Cuban who wished to emigrate, and Fidel Castro released both criminals and patients from the island's mental institutions. Since then, the six-foot-four-inch refugee with the penetrating stare had been arrested for burglary, assault and battery, and domestic violence, among other crimes. Although he and Mia were apparently strangers—neither her friends nor bandmates had ever heard of Mezquia—records revealed that within two weeks of the murder he'd been arrested in Seattle for indecent exposure.

He arrived in Washington State from Florida in 1992 with a woman who'd found employment in the Emerald City. He soon was hired at a hardware store on Rainier Avenue, spending much of his spare time fishing. Neighbors remembered seeing the lanky newcomer adorned in gold chains, bracelets, and rings, lugging a tackle box. Although he spoke enough English to communicate, he was often vague and "shady" when questioned about his past. On the night Mia was murdered, detectives discovered, Mezquia's girlfriend had been out of town.

The girlfriend told a neighbor that Mezquia's temper frightened her, and that she regretted getting involved with him in the first place. The couple broke up but continued to live together until the girlfriend purchased him a car. Mezquia then moved to Southern California and eventually returned to Florida, where he married and had a daughter.

His wife, Niurka, told the *Seattle Times* that she worked to support the family, while Mezquia babysat their two-year-old child and fished from bridges in the Florida Keys. Despite his criminal record, she described him as calm and drug- and alcohol-free. "I don't believe that he did this," she told the *Seattle Times*. "I don't believe it's possible."

Seattle authorities believed otherwise. At their request, Mezquia was taken into custody in the Sunshine State. When Gagnon and Mixsell arrived, they showed the forty-eight-year-old suspect photos of women killed in a number of Seattle cold cases, including Mia. Mezquia denied having ever seen any of them. However, detectives were certain of his guilt. Gagnon told CBS, "There's no way that saliva could be where it was and him not have any knowledge of who this lady was."

Mezquia was charged with premeditated first-degree murder and rape.

Gagnon then called Dick Zapata. "It's a miracle," the investigator said. "But we think we've got him. He's down in Florida. We're bringing him back."

Upon learning of the arrest, Moriarty felt relief over finally being able to walk around the city without wondering whether he was crossing paths with the killer. "I can't say that I felt closure, because it's not going to bring Mia back," he told MTV.com. "But I did listen to Gits albums really loud, and that felt good."

As the defendant listened to a translation of his trial through headphones, Mezquia's defense team contended that the DNA samples were corrupted at the crime scene by paramedics attempting to revive Mia, and that the suspect's saliva might not have actually been on her breasts. But they didn't have much more in their arsenal. After considering the microscopic evidence for four days, a jury convicted Mezquia in 2004. An appeals court overturned the thirty-six-year penalty based on a ruling that it exceeded the eighteen-to-twenty-eight-year sentence generally levied in this type of case. But in 2009, King County Superior Court Judge Sharon Armstrong again imposed a thirty-six-year punishment.

It had been sixteen years since the night Mia was slaughtered in the street.

Seattle is now a very different city, the early-'90s music scene romanticized and encapsulated in the city's Museum of Pop Culture—created by Microsoft cofounder Paul Allen in 2000. Yet Mia's name still garners recognition, as well as feelings of longing and genuine sadness. In 2015, the Gits had their first reunion in more than twenty years, with Rachel Flotard from the group

Visqueen on vocals. "It was magic," Mia's friend 7 Year Bitch singer Selene Vigil-Wilk told *Spark Mag*. "To see those guys get up there and do those songs again, I'm telling you, everybody in the room was crying. It was this healing experience we didn't know we still needed."

17

AIN'T THAT PECULIAR

THE SACRIFICE OF MARVIN GAYE

I don't have any plans at all," "Prince of Motown" Marvin Gaye told British journalist Phil Symes in 1971. "I don't plan anything. I never have and I never will."

The whimsical posture expressed by the singer/composer with the hypnotic, three-octave vocal range belied a desolation that the Motown machine effectively hid. Here was Marvin, smiling and self-confident, acting as if the hits—in the course of his career, he'd post fifty-six singles on the pop charts—spontaneously flowed from him with little or no forethought, when the reality was that Gaye agonized over his work, as well as his life. Whether he was staging a musical protest against the ills of society on "What's Going On" or communicating salaciousness on "Sexual Healing," Marvin was an artist who viewed each single as a thematic piece. In his final years, he not only forecast his death, but orchestrated it—if not deliberately, then subconsciously.

How else could one make sense of Marvin's decision to bestow on his father—a man with whom Gaye had violently clashed his entire life—the gift of a Smith and Wesson .38 Special for Christmas, 1983? Gaye justified the exchange by telling loved ones that his father needed the pistol to fend off burglars who might have had designs on the LA house that the two-time Grammy winner had purchased for his parents.

Marvin's sister Zeola knew better. "He wanted to die," she told the *Daily Mail.*

He hastened this possibility by living under the same roof as his father, ingesting voluminous quantities of cocaine while Marvin Gay Sr. irrigated himself with 100-proof vodka. Nonetheless, when circumstances escalated to the point that the sixty-nine-year-old pastor pulled the trigger on April 1, 1984—one day before the singer's forty-fifth birthday—the news astonished all but Marvin's closest associates.

Even today, the murder of Marvin Gaye is considered one of the most incomprehensible moments in pop music history.

"I think I've got a real love thing going," Gaye told Symes. "I love people. I love life and I love nature, and I can't see why other people can't be like that."

In reality, he understood.

At home in Washington, DC, Marvin grew up watching his mother, Alberta, a schoolteacher and housewife, receive regular beatings from her husband. Marvin Pentz Gay Sr.—his son would add an *e* to the end of his surname after he became an entertainer—grew up hard, working the tobacco fields in Kentucky with his twelve siblings. His family was devoutly religious, but combustible, regularly fighting among themselves and with relatives. But they were devout members of the House of God Pentecostal Hebrew Church, a sect combining fundamentalist Christianity with aspects of Orthodox Judaism. At twenty, Marvin Sr. became a minister, preaching that the modern world was evil and mandating that his children go hungry in order to deepen their connection to God.

"If you do not please the deity," he'd repeat, "you will go to hell."

Neither Marvin nor the other children in the family were allowed to question their father's authority. The singer's sister Jeanne recalled that Marvin Sr. decreed that if any child ever raised a hand to him, the penalty would be death. As an adult, Marvin would describe his father as an odd, erratic, and brutal "all-powerful king."

The kids were forbidden from pursuing secular diversions, like sports and listening to popular music. Yet, Marvin Sr. was hardly a man of virtue. While restricting the activities in his household, he fathered at least one child with a mistress, drank, and cross-dressed. Marvin's second wife, Jan, remembered meeting Marvin Sr. for the first time. "The white-toned pantyhose under his plaid Bermuda shorts and the fact that he was wearing his wife's red flat sandals put him in a category all his own," she told London's *Mirror*. "I don't know the name of that category. All I know is that man was beyond strange."

The elder Gay's outward appearance caused clashes with church members, and bullying for Marvin Jr. As much as Marvin resented his father, he felt obligated to defend him from the insults of neighborhood children, and often returned home bruised, after fighting to protect the family's honor. When Marvin Jr. would explain why he'd been fighting, his father would beat him for daring to imply that people might perceive the minister as feminine.

As a result of his upbringing, Gaye felt disdain for authority, occasionally defying Motown boss Berry Gordy Jr. or manager/producer Harvey Fuqua with a vehemence far out of proportion to the circumstances.

Yet Marvin loved and felt protective of his mother, who doted on him and encouraged his talents. Their closeness enraged Marvin Sr., who accused his wife of spoiling the child and his son of carrying on an incestuous relationship with his mother. Still, it was a bond that could not be broken. "If it wasn't for Mother, who was always there to console me and praise me for my singing," Gaye told David Ritz, author of *Divided Soul: The Life of Marvin Gaye*, "I think I would have been one of those child suicides you read about in the papers."

Despite the musical prohibitions imposed at home, Marvin did manage to listen to early R&B pioneers, and developed a fondness for Ray Charles, Little Willie John, Clyde McPhatter of the Drifters, and the Five Keys' Rudy West. Naturally, the first forum where he could express his talents was the church, where his voice conveyed a deep yearning for some kind of deliverance.

It was during the worship service that he developed his vocal mannerisms—like the "hooo!" Michael Jackson would later consolidate into his routine—along with his skill at performing on a number of instruments, including the drums and keyboards.

"He was very much ahead of his time," his sister Jeanne told the *Daily Mail*. "I used to tell him, 'You are in the next phase of life, even though you live in this one.'"

At seventeen, Marvin gained temporary relief from the family friction by joining the air force. He returned to DC when his service was over, singing doo-wop with one of the city's top groups, the Rainbows. In 1957, he started his own combo, the Marquees. With Bo Diddley's encouragement, the Marquees cut a record, "Wyatt Earp," that began circulating around industry circles. Harvey Fuqua was impressed enough to hire them as the latest incarnation of the Moonglows, an R&B act whose membership shifted regularly. That's how Berry Gordy first became aware of Gaye's skills, hiring him as a Motown house musician in 1961.

Interestingly, Gaye was brought on not as a singer, but as a session drummer and songwriter, working with Smokey Robinson and the Miracles and other groups. Gaye was credited as a cowriter on Martha and the Vandellas' "Dancing in the Street" and as drummer on the Marvelettes' "Please Mr. Postman." In 1962, he made his Motown debut as a vocalist with the single "Stubborn Kind of Fellow."

By the next year, his hit "Can I Get a Witness" was on its way to becoming an anthem for the British mod movement. It would be followed by chartbusters like "Pride and Joy," "You're a Wonderful One"—with the Supremes—"I'll Be Doggone," "How Sweet It Is to Be Loved by You" and his biggest hit of the 1960s, "I Heard It Through the Grapevine."

Despite his reputation as a womanizer, Marvin is said to have enjoyed a deep but platonic relationship with Tammi Terrell—love interest of Temptation David Ruffin—his duet partner on Nickolas Ashford and Valerie Simpson–produced classics "Ain't

No Mountain High Enough," "Your Precious Love," "Ain't Nothing Like the Real Thing," and "You're All I Need to Get By." In 1967, while the two were singing onstage, Terrell suddenly collapsed into Marvin's arms. It was the first indication of the brain tumor that would claim her life three years later. Marvin was so shattered by the loss that he took a hiatus from live performing.

At that point, he'd become disenchanted with the Motown formula of cranking out three-minute hits, primarily love songs that ignored the struggles of the poor and minorities in the United States.

"I spent three years . . . reflecting upon life and upon America especially—because that's where I live," he said, "its injustices, its evils and its goods."

When his brother Frankie returned from serving in Vietnam and shared his stories with Marvin, the singer began to consider making a musical statement about what he saw as the absurdity of the war. Then, in May 1970, four student protesters were killed, and nine injured, by the Ohio National Guard at Kent State University. "I couldn't sleep," he said, "couldn't stop crying. The notion of singing three-minute songs about the moon and June didn't interest me."

What followed was *What's Going On*, an album on which Marvin sermonized not only about the war, but about civil rights and the environment. His chain of hits allowed Marvin the type of artistic control that was rare for Motown headliners, as he composed and produced the record. Nonetheless, Berry Gordy didn't understand the concept album, and attempted to block distribution. But because the Motown president was distracted by film and television projects in Los Angeles, Marvin successfully maneuvered to have it released anyway.

Gordy was livid. But on the first day of its May 1971 release, a hundred thousand copies of *What's Going On* were shipped to record stores. The initial pressing hit the one million mark, while three songs reached the Top 10: the title track, along with "Inner

City Blues (Make Me Wanna Holler)" and "Mercy Mercy Me (The Ecology)."

The Motown founder was pacified. Even Marvin Gay Sr.— who'd previously criticized his son for promoting secular music— expressed admiration for many of the themes. Still, the brief reconciliation did not soothe Gaye's inner torment. In both his personal and professional lives, Marvin sought out surrogate parents to narrow the wide voids in his soul. He loved Smokey Robinson like family and referred to him as "Dad." Even more conspicuous was his relationship with his first wife, Anna. Not only was she Berry Gordy's sister, she was fifteen years older than the singer and reportedly spoke to him the way a mother would a son.

Yet Anna was different than Alberta, who appeared to love Marvin unconditionally. Anna is alleged to have fabricated a pregnancy in order to convince Marvin to adopt her teenage niece's son; as another sign of maladjustment, the child was named Marvin III, after the minister who'd tortured the musician from birth. When the pair finally divorced in 1976, Marvin was ordered to pay Anna a large percentage of royalties from his next album. He agreed to the condition, but shocked Anna with a record he titled *Here, My Dear*, an LP that itemized the problematic marriage so concisely that the singer was sued for invasion of privacy.

By then, he was deeply involved with Jan, whom he'd met when she was a seventeen-year-old fan. As one of jazz musician Slim Gaillard's seventeen children, Jan spent part of her childhood in foster care, and was initially excited by the lifestyle Marvin offered. The affair with Jan inspired Gaye's erotic period, starting with the release of *Let's Get It On* in 1973 and followed up with *I Want You* in 1976.

"It didn't matter to me that he was using me to fulfill his fantasies," she told the *Mirror*. "I was willing to be led."

Nonetheless, she claimed that Marvin's interest in her lessened following the births of their two children. Addressing the complicated ways in which he related to women, Gaye told radio host

Tom Joyner, "Love is miserable. Marriage is miserable. And sex is great."

In his vulnerable moments, Marvin confided to his second wife that he felt like a captive of the entertainment industry, once pointing at a homeless man on the street and expressing envy over the vagrant's anonymity. "I'm an artist," Gaye said. "I'm not made for show business. Show business views artists as products."

With his celebrity firmly established, Marvin had little use for television appearances and concerts, and periodically failed to turn up at either. This irresponsibility was magnified by a growing chemical dependence, which also fueled Marvin's paranoia. He purchased an AK-47 for his home, as well as guard dogs. On one occasion—high on cocaine and magic mushrooms—he allegedly held a knife to his wife's throat.

"I beg you to provoke me," he said, according to Jan's book *After the Dance: My Life with Marvin Gaye.* "Provoke me right now, so I can take us both out of our misery."

Minutes later, Gaye's mood shifted, and he grew remorseful and sad. But his death wish appeared to be ever-present. Following his breakup with Jan, Marvin would tell an interviewer, he attempted to kill himself by consuming more than an ounce of cocaine.

Strung out on drugs, depressed over his romantic failures, and in debt to the IRS, Marvin tried retreating from the grind of the entertainment business. With his mother, he took long sabbaticals in Maui and London. In 1981, he accepted an invitation from a promoter named Freddy Cousaert to relocate to Belgium. "I was really broke and things didn't look too good," he told Joyner. "So I was stuck in this forest. I couldn't see. And . . . I owed the government four million bucks, too. That's enough to leave the country."

In the coastal city of Ostend, Marvin started jogging and boxing, gaining some leverage over his drug habit. When CBS Records representative managed to track down the singer in Europe, Marvin agreed to sever his long relationship with Motown. Insulated from the pressures of the States, he wrote and recorded the album *Midnight Love*, featuring the song, "Sexual Healing," which outsold his prior Motown singles.

Once again, fans in the United States were clamoring for Marvin Gaye. He returned, singing live at the 1983 Grammy ceremony—where he picked up an award for Best Male R&B Vocal Performance—and that year's NBA All-Star game, where his stirring, a cappella rendition of the "Star Spangled Banner" is remembered more than MVP Julius Erving's spectacular dunks and dives. Back on tour, he once again succumbed to cocaine abuse and exhibited unusual behavior. Onstage, he'd sing "Sexual Healing" in a silk robe, stripping down to bikini underwear. Offstage, he outfitted himself with a bulletproof vest, convinced that he was being followed by a murderous stalker.

As gratifying as the European respite had been, Marvin was facing the same problems that he'd left behind. Both of his ex-wives were demanding hundreds of thousands of dollars in alimony, while the state of California and the IRS each insisted that he owed millions.

Seeing few options, he moved into his parents' house. Even when Marvin Sr. was away—at one point, the pastor took an extended trip to Washington, DC—Marvin was preoccupied with his mother's health. Alberta Gay had been diagnosed with terminal bone cancer, and thoughts of losing her possessed him. "I don't want to go to my mother's funeral," he told his sisters. "I want to die before she does."

High on drugs, he'd even come up with a scenario for his impending demise. "I'll be poisoned or shot dead," he predicted.

By and large, Marvin stayed in his room, ruminating about suicide and death. His sister Jeanne contended that she'd seen her brother sitting in three overcoats, with his shoes on the wrong feet, making dire prophesies. In late March 1984, she said, Marvin attempted suicide by leaping from a speeding sports car, emerging with minor bruises.

On April 1, Marvin Sr. was in a foul mood over an insurance policy letter that he maintained Alberta had misplaced. The dispute had started the day before and continued until the singer intervened, ordering his father to stay away from Alberta. Although Marvin Sr. complied, he continued to stomp around the house, shouting from different rooms.

At around 12:30 p.m., Marvin was in his room when he heard his father berating Alberta again. Walking over to the top of the stairwell, Marvin shouted down at his father. "If you have something to say, you better say it to me."

When Marvin Sr. ignored him, the singer cautioned, "You better not come up to my room."

As the singer returned to bed, he heard his father storm up the stairs and enter his own bedroom. There, he continued to rebuke Alberta over the missing document. Infuriated, Marvin rose from the bed and rushed down the hallway. "Get out of this room," he ordered his father.

The minister stood his ground, prompting Marvin to grab his father and shove him into the corridor, unleashing a series of kicks and punches.

"Stop!" Alberta screamed.

Remembering a lifetime of physical assaults, Marvin kicked his father another time, hard. The pastor retreated back into his bedroom, but Marvin followed and kicked him again. At that point, Alberta wedged herself between the two men, and the entertainer huffed away and reentered his room.

As Marvin Sr. gathered his bearings, he grabbed the gun that his son had given him for Christmas.

"I was standing about eight feet away from Marvin when my husband came to the door of the bedroom with the pistol," Alberta would tell police. "My husband didn't say anything. He just pointed the gun at Marvin. I screamed, but it was very quick."

A bullet entered Marvin's right chest, piercing his heart, right lung, liver, diaphragm, left kidney and stomach. The pastor then took a step forward and fired again from point-blank range.

Imagining the family tragedy ending in a mass murder/suicide, Alberta pleaded not to be shot. Her husband appeared not to be listening, instead walking over to a pillow in his room and slipping the .38 underneath.

From their guest house on the property, Marvin's brother Frankie and his wife, Irene, had heard the blasts. As they moved toward the main residence to investigate, Alberta burst out the door, screaming and falling into Irene's arms.

"He's shot Marvin. He's killed my boy."

Tentatively, Frankie entered the house and moved toward Marvin's room. The singer was still alive, but bleeding out. Frankie held him.

"I got what I wanted," Marvin whispered. "I couldn't do it myself, so I had him do it. . . . I ran my race. There's no more left in me."

In the main bedroom, the minister would not tell Irene where he'd placed the gun. She started to search and found it immediately. Hoping to avoid further bloodshed, she lifted the weapon, went outside, and dropped it on the lawn. Marvin Sr. left the house, as well, sitting down on the porch to wait for police.

At California Hospital Medical Center, Marvin Gaye was pronounced dead on arrival. Meanwhile, his father was in the interview room at the police station, telling investigators that he'd fired at his son in self-defense after being attacked. Still, he argued that he hadn't known that the gun was loaded. Instead, he said that he'd believed the pistol would either fire blanks or BBs.

"Do you love your son?" he was asked.

"Let's say I didn't dislike him," Marvin Sr. replied before breaking into tears.

Although Alberta would later post bail, Marvin's murder finally roused her to file for divorce. She'd say that the separation officially began the moment that her son was shot.

Smokey Robinson was in his car when news of his friend's death came over the radio. "I'm thinking to myself, 'That's a lie because this is April Fool's Day,'" he told OWN. "'I know good and well that this is some kind of really morbid, cruel April Fool's joke.'"

When he switched to another station, though, he again heard about the shooting. He drove to a telephone and called Marvin's first wife, Anna.

"As soon as she heard my voice," Robinson recollected, "she said, 'Yeah, baby. It's true.'"

■ ■ ■

Due to the presence of cocaine in Marvin's system, and the photos of the injuries that the singer inflicted on his father, Marvin Sr. was allowed to plead no contest to voluntary manslaughter. On November 2, 1984, he received a six-year suspended sentence and five years of probation. Addressing the court, the tearful minister said, "If I could bring him back, I would. I was afraid of him. I thought I was going to get hurt. . . . I'm really sorry for everything that happened. I loved him."

Despite her dire prognosis, Alberta Gaye managed to live until 1987—the same year that Marvin was inducted into the Rock and Roll Hall of Fame. Marvin Gay Sr. held on until 1998. Although the main players in the heartbreaking tale were gone, peace never descended over the family. There were lawsuits over Marvin's catalogue, and bad feelings between his sisters and second wife, Jan. Yet, everyone unanimously agreed that, in his final moments, Marvin had given his father the retribution that was long overdue.

"Marvin had punished his father by, according to the teachings of his church, ensuring his father's eternal damnation," Jan told the *Mirror*. "This was the last chapter of their poisonous story."

18

ANOTHER SAD AND LONELY NIGHT
TEXAS ROCKER BOBBY FULLER'S CURIOUS HOLLYWOOD DEMISE

They said he'd have been like Elvis Presley," Del-Fi Records owner Bob Keane told the television show, *Unsolved Mysteries*, thirty years after his headliner Bobby Fuller was found dead in a car from apparent gasoline asphyxiation, just up the hill from Grauman's Chinese Theatre in Hollywood. "Everybody that knew him would describe him as a musical genius."

But Fuller's fleeting stardom occurred almost a decade after the release of "Heartbreak Hotel," and within months of the Beatles' first appearance on *The Ed Sullivan Show*. Had circumstances been different, Fuller's Southwestern garage band sounds—merging the Tejano melodies he'd heard back in El Paso with the heavy back-beat of rock 'n' roll and the emerging, reverb-laden surf influences of his adopted city—might have had a greater impact. Even so, his version of "I Fought the Law" would be covered by Hank Williams Jr., Roy Orbison, the Clash, Stray Cats, Dead Kennedys, Bryan Adams, Green Day, and the Pogues. And to his devotees, his other recordings, including "King of the Beach," "Let Her Dance," and "Another Sad and Lonely Night," remain as windows into what could have been—had the British Invasion never taken place, and Bobby's life continued after that strange summer day in 1966.

Although Bobby spent much of his childhood in Salt Lake City, where his father was working in the gas and oil industry, he always considered himself a Texan—by virtue of both his birth in Baytown, home of the state's first offshore drilling operation, and culture. In 1956, his father, Lawson, took a job with El Paso Natural Gas, and the clan returned to the Lone Star State, just as rock 'n' roll was exploding.

Bobby was fourteen and completely taken. He and his younger brother, Randy, would spend the next several years emulating Elvis, the Everly Brothers, Ritchie Valens, Eddie Cochran, and their all-time favorite, Lubbock-born Buddy Holly—another tragic Texas figure. Bobby played drums and keyboards, and is said to have taught himself how to play the saxophone. During a period when Randy was away at military school, Bobby picked up his sibling's guitar and learned that instrument as well. He was so proficient that when Randy returned, he was relegated to performing on bass in the band Bobby headed.

By 1962, the group had garnered two regional hits, "You're in Love" and "Gently My Love," recording much of their music in the studio Bobby had constructed in his parents' den on a Viking reel-to-reel tape deck. Despite the size of their makeshift facility, there was a control room, as well as an echo chamber. "If it was the tape recorder . . . used to do 'La Bamba' with, he got it," Randy told the *Guardian*. "And he would talk my mom and dad into buying it for him."

Bobby was even resourceful enough to found two labels, Eastwood and Exeter, to disseminate his music, particularly on El Paso's premier Top 40 station, KELP.

Yet as upsetting as the 1959 airplane crash that took Holly and Valens had been for the siblings, the loss of their older half-brother, Jack, two years later added a morose—and perhaps foreboding—element to the Bobby Fuller saga.

According to *I Fought the Law: The Life and Strange Death of Bobby Fuller*, which Randy cowrote with Miriam Linna—whose band, the Cramps, also covered "I Fought the Law"—in 2014, the boys' mother, Loraine, had a premonition that something had happened to her oldest son on February 5, 1961. Earlier that day, Jack, an oil field worker, had met twenty-one-year-old Roy Handy at a New

Mexico bus depot. The pair decided to go target shooting and, as they drove to the remote Mescalero Indian Reservation, Handy spotted some gag money in the sun visor. "It was a present . . . Jack had bought for the little boy who lived next door to him," Randy said. Convinced that the cash was authentic, Handy made the spontaneous decision to rob his new companion. In the desert, the pair "took turns setting up targets to shoot at," Randy continued. "When it was Jack's turn, Handy opened fire on him. He shot him four times while Jack was trying to get away. . . . Then, when he could run no more, Handy shot Jack once in the head and killed him, then left his lifeless body there to decay."

It was just one of several morbid incidents that some fans view as a sign that Bobby might have been cursed. As Bobby's popularity increased, his band's hair would be groomed by celebrity stylist Jay Sebring, whose girlfriend was an El Paso beauty named Sharon Tate. Both were massacred by the Manson Family in 1969.

With Bobby as lead vocalist and guitarist and Randy on bass, Fuller and his group, the Fanatics, became stars around the Southwest. During one promotional appearance, according to the *El Paso Herald-Post*, "6,000 screaming and cheering boys and girls" packed into a local shopping center. After a 1963 visit to Los Angeles, Bobby increased his popularity by opening a teen club in El Paso, called the Rendezvous, after a similar venue started by "King of Surf Rock" Dick Dale in Newport Beach, California. The Rendezvous provided a stage for Bobby to refine his act—in front of hordes of high schoolers who shelved their cowboy hats and boots for an El Paso variation of surf fashion. Trumpeted the *Herald-Post*, "England has the Beatles but El Paso has Bobby."

It was during the West Coast sojourn that Fuller met the man who'd help transform him from a regional phenomenon to a national personality. Given his popularity in Texas, Bobby expected to return home with a record deal, but the only company that expressed interest in the group was Bob Keane's Del-Fi Records.

A former big-band clarinetist, Keane transitioned into the business end of the industry in the mid-'50s, naming his label after Delphi, the Greek god of music and inspiration. Among his signees were Sam Cooke and Ritchie Valens, whom Keane first spotted at a Saturday matinee show in a movie theater and managed as well as produced. As a musician himself, Keane appreciated a variety of styles. Del-Fi had two major divisions, Mustang Records—as in the Ford Mustang, which had debuted at the 1964 New York World's Fair—and Bronco, which was devoted to R&B. Over the next several years, Keane would compile an eclectic roster that would include Frank Zappa and Leon Russell.

"I'll listen to anyone," he reportedly said, "even if they bring them in on a stretcher."

Keane—whom Bobby labeled "Big Daddy"—saw potential in the Fanatics but wasn't ready to sign them. He advised Bobby to go back to El Paso and acquire a song or two that Keane could turn into a hit. Following the advice, the band recorded a cover of "I Fought the Law," from the Crickets' 1961 album, *In Style with the Crickets*. It had been written by Sonny Curtis, who replaced Buddy Holly as the band's front man after Holly's death.

In November 1964, the Fuller brothers, guitarist Jim Reese and drummer DeWayne Quirico—a replacement for bandmate Dalton Powell, who was married and hesitant to leave Texas—relocated to LA. Keane liked what he heard, and the quartet was offered a contract. Marketing the band as the Bobby Fuller Four, Keane booked the quartet at clubs all over Los Angeles, in anticipation of their first Mustang album. But Los Angeles wasn't El Paso, and band members didn't receive the rousing response they wanted simply by stepping through the door. As a result, they were forced to ingratiate themselves to audiences by playing a disproportionate amount of cover material.

Still, there was the feeling that the band was circulating among heavyweights. One day, the Fuller brothers' television broke, and Keane instructed them to drive down to Long Beach and meet

Larry Nunes—a Mustang investor who periodically turned up at clubs with call girls—at a warehouse. They returned to their apartment with a free RCA color television, a luxury item at the time.

Nunes also arranged for LA music stores to feature life-size cutouts of the band members, elevating them to the status of the British Invasion groups that were dominating the charts. In 1965, the Bobby Fuller Four had a Top 40 hit with "Let Her Dance"—a song written by Bobby. The track received regular airplay on popular KRLA—no surprise, since it appeared on a hot-rod-themed album called *KRLA King of the Wheels*, as Keane knew this would entice the station to publicize it.

In 1966, "I Fought the Law" vaulted the group to an even higher level. Keane arranged for the group to lip-synch the hit on national television, surrounded by go-go dancers with cowboy hats and faux pistols.

Hoping to cross over to the R&B crowd, Keane arranged for future three-time Grammy Award winner Barry White—whose baritone voice would be heard on such '70s hits "You're the First, the Last, My Everything" and "Can't Get Enough of Your Love, Babe"—to produce "The Magic Touch." While the intention was to widen the Bobby Full Four's appeal, Bobby complained that the added drums and remix made the song sound like it was performed by an entirely different act.

"Bobby was furious," Randy said in the book *I Fought the Law*. "Bobby hated the Motown thing they did to the song. He was real proud of his West Texas sound, and could not understand why Keane had gone ahead and made a major decision like this without his approval. He didn't like recording a song [the band] couldn't duplicate live, and 'The Magic Touch' was overdub over overdub over overdub."

Keane was unapologetic. "Buddy Holly was his god, and he wanted to play like Buddy Holly," the Del-Fi owner told *Unsolved Mysteries*. "And I was constantly saying, 'No. Don't do that, because you're Bobby Fuller. You have your own talent.' We were at odds sometimes."

The tension did not dissipate. Bobby resented Keane's edict that the band traverse the country, sometimes playing high school dances, to promote their records, when the singer wanted to be in the studio, creating new ones. He was appalled over having to appear in a lowbrow horror movie, *The Ghost in the Invisible Bikini*, alongside Nancy Sinatra and Dean Martin's daughter, Claudia. Meanwhile, band members bristled about being instructed to maintain a wholesome look—short hair and matching tricolor outfits—in order to differentiate themselves from newer, unkempt rock acts whose seemingly improvised clothing choices symbolized originality and freedom.

When Jim Reese received his draft notice, it was clear that the Bobby Fuller Four was about to splinter. After an abominable show in San Francisco, Bobby announced his plans to begin performing as a solo with new backup musicians and, most likely, another label. Hoping to shed his teen idol image, twenty-three-year-old Bobby fantasized about taking his act to casinos in Las Vegas and Lake Tahoe.

Still, the band managed to work well together, gathering material for a new album in the studio, and discussing a possible UK tour. Although uncertain about the future, Bobby appeared in buoyant spirits in July 1966 when a group of friends visited him from El Paso. As they drove around Los Angeles, Bobby chatted about a Corvette he planned to purchase, and posed for photos in front of Hollywood landmarks.

"He was in a good mood, a great mood," Robin Vinikoff, a guitarist the Fullers knew from home, told the *El Paso Times*.

On Sunday night, July 17, Bobby was lounging in apartment 317 of the Sycamore Apartments in Hollywood, chatting with his mother, Loraine—who'd flown to LA to visit with her sons—while drinking beer with road manager Rick Stone and two female friends. The girls left around 11:30 p.m., and Rick made himself comfortable, eventually falling asleep on the couch while watching TV. At a certain point, Bobby left—apparently to meet a girl he knew named Melody.

Not much was known about Melody. Bobby's friends believed that she was from Chicago and associated with Larry Nunes. Randy recalled Bobby mentioning that Melody was bringing him to a party. "Melody was going to drive him there and introduce him to a lot of big-time people," he told *Unsolved Mysteries*. The psychedelic era had arrived in Los Angeles and—despite the band's innocent appearance—Bobby occasionally experimented with acid. "He said that there'd probably be a lot of, you know, drinking and everything else going on. And I told him not to do anything that would get him in trouble."

It was not uncommon for Bobby to go out in the middle of the night. But since there was a band meeting scheduled for nine-thirty the next morning, everyone assumed that the singer would come home to shower and change beforehand.

When Loraine woke up, though, there was no sign of her son. In addition, the family's blue Oldsmobile was missing from its parking spot. Rick Stone left the apartment and headed to the studio. One by one, the other band members and Bob Keane arrived. When Bobby didn't show up by noon, the group ordered hamburgers, and Keane joked that the "prima donna" was running particularly late. At two-thirty, it was clear that nothing was going to get accomplished that day, and everybody left.

At around 5 p.m., two of Bobby's musician friends from El Paso, Ty Grimes and Mike Ciccarelli, drove up to the Sycamore Apartments. They noticed that the Oldsmobile was not in its usual spot, but decided to ring Bobby's bell on the off chance that someone else was driving it. As they climbed the stairs, Ty heard a car pulling up behind them but didn't turn around to look. Around this time, Loraine walked down the back stairs to retrieve the mail. As her eyes scanned the parking lot, she spotted the

Texas license plate on Mike's car, then saw the Oldsmobile parked close by. She rushed over and opened the door.

The smell of gasoline filled her nostrils. A bedraggled Bobby appeared to be napping inside. "He was lying on the front seat," Loraine told the *El Paso Times*. "The keys were in the ignition, and his hand was on the keys, as if he had tried to start the car. . . . I called his name. When I looked closer, I could see he wasn't sleeping. He was dead."

Loraine ran past Mike and Ty, ascending the stairs to phone the police. The pair's attention shifted to the Oldsmobile and its open door. "Mike and I went over to see," Ty said in the *El Paso Times*. "Bobby was obviously dead. I noticed dried blood on the front of his shirt." He also seemed to have been beaten up.

Police arrived and began to survey the vehicle. Road manager Rick Stone pulled up a short time later. Squeezing past the officers, he said that he noticed an object in Bobby's hand: a hose attached to a gasoline can sitting on the vehicle's floorboard. It appeared that Fuller had been drenched in petroleum.

The singer also appeared to be burned. The police told Rick that the gasoline had singed Bobby's skin. Rick's eyes shifted to Bobby's feet. His slippers looked dirty and worn, as if he'd been dragged somewhere.

A call went out to Randy, who was visiting a friend's art studio. "My mother said, 'Bobby's dead,' and hung up," he recounted to the *El Paso Times*. "I hurried home and somebody in the crowd grabbed me and said, 'Your road manager's been murdered.' I had strange mixed feelings. I was sorry to hear Rick Stone had been killed . . . but I was relieved it wasn't my brother."

As Randy went upstairs to speak to his mother, he saw Rick leaving the apartment. The two men made eye contact, and Rick uttered two words: "It's Bobby."

Police questioned Mike and Ty, since the car had presumably been missing until they turned up. The pair detailed their movements and were told that they'd be contacted if detectives had further questions. Loraine mentioned that Bobby had been troubled over the band's impending breakup, but he didn't appear to be overwrought in any way.

Nonetheless, newspaper stories the next day suggested that Bobby had committed suicide, citing the plastic hose and the gas can, and quoting Loraine as saying that her son had recently been "despondent."

According to one theory, Bobby had been sniffing gasoline to get high, blacked out, kicked the can over, and suffocated.

Whether the LAPD investigators subscribed to the suicide hypothesis or had been told not to probe, police appeared to treat the case with relative indifference. The car was neither impounded nor dusted for fingerprints. A detective was seen throwing the gas can into a dumpster at the scene.

An autopsy report—released three months after the death—concluded that Bobby had died from "asphyxia due to inhalation of gasoline." Despite Loraine and Rick's insistence that they'd seen abrasions on Bobby and the car keys in the ignition, the report stated otherwise.

Loraine was adamant that the Oldsmobile had not been in the parking lot thirty minutes before it was found. Hence, she believed that it was implausible that, in that small stretch of time, Bobby could have driven up and found a way to end his life. Therefore, it appeared that the musician had been murdered elsewhere, then driven back to the Sycamore Apartments. The questions were why the body had been carted back to Bobby's residence, and how the perpetrators had managed to flee without detection.

When Bobby's father and uncle attempted to broach these topics with authorities, Randy said, the chief of police warned them, "If you know what's good for you, you'll keep your mouth shut."

To some fans, Randy should have been scrutinized further, since Bobby's decision to break up the group threatened to adversely affect him. As the Crickets had after Buddy Holly's accident, the band attempted to repackage itself in the wake of Bobby's death—this time as the Randy Fuller Four. But it was unable to capitalize on whatever interest lingered, and broke up within months. Still, it seemed unlikely that Randy would actually murder his brother to fill his spot. The pair were close, and Randy was never evasive or inconsistent when questioned about Bobby's death in the years after the incident.

Those who knew about Bobby's experimentation with LSD came up with a number of other theories. In one, Bobby experienced a bad trip, doused himself with gasoline, drove home, and died before anyone could save him. In another, an impaired Bobby was killed in either a fight or a fall in the home of a fellow celebrity and was shuttled to the Sycamore Apartments to remove him from the actual crime scene. The most bizarre hypothesis of all suggests that Bobby turned Nancy Sinatra on to acid on the set of *The Ghost in the Invisible Bikini,* angering her father, Frank, who put in a request to underworld friends to eliminate the pop star.

The woman Bobby was supposed to meet on the last night of his life, Melody, would later deny that she was in the singer's company when he died. But several of Bobby's associates believed that she was somehow responsible for his demise, maintaining that she was the girlfriend of a dangerous mobster who killed the musician in a jealous outburst. Some have gone so far as to suggest that the boyfriend forced Bobby to drink gasoline, despite the autopsy results indicating otherwise.

Until his death in 2009, Bob Keane argued that the indifference of detectives demonstrated official involvement in the killing. Yet some fans believed that it was Keane who had Bobby murdered as retribution for going solo and leaving the record label. In 1966, Keane had signed a deal with mob-tainted record boss Morris Levy to distribute Bobby's music. Levy regularly threatened the lives of musicians he suspected of disloyalty, and was once indicted for an assault that led to an off-duty police officer losing an eye. Depending on who's telling the story, Levy wanted Bobby dead for any number of reasons. The first is the most obvious: Morris was mad about all the potential revenue that would be lost after Bobby severed ties with Keane. But some suspect that the singer was murdered to punish Keane, after the label head did something to anger the criminally connected entrepreneur.

Levy died in 1990, the same year that he was convicted of extortion following an FBI investigation into mob ties in the record industry. Yet he still wielded considerable power in 1982 when Randy told the *El Paso Times*, "If it was foul play, then the guy who did it is still running loose. I'm afraid to talk too much about it. I don't want him to come for me next."

Two months after Bobby's death, radio listeners phoned into stations around the United States wondering if newcomer Neil Diamond's single "Cherry Cherry" was the final release by the Bobby Fuller Four. But the handsome singer from Texas quickly faded from public consciousness, as tastes shifted to the heavier sounds of the Jefferson Airplane, Jimi Hendrix, and the Doors. As for the people who Bobby emulated, Gene Vincent, Buddy Holly, and Ritchie Valens all have stars on the Hollywood Walk of Fame mere blocks from where Fuller's body was found. Sadly, Bobby wasn't around long enough to earn the same honor, and is largely remembered in the town he tried to conquer as being the prime player in yet another wretched Hollywood calamity.

19

"I Just Killed John Lennon"

After a lifetime of anonymity, he really followed through on something. He'd been planning it for months, and almost backed out a few times, and, now it had happened. Now it couldn't be undone. Now immorality was his.

Yet, as he stood there, waiting for the police to arrive, it was hard to revel in the realization of his private fantasy, firing four shots into arguably the greatest music icon of the twentieth century. In fact, at one point, he'd even considered slipping the gun into his mouth and capping off the experience with a bullet to the back of the throat. But he knew that he wasn't going to do it. "I'm too much of a coward to take my own life," he'd later claim.

But was it cowardice that prevented him from joining his one-time idol in the afterlife, or the understanding that, in the physical world, everyone who'd ever set the record needle down on a disk would remember him—even as the most avid of the victim's fans refused to utter the killer's name aloud, the way certain religious factions avoided saluting a graven image or looking at an illustration of their deity?

They could omit his name all they wanted, not say it on the radio, leave it out of fan bulletins, but, really, it wouldn't matter. Everyone knew it anyway. Everyone from the president of the United States to the tribesmen grazing their cattle along the African Great Lakes. They knew John Lennon and they knew the bespectacled, pudgy former security guard who'd permanently amended the Beatles saga.

Mark David Chapman.

"I don't think I'm a celebrity," he'd insist. "A chimpanzee could have done what I did. . . . Anyone could have pulled the trigger, and I'm nobody special. . . . But I do wish I was a big nobody again. That's true. I wish that this had never happened."

If it hadn't, though, he wouldn't have the opportunity to address the court and the world every two years when he came up for parole, expressing regret while seeming to relish the impact of having blasted his former hero in the back.

"I'd like the opportunity to apologize to Mrs. Lennon," he'd said at one hearing, mindful that the famous woman once derided for breaking up the Beatles had taken the effort to contact authorities and demand that he—Mark David Chapman—never taste freedom again. "I've thought about what it's like in her mind to be there that night, to see the blood, hear the screams, to be up all night with the Beatle music playing through her apartment window."

Post-assassination, Yoko Ono was no longer perceived as the creepy woman in black, sitting on John's amp and whispering conspiracies into his ear during the Beatles' final recording sessions. Today, by and large, people liked her. But when Chapman spoke in court, the media flocked. He wasn't more popular than the Beatles, of course, but, since killing John, he sometimes felt more popular than Yoko. And he was only too pleased to accommodate the curious, using each forum as a live streaming therapy session. "I was feeling like I was worthless," he'd reveal, "and maybe the root of it is a self-esteem issue. I felt like nothing, and I felt that if I shot him, I would become something."

And he did. Despite all the public repentance, Chapman got what he wanted. "I needed a lot of attention," he articulated in a 2014 hearing. "That bright light of fame, of infamy, notoriety was there."

At one time, Lennon had been Chapman's favorite Beatle. Alone at home, Mark pretended to garner the same adulation, while his imaginary friends, the "little people," followed his exploits on their miniature televisions and in their newspapers. But shortly before *Sgt. Pepper's Lonely Hearts Club Band* was released in 1967, Lennon began to annoy him. The feelings would waver, but something had changed. Just as Chapman turned on the little people, blowing certain adherents up by pressing down on the button in the sofa, he'd occasionally think about Lennon, and feel contempt, fury, even hate.

In 1971, Chapman listened as John asked the world to imagine there was no heaven. What an offensive thing to say! Mark wasn't just a devout Christian, but a prayer warrior, a crusader. Friends later heard him sing the song with different lyrics: "Imagine if John were dead."

More recently, the sight of Lennon lounging at the Dakota, the landmarked building where he and Yoko moved in 1973, was especially galling. Why should John live in luxury when Chapman could barely get by? It was a con, Chapman concluded. The man who preached about love and peace and equality was another rich glutton—a "phony," as Holden Caulfield, the main character in Chapman's favorite book, *Catcher in the Rye*, would contend. "Wouldn't it be something," Chapman asked himself, "if I killed this individual?"

In the fall of 1980, Chapman—claiming that his Honolulu home had recently been burglarized—applied for, and received, a pistol permit. But he wasn't sure if he was going to exercise his right to bear arms. Then, on October 20, the *Honolulu Star-Bulletin* ran an interview with Lennon about his new album, *Double Fantasy*. There were the requisite questions about the Beatles years, the breakup and the life Lennon had been living as a stay-at-home father since his last public performance in 1975. But there was also a mention of the guilt he felt over becoming wealthy, and an introspective discussion about whether or not some of the political positions of his recent past had been heartfelt.

This validated the suspicions that Chapman had been harboring. When Lennon spoke, he did so with an impure heart. He was a Judas, untrustworthy, treacherous.

He had to go.

Three days later, Mark quit his security job. John Lennon wasn't the only one whose actions could change society. Chapman was going to New York to alter the culture. Generally, he signed out under the nickname "Chappy." But on this particular day, he wrote "John Lennon," then symbolically crossed it out.

A long, circuitous journey followed, ending with Chapman in front of the Dakota, the building where Lennon and Ono lived on Central Park West, a .38 burning in his pocket, a copy of *Catcher in the Rye* in his hand. "It started with anger," he said of his quest to extinguish the singer. "But I wasn't angry the night I shot him." Indeed, he should have been happy. While John had been raising a family and familiarizing himself with the individual fans who came to venerate him each day outside the Dakota, Chapman was doing okay, too, finding love and showing signs of beating the demons who'd possessed him since childhood. . . .

■　■　■

Chapman received his first guitar lesson from his father, an air force sergeant who'd left the military to work in the oil industry. But Mark hadn't been particularly happy at home, and tended to lose himself in rock music, drugs, and—often when he was drying out from the other two—fundamentalist Christianity. By his senior year of Columbia High School in Decatur, Georgia, he was known for carrying around a Bible and a special "Jesus notebook" he used to record his spiritual observations. In 1975, the same year that Lennon took himself out of circulation, Chapman traveled to Lebanon to work in the YMCA's International Camp Counselor Program. It should have been great, but it wasn't. Mark found himself besieged in Beirut at the start of the country's fifteen-year civil war, and felt fortunate to escape with his life.

Back in the US, he took a job in a program for Vietnamese refugees at Fort Chaffee, Arkansas. The kids apparently loved him, and Chapman grew attached to them, as well as to a girlfriend who shared his Christian worldview. But when he tried attending Covenant College in Lookout Mountain, Georgia, he was reaching too high. He failed out, and his girlfriend left him. True to form, he blamed the breakup on himself.

He was probably right.

During a visit to a public library in 1977, he studied a map of Hawaii and determined that the volcanic archipelago would have a soothing effect on his soul. It was pretty good there for a while. Yet, even in the central Pacific, his old problems and destructive thoughts managed to find him.

So after an indulgent dinner in a Honolulu steak house, he drove a rental car to a beach on the north shore, connected a vacuum hose to his exhaust pipe, and twisted the apparatus through his window. Turning on the engine, he leaned back in the driver's seat and closed his eyes, becoming groggy from the fumes. When the Japanese fisherman knocked on his window, Mark realized that, once again, he'd failed at something. Leaving the vehicle, he discovered that the heat from the exhaust pipe had melted the plastic hose.

He rolled down the windows, letting the fresh sea air purge the deadly vapors from the car, and began to drive. There was a reason why the fishermen had intervened, he concluded. God had plans for him, and needed Chapman to be alive.

Assenting to the will of his creator, Chapman checked himself into Castle Memorial Hospital, where he was placed in the psychiatric unit under suicide watch. But he wasn't an average patient. The doctors liked him, and found him intelligent. He easily befriended the other patients. When he was released, he continued to visit, playing Hawaiian songs on his guitar not just for the psych patients, but for the elderly. He moved in with a Presbyterian minister and found a job in a gas station. Spare time was spent at church, or volunteering at Castle Memorial and socializing with staff. He was feeling as confident as he had when the Vietnamese kids would follow him around at Fort Chaffee. The suicidal thoughts receded. Now, he wanted to live.

After catching an adaption of Jules Verne's *Around the World in 80 Days* at a Honolulu movie theater, he began devising a journey, not in his mind, but a legitimate trip that would take him all over the globe.

It was a complicated itinerary—China, Japan, South Korea, Iran, Israel, and other locales—but Chapman had the help of a conscientious Japanese American travel agent named Gloria Abe. When he returned to Hawaii, they began seeing each other. At Mark's church, the Buddhist-reared Gloria responded to the pastor's altar call and accepted Jesus Christ as her personal savior. In 1979, during a walk on the beach, Chapman asked her to marry him by writing the proposal in the sand.

Gloria bent forward and used her finger to gleefully reply with the word *Yes.*

They'd been married for eighteen months when John Lennon was killed.

Mark took a job in the print shop at Castle Memorial, but couldn't get along there. He was fired, then rehired, then quit after an argument with a nurse. He also interfered at Gloria's job at the travel agency, forcing her to quit. He threw out his record collection, regretted it, and began perusing music shops in an effort to restock. Before he could, he had an episode and smashed his turntable. At one point, he wrote to the Hawaii attorney general about legally changing his name to Holden Caulfield.

He thought about traveling to a small city and setting off a nuclear device. But he didn't exactly have the resources to acquire one. Anyway, he'd probably make a greater impact by killing a person idealized by millions of people. If he couldn't get to Lennon, he pledged to hunt down either late-night TV host Johnny Carson or Elizabeth Taylor.

It cost $169 to purchase the .38. Chapman sold one of his father-in-law's Norman Rockwell paintings to pay for the airfare to New York, along with lodging. He told Gloria that he needed to go to the city to write a children's book. Due to the lack of vigilance of that era, he was able to pass through security at Honolulu International Airport without anyone noticing his weapon.

On October 29, 1980, Chapman stood in front of the Dakota, trying to get a sense of Lennon's movements. He was not alone.

Every day, Beatles fans, tourists, and high school kids playing hooky lounged in front of the building, hoping for a glimpse of John. Lennon knew some of them by name and many others by sight. Most likely, until that point, Mark was the only one who'd come to the Dakota to murder his hero.

It was going to be harder than Chapman had anticipated—not because John, Yoko, and their five-year-old son, Sean, weren't accessible, but because the aspiring killer had neglected to bring along bullets. He called up a local gun dealer, amusing the man with the request. This was New York City, not the American heartland, and gun laws were tight. So Chapman contacted an old friend from Fort Chaffee, a police officer in Georgia, and asked for a favor. He was in New York and needed protection—something with "real firepower." Soon, Mark was on a flight to the Peach State to pick up five hollow-points—projectiles that expanded when fired into a victim's body.

Chapman loaded the gun and packed it in his bag. He checked it at the airport, and reclaimed it when he landed.

Halloween was fast approaching in New York. The area around Central Park was bedecked with woolen cobwebs and cardboard ghouls. The gargoyles molded into the side of the Dakota screeched and menaced. Chapman was ready to kill, but it was chilly outside, so he retreated into a movie theater for a few hours to see the film *Ordinary People*. The story, about a young man battling mental illness and suicidal impulses, tore at his emotions and made him rethink his mission.

"I came here to kill John Lennon," he confessed to Gloria during a conversation from a pay phone.

"Come home," she pleaded. "Come home."

His mind cleared. "I'm not going to do this," he said. "This is a great victory. Your love has saved me, Gloria."

Feeling renewed, he made the long journey back to Hawaii. "I thought it was over," he said of the homicidal expedition. "I thought I was able to get that out of me."

Either way, she specified, he needed to sign up for psychiatric treatment. He tried, but there was a waiting list. Try as he might to distract himself, the fixation with Lennon returned.

One day, he was eating lunch with his mother when he blurted out his desire to return to New York. "You're not going to do anything funny, are you?" Diane Chapman asked.

"No, Mom. No way."

On December 6, he was at the airport again, accompanied by Gloria. She walked him to the gate, crying.

"I need to be alone for a little bit," he said. "I need a bit of a time-out."

Chapman would contend that Gloria believed that he'd tossed his .38 in the ocean. But in another version of the tale, he claimed to have laid out the gun and bullets in front of his wife, precisely outlining what he intended to do. "My God, I still have deep-seated resentment that she didn't go to somebody, even the police, and say, 'Look, my husband's bought a gun and he says he's going to kill John Lennon,'" Mark told reporter Jim Gaines.

Chapman offered the first cabbie he met a hit of cocaine. Another cab driver was told that the visitor had come to New York to help John Lennon record a reunion album with his old bandmate Paul McCartney. He worried about John being killed in a car wreck before there was a chance to kill him. At the Sheraton—where Mark had transferred after being revolted by the sounds of gay sex in an adjoining room at the YMCA—Chapman ordered a prostitute, just like Holden Caulfield in *Catcher in the Rye*. But he was too concerned with Lennon to have intercourse.

As confused as his thoughts were at the time, Chapman was aware of the likelihood of being gunned down by police in the course of slaying Lennon. So he left a shrine to speak posthumously for him at the Sheraton. There was a leather Bible opened to the Gospel of John; Mark added the word *Lennon* to the end of the title. A copy of *Catcher in the Rye* was also open, with the inscription, "This is my statement" over the name "Holden Caulfield." Other items included a letter of commendation from his bosses at Fort Chaffee, a *Wizard of Oz* poster acquired at a Manhattan souvenir shop, and the album *The Ballad of Todd Rundgren*. The last was particularly important because Rundgren and Lennon had been feuding in the press. Among Rundgren's claims: John took up causes to grandstand. Essentially, the singer maintained, the Beatle was no ideologue. He was a phony.

"This wasn't a, you know, naïve crime," Mark would say. "It was a serious, well-thought-out crime."

Staring at his reflection in the mirror, Chapman smoothed out his tan sweater and took aim with his .38.

On the morning of December 8, Chapman left his hotel with a copy of *Double Fantasy* under his arm. He'd traveled too far and waited too long to procrastinate any longer. Today, he vowed, John Lennon was going to die.

As he walked along Central Park West, he realized that he needed a crucial item to get through the day: another copy of *Catcher in the Rye*. Riding the crowds of pedestrians like a wave, he drifted over to Broadway and picked up the red paperback in a bookstore. By 9 a.m., he was stationed in front of the Dakota, nodding at both neighbors and building employees who'd come to recognize him. Whenever a wave of anxiety hit him, he'd open his book and reread a passage.

It was going to be a long day, and Chapman was prepared for it, more confident than ever about accomplishing his task. It was close to 2:30 p.m. when he saw Sean Lennon, accompanied by a nanny, talking to Jude Stein, a superfan well-known outside the Dakota. "Oh, isn't he a cute, sweet boy?" Mark declared, bending down to observe the child. Smiling, the five-year-old looked up and accepted a handshake.

At the height of Beatlemania, each member of the Fab Four contemplated the likelihood of assassination. At a Montreal show, Ringo Starr raised his cymbals high to protect himself from a possible fusillade. George Harrison refused to appear in a San Francisco parade, fearing a repeat of the JFK murder. When asked about how he envisioned his life ending, John theorized, "We'll either go in a plane or we'll be popped off by some loony."

In recent years, though, Lennon had tempered his attitude. "I've been walking these streets for the last seven years," he said, describing his New York experience to BBC Radio. "I can go right out this door and go to a restaurant. You know how great that is? Or go to the movies. I mean, people come up and ask for autographs or say hi, but they won't bug you."

Indeed, John had actually befriended a fan who snuck into his apartment under the guise of being a VCR repairman. After learning that Paul Goresh, an amateur photographer from North Arlington, New Jersey, had no motive rather than making some kind of personal connection with a Beatle, Lennon set down some ground rules. He'd be happy to chat with Goresh when he saw him outside the building, but the relationship had to be honest. No more ruses, Lennon emphasized. And no pictures that could end up in the tabloid press.

Goresh agreed to the terms, and from that moment forward, John seemed to view the fan as a personal favorite. When John and Yoko needed a photo for the sleeve of "Watching the Wheels," the first single released from *Double Fantasy*, they chose an image Goresh had taken of the couple walking past the front gate of the Dakota.

From his vantage point, Chapman had noticed Goresh and the status he seemed to enjoy among both fans and workers at the Dakota, and made an effort to engage the New Jersey native in conversation. In fact, Goresh was standing nearby when John suddenly made an appearance outside the building. Taken off guard, Chapman rushed toward the ex-Beatle and held out his album. Goresh lifted his camera and snapped a photo of John signing the LP cover as a satisfied Chapman watched.

Thinking back, Chapman would remember Lennon as being "extremely gracious and kind to me. That's something I often reflect on, how decent he was to just a stranger."

It had been a busy day for the former Beatle. He and Yoko had done a photo shoot with their friend Annie Leibovitz, the one in which a naked John curled his body around a black-clad, reclining Yoko, his mood suggesting a near worship of the woman he called "Mother," hers a meditative fatigue. And John had done an interview with California radio personality Dave Sholin, in which he talked about surviving both personal and cultural challenges. "The whole map's changed, and we're going into an unknown future," he said. "But we're all still here. And while there's life, there's still hope."

Once darkness fell, Goresh gathered his belongings and started home. Although Chapman had acted a little skittish around the photographer—refusing to answer when Goresh casually asked where the visitor was staying in New York—Mark felt a certain affinity with him, and didn't want him to leave.

"You never know," Chapman reasoned. "Something might happen to him and you'll never see him again."

"What do you mean?" Goresh said. "I see John Lennon all the time."

Chapman chose his words carefully. He'd come this close—meeting both John Lennon and his kid—without anyone telegraphing his intentions. He didn't need Goresh or any of the other fans reporting him to the police.

"Well, you never know," Mark answered quickly. "He may go to Spain and you'll never see him again."

In reality, John was at the Record Plant studio, working on Yoko's song "Walking on Thin Ice." He was feeling good about it. It had depth and sensuality, like her other material, but it was danceable and crossed several genres. He imagined it becoming his wife's first number-one single. As the night wore on, his head swirled with ideas of little things he could do the next day to enhance the song. But he wanted to sleep on it.

When producer Jack Douglas walked the couple to the elevator, a smiling John promised to return to the Record Plant at nine the next morning.

On the limousine ride home, Yoko asked her husband if he felt like going to dinner. John declined. He preferred to go home and see his son.

Outside the Dakota, Chapman prayed. He'd claim to have prayed for a full hour, waiting for God to dissuade him from killing the celebrity. But the entreaties weren't working. "I was obsessed with one thing," Chapman said, "and that was shooting him so that I could be a somebody."

It was 10:50 p.m. when the limo turned from Central Park West onto West Seventy-Second Street. Without even seeing the occupants, Chapman knew that his moment had arrived. His heart raced, but he was able to steady his nerves. "Do it," an inner voice told him. "Do it. Do it."

The vehicle slowed to a halt alongside the sidewalk in front of the building. Often when cars discharged Dakota residents, drivers were ushered into the courtyard, away from the public. But Lennon had grown to appreciate the interactions with his fans and tended to exit at the curb. As soon as Chapman saw Yoko emerge from the limo, he knew that he was going to empty the entire gun.

Seemingly anxious to get inside, Yoko walked about thirty feet in front of her husband. Holding the session tapes, John passed Chapman and made eye contact, apparently remembering the fan from earlier in the day. Mark looked away, embarrassed to return his former idol's gaze. He turned toward the street, as if he were ready to go back to the Sheraton, took five small steps, then abruptly spun around and went into a combat stance.

One bullet flew over John's head, splintering a window in the building. Four more hit their target. Two penetrated Lennon's back, while another two punctured his left shoulder. At least one of the hollow-points hit the former Beatle's aorta.

As Yoko ran for cover, John stumbled up the six stairs into the Dakota's security area, gasping, "I'm shot." Screaming, Yoko cradled her husband in her arms. Concierge Jay Hastings used his uniform jacket to absorb the blood pouring from John's chest. With the life seeping from the musician's body, Hastings removed John's glasses.

Chapman watched, as if the attack were part of a play, his gun hanging at his side. No one even bothered looking at him at first, indifferent to his role in the shooting. Could he really be that insignificant? And, if so, would anyone even remember him?

Eventually, doorman Jose Perdomo walked up to Chapman and swatted the gun out of his hand, as if he were a child with a water pistol. The .38 hit the pavement, and Jose kicked it to out of the gunman's reach. There wasn't fear in Jose's eyes, but a mixture of disgust and sadness. Unlike Chapman, Jose knew John as something other than a rock star. This was the father of a five-year-old child who some miscreant had just gunned down for no rational reason.

Knowing that the police were on their way, Chapman turned his thoughts to himself. What if they believed that he had other weapons, and roughed him up? To avoid this possibility, Mark took off his coat, eliminating the number of bulges protruding from his clothing. He also removed his hat, but continued to clutch his copy of *Catcher in the Rye*.

For the last several days, Jose had been tolerant of Mark as he loitered outside the building. Now, this nut had shot the building's most famous resident. "Do you know what you've done?" the doorman shouted incredulously.

"Yes, I just shot John Lennon."

Cracking open the book, Chapman attempted to read. But everything was going too fast. Yoko was still shrieking and the smell of gunpowder wafted in the air. When the first officers arrived, Chapman held up his hands to block his face, scared that he was about to be beaten. But the police simply frisked and cuffed Mark, bewildered that someone so meek was capable of such violence. Before he was even in the cruiser, Chapman was talking, eager to establish his mark on history. "I acted alone," he offered.

In the squad car, Chapman babbled, talking about the devil and Holden Caulfield. Still, as the press corps gathered for a press conference at the nearby Twentieth Precinct, NYPD chief of detectives James Sullivan looked past all that and spoke with a psychologist's insight. "It's an old rule," he said. "You become as famous as the guy you kill. From now on, anytime there's something with the name Lennon, it's got to have the name Chapman with it. This kind of killing brings names closer together than marriage."

Chapman's attorney Jonathan Marks was prepared to call a succession of mental health professionals to the stand to affirm that the killer was indeed psychotic and not responsible for his actions. But Mark wanted to take ownership of his crime. Against his attorney's advice, he pleaded guilty to second-degree murder on June 22, 1981.

Sentenced to twenty years to life, Chapman had his first parole hearing in 2000, retelling the story of the murder to both those who lived through it and people too young to remember. "I needed a lot of attention at that time, and I took it out on him," he stated. "It became very notorious. . . . I still get letters."

Seeming to enjoy the forum, Chapman emphasized that he didn't expect to be set free, nor did he want to give the impression that he was "playing my violin. I don't have a violin. I don't want one. I'm not asking for anything. I'm lucky to be sitting here alive, and I really mean that."

As the decades passed, Chapman's hair thinned but remained relatively dark. His face was still round, but seemed to lose the bloated appearance it had had in 1980. In fact, he looked very good for his age, exceptional for a man with his psychological history.

Being a ward of the state apparently suited him.

Much of his time was spent alone in a fifty-square-foot cell, reading the Bible and commentary on scripture, particularly passages that dealt with incarceration. One of his Bible study courses that he took was titled "Uprooting Anger: Destroying the Monster Within." His prison jobs varied: porter, kitchen duty, law library clerk, repairer of wheelchairs. Despite his protests, officials mandated that he remain in protective custody. He knew there were Beatles fans in prison, but claimed that he'd never been attacked or threatened.

More than thirty years after Lennon's murder, Gloria still made the five-thousand-mile trek to upstate New York for the forty-four-hour conjugal visits she and Mark were allowed to enjoy in a trailer on prison property. "Our love has grown and grown," she told the *Daily Mail* in 2014. "He tells me to remember that love and intimacy come first."

The years immediately after the murder were a struggle for Gloria. Friends urged her to annul the marriage. But she took comfort in Malachi 2:16: "The man who hates and divorces his wife," according to the New International version of the Bible, ". . . does violence to the one he should protect." "It says, 'I hate divorce,'" Gloria explained. "And that made my decision for me."

During his 2014 hearing, Chapman spoke about the strength of his marriage. "I can't believe she has stuck with me all these years, but she has," he told the parole board. "We're closer to the Lord now than we were on the street, so I am going to credit him with keeping our marriage together and our sanity. . . . For our anniversary, I got her a gold cross with a ruby heart in the center and it's not, you know, just to say, 'Thank you, honey.' It's to tell God thank you for his love for us, for sticking with us."

From behind prison bars, Mark and Gloria started a ministry, counseling young people to choose Christ over gangs, drugs, and other antisocial undertakings. The project resonated throughout the Christian world, and impressed one minister enough to offer Chapman housing if he were ever released.

For more than thirty years, Pastor Ken Babington had been writing to and visiting with the shooter, and was convinced that, through his genuine acceptance of the Word, Chapman had sincere regret about killing the rock legend. "To this day, he refers to John Lennon as 'Mr. Lennon,' with tears in his eyes," Babington was quoted as saying in the ministry's promotional material. "He is remorseful."

Aware that he'd reenter a society perhaps more hostile toward his actions than the prison environment, Chapman admitted to worrying about facing the same type of violence that had resulted in John Lennon's death. But, like the biblical Daniel, delivered from the lion's den after God sealed the beasts' jaws, he felt protected.

Jesus had forgiven him, Mark maintained, even as the New York State Parole Board denied his quest for liberty eight times.

He was convinced that John would forgive him, as well.

As convinced as he'd been that murdering John would make him famous.

20

The Great Rock 'n' Roll Swindle

The Myth of Sid and Nancy

It was a long ride from New York to Bensalem, Pennsylvania, particularly in a snowstorm, but Howie Pyro felt he had no choice but to go. Just a few years ago, before he'd adopted the "Pyro" moniker, he'd been another kid from Bayside High School in Queens, beguiled by the gruesome theatricality of Alice Cooper, wandering around the East Village and wondering if this was the place where he could fit in. At the same time, on the other side of the Atlantic, John Simon Ritchie was going through the same thing, hanging around bands, teaching himself to play bass, getting fucked up on drugs, and cultivating his own legend. In New York, Howie became a founding member of the Blessed—he would later cofound D Generation—a few months before Ritchie, now branded "Sid Vicious," was admitted into the Sex Pistols in London.

Howie had found the punk-rock lifestyle so intoxicating that he stopped taking the 7 train and Q16 bus home to his parents' apartment. But now here he was, hanging out with Sid's mother on that ride to Pennsylvania. Howie had been there the night Sid died, and the performer's mother, Anne Beverley—saddled with the same chemical addictions as her son—needed to be around friends who'd shown loyalty to the former Pistol. A lot of people had turned on Sid when he was arrested for the murder of his girlfriend, Nancy Spungen. But Howie knew that Sid was innocent.

Despite his own drug issues, he supported Anne, even moving in with her after she'd come to New York from the UK, and promised to accompany her as she fulfilled one of her son's dying wishes.

"We had a death pact," Sid had written on a piece of paper Anne had found in his pocket after the overdose, "and I have to keep my half of the bargain. Please bury me next to my baby. Bury me in my leather jacket, jeans and motorcycle boots. Goodbye."

Although Anne had cremated her son, she hoped that he could rest eternally with the peroxide blonde whom both the tabloids and punk scene denizens called "Nauseating Nancy." The Spungen family had placed Nancy in a grave at King David Memorial Park in Bensalem, below a plaque that bore her English and Hebrew names. When Anne asked if Sid could join her at the Jewish cemetery, the Spungens recoiled, refusing with a vehemence that surprised and hurt.

But Anne didn't need anyone's sanction. Sid had never asked for permission for anything—and neither had Nancy. As the car turned onto the Pennsylvania Turnpike, Anne was determined to fulfill her son's wish.

Before they arrived in Bensalem, driver Jerry Only, the bassist for the Misfits, pulled over at a truck stop. Sid's urn was produced and passed around. Howie remembered, "I snorted some of Sid's ashes, so I have some of his DNA in me."

Then they were on their way to complete the mission. When they pulled up at the cemetery, though, it was closed. As the harsh winter winds pushed against her, Anne clutched onto the urn and advanced toward the fence. Then she started to scale it. "What was I at the time, eighteen?" Howie asked. "She seemed so old." Indeed, Anne was forty-eight. "And there she was in a snowstorm, climbing a fence."

The group stood outside the car, smoking cigarettes and rubbing their hands to ward off the chill while Anne disappeared on the other side of the enclosure. Then she was back, climbing back over the gates.

Her face was flushed but satisfied.

Sid and Nancy would be together forever.

"It was so Romeo and Juliet," Howie said. "He didn't care that nobody liked her. He loved her."

The only part that would have bothered Sid was that no one was around to photograph the ash spreading for London's *Mirror* or the *New York Post*. As much as he often claimed to detest the media—threatening to smash the cameras of the assembled paparazzi during his perp walk—he also knew how to play to them, once cutting himself and mixing his blood with his breakfast cereal as a reporter watched in awe.

"Sid was everything everyone else was not," the Pistols' Svengali-like manager, Malcolm McLaren, wrote thirty years after the musician's death in the *Daily Beast*. "Sid proved that you don't have to play well to be a star. You can play badly or not even at all. . . . What matters is this . . . being fearless of failure. . . . In doing so, you may change the culture."

Certainly, the culture of punk rock would have been very different without Sid. To his followers carelessly thrashing about while jumping in place from leg to leg—the "pogo dance," by the way, was a Sid Vicious creation—their clothes deliberately shredded and cheeks punctured by safety pins, he represented nihilism and self-destruction. The whole thing wasn't supposed to last. *"There's no future for you,"* the Pistols famously sang. And Sid made sure that he wasn't around once the initial phase was over.

Although he was dead at twenty-one, he achieved far more than anyone would have predicted. Shortly after his birth in 1957, Sid and Anne moved to Ibiza, Spain, awaiting the arrival of the boy's father. But John Ritchie Sr., a Buckingham Palace guard and trombone player who'd met Anne when they were both in the Royal Air Force, never turned up. Returning to England, Anne married again, in 1965. But her second husband, Christopher Beverley—who allowed his stepson to use his last name—succumbed to cancer six months later.

At a certain point, heroin overtook Anne's life to the extent that she lost track of where her son attended school, and she kicked him out of her home when he turned sixteen. "I remember saying to him, 'It's either you or me, and it's going to be me,'" she told Jon Savage, author of *England's Dreaming: The Sex Pistols and Punk Rock*. "'I have got to try to preserve myself and you just fuck off.'"

Yet Howie Pyro would always defend Anne: "People say Sid's mom didn't love him. She fuckin' loved him very much. She was just a fucked-up person too."

During one of the sporadic times Sid attended class, he met future Pistols lead singer Johnny Rotten, then known as John Lydon. The pair would pick up small change by busking around London, singing Alice Cooper covers so obnoxiously that they were occasionally paid to stop. For Sid, it was better than showing up at a job. "I always hated work," he told Judy Vermorel, coauthor of *Sex Pistols: The Inside Story*. "I never did anything at all. I didn't do a single thing. . . . I wasn't interested in it."

Deciding to become a musician instead, Sid attempted to teach himself bass after shooting speed and listening to the Ramones for forty-eight straight hours. He'd later apply the bass pattern from the group's single "I Don't Wanna Go Down to the Basement" to virtually every song he played.

He also tried playing drums, wielding the sticks during one now-immortalized Siouxsie and the Banshees show. His tenure lasted all of one night.

When he heard about an opening for a lead singer in the Damned, he was excited to audition. But he blamed the eventual pick, Dave Vanian, and his friends for passing along erroneous information about the time and place of the session. It was a slight Sid never forgot, once hurling a glass at the stage while Vanian was performing. Missing its target, the object hit a pillar and shattered into pieces, one of which partially blinded a female spectator.

Sid was a fan of the Sex Pistols before he was a member. Malcolm McLaren had organized the group in 1972, but it wasn't until 1975, when Johnny Rotten joined, that the band began receiving attention. Allegedly, Sid had attempted to audition for the lead singer role as well, but his friend turned up first. McLaren maintained that had he known about the charismatic Sid at the time, the job would have been his.

When Glen Matlock left as bassist in February 1977, Sid filled the void. Since there was already a "John" as lead singer, the newcomer adopted the name of Rotten's pet hamster, Sid. Although Sid would perpetuate the myth that he'd earned the "Vicious" surname by attacking a police officer, Rotten claimed the moniker was born after the small rodent bit the bass player's finger. Observed Rotten, "Sid is really vicious."

Spiking his hair with Vicks VapoRub, Sid antagonized the public by deliberately including Nazi symbols in his wardrobe. Although he'd pretend to be so dim that he didn't grasp the history of the insignia, Slits guitarist Viv Albertine—who once shared an apartment with Vicious—told the *Guardian*, "He was clever. He understood concepts."

And he was willing to risk his body to fortify his image, cutting himself onstage and slugging antagonists in public with his belt buckle wrapped around his knuckles. Rotten later said that he realized that Sid had never been taught how to cope with lifestyle shifts, and was unequipped to deal with the group's growing popularity. "I'm sorry, God, for the day I brought Sid into the band," Rotten told the *Independent*. "He felt so isolated, poor old Sid."

While visually he was as much a part of the Pistols as the orange-haired Rotten, Sid was all but absent from the band's debut album, *Never Mind the Bollocks*. He missed recording sessions due to hepatitis, the likely result of his intravenous drug use. Even when he did show up, guitarist Steve Jones was forced to play bass to compensate for Sid's inexperience. The song "Anarchy in the

UK" was recorded while Matlock was still in the band, and had been out in England as a single.

When the Pistols met the members of Motörhead, Sid asked the group's legendary bassist, Lemmy Kilmister, for lessons.

"I can't play bass," Vicious confessed.

"I know," Lemmy answered.

One night, a groupie from the States followed the Pistols back to the place where they were crashing and crawled into bed with Johnny Rotten. He rejected her, taunting, "You want it, but you're not going to get it." The next night, the same scene was repeated. The night after that, the girl, Nancy Spungen, became Sid's girl-friend.

According to McLaren, Sid was a virgin at the time. "On the first night, we screwed, me and Sid," Nancy told UK's *Record Mirror* music weekly. "He had smelly feet and he wet the bed. . . . I've taught Sid everything he needs to know. . . . I've put that sexual aura into Sid."

Nancy had been born in Philadelphia and raised outside the city, in Lower Moreland Township. Her parents, Frank, a traveling salesman, and Deborah, an organic-food shop owner, were middle class with aspirations of upward mobility. But from the very start, Nancy didn't fit into the suburban blueprint.

Born in 1958 with her umbilical cord wrapped around her neck, Nancy likely was oxygen-deprived: this condition can lead to mental illness and aggressive behavior. At home, she threw tantrums and terrorized her younger sister and brother. "A seven-year-old ran our household," Deborah wrote in her memoir, *And I Don't Want to Live This Life: A Mother's Story of Her Daughter's Murder*. "When she wanted something, no matter how big or how small, she hollered and screamed and backed us into a corner until we were the ones to back down." Nothing seemed to satisfy the child. She went after her babysitters with scissors and tried to bash Deborah with a hammer. Despite her natural intelligence, Nancy had few friends and was sent to a boarding school for problem children. The alternative curriculum did nothing to calm her; Nancy ran away and slit her wrists with scissors. At fifteen, she was diagnosed with schizophrenia.

Two years later, she was in New York, where she worked as a topless dancer, turned tricks and supplied drugs to bands. To ingratiate herself to the musicians, she cooked for them and made herself sexually available. "I'll kill myself when my first wrinkle appears," she boasted to the *Record Mirror*. "I don't want to lose my looks."

The other groupies resented her. She didn't follow the same fashion guidelines, and was so loud that she pulled all the attention to herself. Even the performers began avoiding "Nauseating Nancy."

In 1977, the Heartbreakers announced a series of gigs in London. Nancy followed them there. Members Johnny Thunders and Jerry Nolan weren't pleased, warning people on the scene not to inform Nancy of their whereabouts.

That's when she decided to go after the Sex Pistols instead.

According to rock 'n' roll folklore, Nancy introduced Sid to heroin—though he consistently denied the claim. "I've been doing every fuckin' thing they reckon she turned me onto two years before I met her," he told *New Music Express*.

Sid was a handful without Nancy. Now he had a partner to encourage his every antisocial impulse. Johnny Rotten wasn't the star of the Sex Pistols, Nancy told her boyfriend. Sid was. "She was a very, very, very, very, very, very bad influence on people who were already a mess," said Heartbreakers manager Leee Black Childers in the book *Please Kill Me: The Uncensored Oral History of Punk*, by Legs McNeil and Gillian McCain.

Every day, there was another episode. Sid threw Nancy out of the apartment, and she ran up and down the street in her G-string, screeching out her love for him. If Sid would punch somebody, Nancy made sure to kick the guy in the balls. Once, a female fan offered Sid her phone number. On Nancy's orders, he pushed the girl down the stairs.

Singer Chrissie Hynde, of future Pretenders fame, had worked at McLaren and partner Vivienne Westwood's seminal clothing shop SEX before becoming friendly with Sid. Meeting Nancy, Hynde was shocked at the way she seemed to control the bass player. On one occasion, a musician from Paris accidentally slammed a door on a few tufts on Nancy's hair. As Nancy shrieked for her boyfriend, Sid raced forward, waving an eight-inch knife. The very tip clipped the man's neck, drawing a dribble of blood. Sid "surprised even himself this time," Hynde wrote in her auto-biography, *Reckless: My Life as a Pretender*. "Not because of the knife wielding or the obnoxiousness of his actions, but because of what he had become: pussy whipped, cowed."

At one stage, McLaren contemplated kidnapping Nancy off the street, bundling her into a van and dropping her off at Heathrow Airport with a one-way ticket home. But when he thought the plan out, he realized that if he lost Nancy, Sid would leave with her.

Remarkably, the band managed to ban her during a 1978 U.S. tour in which the Sex Pistols' partnership dissolved night after night onstage. No one was getting along, and the venues seemed to draw spectators who lacked both the appreciation and the knowl-edge of punk rock. When an audience member in San Antonio, Texas, loudly threatened Sid, the musician screamed out, "Faggot fucker!" and smashed his bass into the man's head. In Dallas, Sid was so strung out from heroin withdrawal that he carved the words *Gimme a Fix* onto his chest before taking the stage at the Longhorn Ballroom.

"All that heroin shit got on my nerves," Rotten told *Melody Maker*. As it was, he pointed out, Sid could barely play the bass. "It made doing gigs a waste of time 'cause I had no idea what was going on behind me. There was no one tune that I could pick up on. One song sounded very much like the other one. It all became pointless."

After a disastrous show at San Francisco's Winterland Ballroom, the band ended the tour early. Landing at New York, Rotten in-formed the *New York Post*, "I am sick of working with the Sex

Pistols." His frustration appeared justified, given that Sid was taken off his flight in a Valium and methadone coma, and rushed to Jamaica Hospital, near John F. Kennedy International Airport.

After his discharge, Sid and Nancy decided to stay in the city, eventually settling into a $35-a-night room at the famed Chelsea Hotel, where Eugene O'Neill, Dylan Thomas, Janis Joplin, Jerry Garcia, Bob Dylan, and Leonard Cohen had all stayed at one time or another. There were arguments, beatings, and deliberate cigarette burns. The pair were transferred to room 100 after Sid set fire to their first domicile. Their socializing centered around drugs and music, although, at that point on the punk scene, neither seemed to be exclusive from the other.

Howie Pyro remembered hearing about Nancy—and her sexual adventures with Aerosmith and the New York Dolls—before the term *punk rock* was regularly in use. "I disliked her before the Sid stuff because of public opinion in the scene. When she returned with Sid, 'the prize,' I understood why, but I liked Sid. He was a kid on drugs, I was a kid on drugs, and that's how that worked. But I saw another side to him, too. He was funny and normal and working-class, like people I knew."

In the wake of the Pistols' breakup, Nancy announced that she was the manager of her boyfriend's solo career. If Rotten was interested in participating, Nancy said, the lead singer could back Sid up on drums. "I remember Nancy wanted good pictures of her and Sid," Pyro said. "It was like, 'Ha, ha, everybody. Look what I got.'"

Indeed, she seemed to be gloating when the couple appeared on a small New York City cable show, taking questions from callers. When a viewer dared to describe Sid's music as "derivative," Nancy yowled, "He's about as original as you can get. He's not derivative of anything. If you don't believe me, you can ask the old-wave musicians in England, because they believe the same thing."

A young woman phoned in to compliment Sid on his looks. Cautioned Nancy, "Well, you better keep your hands off him, dearie, or I'll kill you."

Another woman referred to Sid as a "spoiled brat" and Nancy as "a blonde bitch." The provocation seemed to turn Nancy on. "Oh, yeah? Come here and say that."

"You're an asshole."

As usual, Sid, who'd previously appeared lethargic, rose to defend his girlfriend. "Not as much of an asshole as you are, you fuckin' cow."

"Cow!" Nancy harmonized with a grin.

All this theater seemed to inspire fans to see Sid's live performances. Large crowds turned up at Max's Kansas City in Manhattan, as Sid played with Mick Jones from the Clash, Rat Scabies from the Damned, Glen Matlock, and Nancy's old Heartbreaker intimates, Johnny Thunders and Jerry Nolan. "My Way" lyricist Paul Anka would later say that Sid's version of the song was even better than Sinatra's.

But the heroin and other drugs still blunted the couple's spirits. Days blurred together as the two zoned out at the Chelsea. "They didn't really go out that much or do anything," Pyro observed. "Everything was getting bad. They were so annoying that most people didn't want to be around them."

Sid was worried about being attacked and robbed when he went out to score dope. So Dee Dee Ramone—who shared the same proclivity for hard drugs—recommended that Sid always carry a knife to protect himself. On October 11, 1978, according to one report, Nancy went up to Times Square and purchased her boyfriend a five-inch folding blade with a jaguar carved into the handle. Other sources list the weapon as a "007" hunting knife that Sid had recently seen Dee Dee give to Stiv Bators of the Dead Boys.

At around 9:45 that night, the couple dropped in to visit another Chelsea couple, "Neon" Leon Webster, lead singer of an African American punk band, and his girlfriend, Cathi O'Rourke. At one point, Nancy made a muscle and asked Cathi to feel her arm. Cathi told the *Soho Weekly News* that Nancy boasted, "I'm strong. I carried Sid up from the restaurant. I can carry him, but he can't carry me."

As Nancy pondered the most productive way to score drugs, Sid sat on the bed, turning the pages of a portfolio featuring various Sex Pistol photos. "I've lost my looks," he lamented. "I really used to look good."

Cathi noticed him using his new knife to scratch his face. Quoting the Sex Pistols song, Sid told his friends that he had "no future."

At about 2:30 a.m. on October 12, Nancy asked Rockets Redglare, a stand-up comedian and actor who'd later appear in *Desperately Seeking Susan* and *Stranger Than Paradise*, among other movies, to score some Dilaudid, a powerful opiate containing morphine. Redglare occasionally worked as a bodyguard for Vicious. "I'm an ex-addict," he told the *Soho Weekly News*. "I would shoot [up] Sid because he's got collapsed veins and, anyway, he's not too good."

After sending Redglare on his quest, the couple made do with whatever drugs they had lying around the room.

At around 7:30 a.m., a neighbor heard a female moaning in room 100. This was a common occurrence at the Chelsea, and no one came out into the hallway to investigate.

Another three and a half hours passed before the desk clerk received a call from Sid: "Get an ambulance up here quick. I'm not kidding."

A bellman was dispatched. Moments later, the front desk was contacted by another unidentified male: "Someone is sick. Need help."

When the bellman finally arrived, he spotted a bloodstain on the bed and a red, wet trail leading into the dingy bathroom. There, Nancy lay slumped against the toilet in a black bra and panties, her head below the sink.

Racing out of the room, the bellman instructed the front desk to call for an ambulance. Paramedics arrived and confirmed that twenty-year-old Nancy was dead from a single knife wound in the lower abdomen. Police would find the couple's drugs, as well as the bloody knife.

Outside the room, they located a distraught, crying Sid, wandering the corridor and muttering. "She must have fallen on the knife," he apparently said. But police maintained that he also blurted out, "I killed her. . . . I can't live without her."

Sid claimed that he'd taken some thirty Tuinals—a potent sedative—and fallen into a deep sleep, waking up at one point to see Nancy on the bed, touching his new knife. He intended to ask her about her intentions, but was so stoned that he nodded off again. When he next woke up, he said, he saw blood soaking Nancy's side of the bed. "My first thought," he told police, "was that she had been killed."

Officers were certain that Sid was the perpetrator. "Listen, kid, why'd you do that?"

"Why'd I do what?"

"Why'd you kill the girl?"

"I didn't kill her."

"If you didn't kill her, why can't you look me straight in the face?"

Vicious stared at the officer. "All right. I'm looking you straight in the face. I didn't kill her, mate."

Incredulous, the policeman turned Sid around, pressed him against the wall, and handcuffed him.

The press immediately reported that Sid had confessed to murder, quoting NYPD sergeant Thomas Kilroy as saying that the homicide occurred "during a dispute." It's a charge that Sid vehemently refuted. "When the fuck did I make a confession?" he challenged Joe Stevens of the *New Music Express*. "I was well out of it, mate."

Before a pretrial hearing, a Hofstra University journalism student named Larry Jaffee asked Sergeant Kilroy about the veracity of Sid's confession. The lawman replied that the punker never admitted to the crime. The revelation appeared in a small Connecticut magazine called *Imagine*, but remained largely unknown until the *Guardian* reprinted Jaffee's article in 2013.

"Undesirable people have no rights," Pyro said. "No one liked Nancy, and Sid was the easiest person to blame. He's a junkie, he has a violent reputation, and the Sex Pistols weren't only hated, but the people in the music industry were afraid of them."

Malcolm McLaren was quick to fly to New York. Contractually, Sid was still his charge—the two were working on a punk-rock film at the time called *The Great Rock 'n' Roll Swindle*—even if Nancy said she was his manager and had actually helped score a couple of good deals for him. When McLaren entered the courtroom, he saw a disconnected, addicted twenty-one-year-old being led by court officers. Sid staggered to the defendant's table, and his knees buckled as he was helped to his chair. As his court-appointed lawyer, Joseph Epstein, argued that the alleged confession had never occurred, Sid's head sank to the table. He perked up slightly when he heard that he faced a sentence of twenty years to life. With good behavior—a goal Sid had never been able to accomplish— and parole, he might be released after seven years.

The moment that the hearing ended, Sid was transferred to the hospital ward at Rikers Island, New York City's sprawling jail complex. The judge had been sensitive enough to mandate that, before any trial started, the rocker needed to detox from heroin.

Even those who'd grown weary of Sid were quick to defend him. "He isn't capable of killing her," Rotten told *Melody Maker*. "It's not possible."

"Not even in an extreme moment?" he was asked.

"No. It is not possible. Full stop."

McLaren was just as adamant. "Sid was capable of a wide range of self-destructive acts," he wrote in the *Daily Beast*, "but I didn't think that he could kill someone, especially his girlfriend, unless it was a botched double suicide. No! I don't believe Sid killed Nancy."

The fact that he had consumed thirty Tuinals left friends who were familiar with the barbiturate astonished that Sid was even able to wake up the next morning. To rise to his feet and tussle with a woman as feisty as Nancy seemed all but impossible. McLaren was among those contending that, while Sid was unconscious, drug associates wandered through room 100, helping themselves to the couple's possessions. Indeed, the fingerprints of six of Sid and Nancy's acquaintances were found at the scene; police opted not to interview any of these people. And $2,400 in cash—payments from recent gigs and other projects—was reportedly missing.

"Money was stolen and Sid's knife . . . was taken from the wall, where it was hung, and seemingly [was] used by someone defending themselves in a struggle with Nancy," McLaren wrote. "Nancy was no pushover. . . . Probably, she caught this person stealing money from the bedroom drawer."

According to one theory, the perpetrator was Rockets Redglare, who was alleged to have boasted about killing Nancy in a struggle to some regulars at CBGB. The actor, who died from liver failure and hepatitis C in 2007, always denied this to reporters, blaming the murder instead on a dealer named "Michael," who some said had been seen with a wad of cash tied with Nancy's purple hair band.

Pyro speculated that after Sid fell back asleep after seeing Nancy on the bed, fingering the knife, she cut herself. "She had one tiny stab wound in her abdomen," Pyro said. "I think she stabbed herself to get attention. 'Sid, I'm bleeding.' It's the kind of thing she would have done. But Sid didn't wake up, and she bled to death."

Deborah Spungen believed that Nancy told Sid to kill her to alleviate the mental torment she'd been enduring since infancy. From jail, Sid wrote Deborah that he soon hoped to meet Nancy again in the afterlife. "No one should expect me to live without her," he said.

On the day of Nancy's funeral, Anne Beverley arrived in New York, swiftly telling any reporter who wanted to hear her story that it was going to cost money. By now, McLaren had done his own version of crowdsourcing, raising $50,000—part of it from Virgin Records head Richard Branson—for bail.

A freshly released Sid was photographed walking through Manhattan with his arm draped around Anne. At the Seville

Hotel on Madison Avenue, he repaired to the bathroom and slashed his wrists with a broken light bulb. McLaren told the press that the musician was suffering from methadone withdrawal, having exhausted his supply of the heroin substitute two days before. What the punk entrepreneur didn't mention was Sid's declaration, "I want to be with Nancy!"

Sid drifted through New York, zonked out, miserable, in transition between life and death. At a show by Chicago punk band Skafish, Patti Smith's brother, Todd, confronted Sid after the former Pistol allegedly pinched the man's girlfriend. Vicious responded by smashing a beer mug in Todd's face: the act earned the punker an additional two months at Rikers.

"I remember going on the bus with Anne and another friend, the photographer Eileen Polk, to Rikers," Pyro said. "Sid was bummed out, trying to kick methadone, getting abused in jail by hardened criminals. He was defenseless as a puppy. Last thing he knew, he was in a big rock band. Now, here he was in America, in jail, waking up from a fuzzy drug dream into a total nightmare. It was, 'How did I get here?' Crushed dreams."

Along with "My Way," Sid's brief solo career had yielded such offerings as Eddie Cochran's "C'mon Everybody" and "Something Else," cacophonous variations of recognizable pop tunes that appealed to people who weren't necessarily punk fans but admired the attitude. Given Elvis Presley's recent death, McLaren was convinced that Sid could step in for "the King" on the Las Vegas Strip and was talking to promoters about the possibility. Capitalizing on the charges against Sid, the repertoire would include renditions of "Mack the Knife" and "I Fought the Law." With a new album paying for the musician's legal bills, McLaren was confident of an acquittal. Until then, he and Westwood were mass-producing a Sid Vicious T-shirt with the slogan "She's dead. I'm alive. I'm yours."

After seven weeks of detox, Sid was released from custody a second time on February 1, 1979. Pyro was among the greeting party, along with Anne, Jerry Only, and a new girlfriend, aspiring actress, Michelle Robinson. The group repaired to Robinson's apartment on Bank Street: records were played and spaghetti Bolognese prepared. For a group of punk rockers, it was a pretty wholesome scene.

"At first, Sid was in a good mood," Pyro said. "There were no drugs. Sid was normal and clean, childlike, playing air guitar, listening to the first New York Dolls album. He was just another kid like me. Not Sid Vicious. John Beverley. He seemed to be pretty fuckin' happy. And then the doorbell rang and the happiness ended. But that was going to happen sooner than later."

Even though he was technically drug-free, Sid had no intention of remaining that way. By sheer circumstance, photographer Peter Gravelle had run into Sid shortly after his release. Peter enjoyed a robust sideline as a rock 'n' roll drug supplier, particularly for the Rolling Stones' Keith Richards. Sid had been looking to score, and Gravelle had promised to do his best to accommodate the punk rocker. The photographer stepped into Michelle's apartment and he and Sid huddled, with Gravelle passing over $200 worth of unusually pure heroin.

"When you're an addict," Pyro explained, "anything is a good excuse to get high. When you've been denied it for a long time, the mental craving is worse than the physical one. You physically get sick before you even do the drugs, from anticipation. Just having it in your hands will make you crazy."

Sid retreated into the bedroom. The weeks in Rikers had lowered his resistance to the drug, and Sid instantly overdosed. "Everyone freaked the fuck out," Pyro said. "The decision was, 'Don't call an ambulance. Don't call the police. We'll figure it out.'"

Incredibly, Sid woke up. "And he was nice again," Pyro stated. "And he was apologizing."

The party continued. Eventually, Pyro, Eileen Polk, and Only left together. "Within a few hours, we were back at the apartment," Pyro recalled. "He'd OD'd again. But this time, he was dead."

Authorities saw no reason to continue to examine the circumstances of Nancy Spungen's death. According to the police and district attorney's office, the perpetrator had died. As people in the straight world saw it, Nancy had kind of brought it upon herself.

Deborah Spungen knew this because she'd been told just as much. In Pennsylvania, the Spungen home was bombarded with phone calls from strangers. Almost all of the messages were hateful.

As would the murders of Biggie Smalls and Tupac Shakur, the deaths of Sid and Nancy helped mainstream music and fashion previously associated with society's outlaws. Tourists regularly appeared at the Chelsea, creating makeshift shrines to the marginal couple outside room 100 until the hotel tired of the visits and renovated the floor. The place where Nancy Spungen died was divided into a stairwell and laundry chute, the room numbers skipping from 99 to 101.

In 2006, Vicious was inducted into the Rock and Roll Hall of Fame, along with the four original members of the Sex Pistols. None of them attended. Nor did Anne Beverley, who committed suicide in 1996.

Asked if there's a lesson to the Sid and Nancy saga, Howie Pyro answered with a cynicism steeped in punk rock. "Does there have to be one? It's a lesson of life and death. It happens. People die. People OD. And, sadly, there are many more to come."

"I Hate Myself and Want to Die"

Did Kurt Cobain Really Off Himself?

The electrician hired to install security lighting at the house one block from Lake Washington thought Kurt Cobain was asleep on the floor. He was a rock star, after all, and that's where they ended up sometimes. But as Gary Smith approached the Nirvana lead singer, the workman noticed that blood was trickling from Cobain's ear. Now, Smith stepped back and surveyed the full picture. A rifle lay across Kurt's chest, and a good deal of his face was missing—so much that authorities would have to identify him through fingerprints. A note, with a pen plunged through it, had been placed in a flowerpot, providing an explanation as to why Kurt had taken it upon himself to join the iniquitous 27 Club.

"Even though Kurt died in the most horrific way possible, there is this mythology and romanticism that surrounds him because he's twenty-seven forever," his daughter, Frances Bean Cobain, would tell *Rolling Stone* in 2015, twenty-one years after her father's death in Seattle's Leschi neighborhood. "The shelf life of a musician or artist isn't particularly long. Kurt has gotten to icon status because he will never age. He will always . . . be beautiful."

In the three years since Nirvana became international superstars, Kurt had grown weary of the responsibility of having to speak for his generation. He resented the way that his lyrics were searched for hidden meanings, as well as the relentless media scrutiny and the animosity fans and social critics directed toward his wife, Hole lead singer Courtney Love. The pressures were aggravated by Cobain's struggles with depression and drug addiction. While others fantasized about trading places with Cobain onstage, Kurt just wanted to disappear, leaving more than a few hints about the way it was going to end.

It was Kurt, after all, who'd written the song "I Hate Myself and Want to Die."

But certain relatives, friends, and devotees refused to accept the official cause of death. Kurt did not kill himself, they said. Someone killed *him*.

Along with a predisposition toward suicide, Kurt's family boasted an artistic streak. His grandmother, Iris Cobain, was a professional artist, while her brother-in-law Delbert Cobain had performed as an Irish tenor, and appeared in the 1930 movie *King of Jazz*. An uncle on his mother's side, Chuck Fradenburg, was in a group called the Beachcombers, whose boisterous version of the single "Farmer John" circulated around the Northwest. In 1969, at the age of two, Kurt was singing. Within a few short years, he'd be playing the piano, writing songs, and drawing impressive sketches of his favorite cartoon characters.

By most accounts, he was a relatively happy child until his parents divorced when he was nine. "I was ashamed of my parents," he told journalist Jon Savage. "I desperately wanted to have the classic, you know, typical family."

Years of instability followed. Kurt's mother, Wendy, a waitress, began dating a man with abusive tendencies. Kurt seemed to be closer to his father, Donald, a mechanic, who'd pledged not to remarry. But Donald reneged when he met Jenny Westby, and moved the boy into an Aberdeen, Washington, home with the woman and her two daughters. At first, Kurt liked the arrangement. But when Jenny gave birth to Kurt's half-brother, Chad, in 1979, Cobain lost his status as the only boy in the family. At one point, he moved into his friend's born-again-Christian household.

Dispute the bitter criticism he'd later level at Christian institutions, Kurt briefly embraced the family's faith and attended church.

Donald tried to find a way to bond with his oldest child, but Kurt worked hard to sabotage the relationship. Although a gifted wrestler, he once deliberately lost a match in order to disappoint his father.

Recognizing signs of depression in himself, Kurt developed a fixation with Seattle-born Frances Farmer, known as much for her paranoid schizophrenia and stays in mental asylums as for her work as an actress and television host. Besides naming his daughter Frances, Cobain would pen a song titled "Frances Farmer Will Have Her Revenge on Seattle."

Growing up on his aunt's Beatles collection, Kurt related to the rebelliousness and inner torment of John Lennon. Upon receiving a used guitar as a fourteenth-birthday present, he began playing Beatles tunes, as well as songs by Led Zeppelin, Queen, Black Sabbath, Aerosmith, and Kiss. He eventually became part of the Seattle punk scene, expressing a particular affinity for the Clash, Black Flag, Bad Brains, and fellow Aberdeen natives the Melvins.

By the time high school graduation approached, Kurt realized that he hadn't accumulated the proper credits and dropped out. At that point, he was living with his mother, who demanded that he find a job. Instead, he left home. According to a legend he cultivated, his exodus included a stint camping out under a bridge on the muddy banks of the Wishkah River. Eventually, he found a girlfriend, Tracy Marander in Olympia, Washington, who supported Kurt's art by working in the cafeteria at Seattle-Tacoma International Airport.

Tracy would have an enduring influence on Nirvana. A photograph she had taken appeared on the cover of the band's debut album, *Bleach*, and the couple's arguments over Kurt's reluctance to find proper employment inspired the song "About a Girl."

A subsequent girlfriend, Tobi Vail, a founding member of the band Bikini Kill, would inadvertently help influence the title of

Nirvana's most well-known hit. Alluding to Tobi's deodorant of choice, Bikini Kill bandmate Kathleen Hanna spray-painted the slogan "Kurt Smells Like Teen Spirit" on his wall. Unaware of the brand-name reference, Kurt later composed "Smells Like Teen Spirit," hoping to convey some type of revolutionary message.

Nirvana was formed in 1987, with Kurt on guitar and Krist Novoselic on bass. Aaron Burckhard was the first in what would be a succession of drummers until Dave Grohl took over in 1990. In what may have been a window into his motives for committing suicide, Kurt favored the name Nirvana because of its definition as the Buddhist concept of "freedom from pain, suffering and the external world."

Courtney Love first saw Kurt onstage in 1989 in Portland, Oregon. They had much in common. Each headed a rock band with a growing following, and both struggled with drug issues. After running into Kurt again a few months later, Courtney attempted to pursue a romance. Determined to remain single, he was elusive. Eventually, though, they became a genuine punk-rock couple—with all the drama that the label implied. In 1992, they married just after Nirvana completed a tour in Hawaii. In keeping with Kurt's obsession, Courtney wore a dress once owned by Frances Farmer.

By this point, Nirvana was one of the most popular bands in the world, riding a wave that began with the release of "Smells Like Teen Spirit" from their second album, *Nevermind*, in 1991. Suddenly, the Northwestern grunge scene was no longer an underground secret. With the media describing Nirvana as the mothership of the grunge movement—and Seattle becoming a destination for rock pilgrimages—bands like Pearl Jam, Alice in Chains, and Soundgarden were soon receiving extensive airplay.

Unprepared to play the role of Generation X spokesman, Cobain bristled as strangers foisted accolades upon him. "My dad was exceptionally ambitious," Frances told *Rolling Stone*. "But he had a lot thrown on him, exceeding his ambition. He wanted to be successful. But he didn't want to be the fucking voice of his generation."

The magnified visibility induced the press to examine every aspect of Kurt's personal life. Love was rebuked for using heroin while pregnant, and Cobain's flaws and insecurities were constantly exposed. The song "Rape Me," on the group's third album, *In Utero*, was Kurt's statement about the treatment he claimed to receive from the media.

"Kurt got to the point where he eventually had to sacrifice every bit of who he was for his art because the world demanded it of him," Frances said in her interview. "I think that was one of the main triggers as to why he felt he didn't want to be here."

Symptoms of the stress revealed themselves both on tour and in the studio. "Kurt could be very outgoing and funny and charming," *Nevermind* producer Butch Vig told *Rolling Stone*. "And a half hour later, he would just go and sit in the corner and be totally moody and uncommunicative."

On one occasion, Novoselic acknowledged the demands placed on his lead singer and offered to buy Cobain dinner. Instead, Kurt instructed the bassist to drive him to a location where a heroin dealer was waiting. Cobain maintained that he had a chronic stomach condition that could only be relieved by the opiate. Some friends countered that it was the heroin that was causing the illness in the first place.

In 1993, Kurt suffered an overdose while visiting New York to perform at the New Music Seminar. Rather than dialing 911, Courtney injected her husband with naloxone, a medication used to soften the effects of an overdose, enabling him to take the stage without anyone knowing what had transpired earlier in the day.

During a 1994 European tour, Kurt came down with bronchitis and laryngitis, and was unable to perform. The band canceled the remainder of the tour, and Kurt flew from Munich to Rome for treatment. On March 3, Love joined him there. At 4 a.m., she said, she woke up to discover Kurt unconscious after mixing champagne with her prescription Rohypnol, a tranquilizer said to be ten times more powerful than Valium. He was apparently upset that Courtney had fallen asleep after they'd begun kissing earlier in the night. In a note left behind, Love said that Kurt had written, "You don't love me anymore. I'd rather die than go through a divorce."

After she phoned police, the singer was revived.

Two weeks later, Love called authorities again. This time, the couple was back in Seattle. When police arrived, Courtney told them that Kurt had locked himself in a room with a .38-caliber pistol, threatening to kill himself. Cobain said that he had no intention of taking his life. The officers resolved the matter by confiscating the revolver, along with three other weapons and a bottle of pills.

However, Love claimed that she realized that both she and Kurt needed help. On March 25, she brought an intervention counselor to their home, along with Nirvana bandmates Novoselic and Pat Smear, Cobain's close friend Dylan Carlson, and various others. Cobain was furious, locking himself in the upstairs bedroom at one stage and insulting his visitors. Smear told Cobain that if he didn't clean up, Nirvana would have to disband. After two days of prodding, Kurt agreed to enter rehab. But first, he arranged for Carlson to bring over a shotgun—in case it ever had to be used to ward off intruders on the rock star's property.

Love was also supposed to stay at the Exodus Recovery Center in Marina Del Ray, California, but opted to situate herself at the Peninsula Hotel in Beverly Hills and attend an outpatient program. At Exodus, the counselor saw no indication of suicidal thoughts in Kurt as he played with his daughter and openly discussed his drug and personal issues. He appeared to be a man who wanted to help himself.

But after two days of counseling, Kurt stepped outside to have a cigarette, then scrambled to the six-foot fence that ringed the facility and climbed over. He took a taxi to the airport, and sat with Guns N' Roses' Duff McKagan on a flight to Seattle.

Family and friends desperately tried contacting the AWOL musician, but Kurt was unresponsive, prompting his mother, Wendy, to file a missing-persons report. Unable to leave her detox program, Love hired a private investigator to find her husband.

But it was electrician Gary Smith who located him first, as well as the gun Dylan Carlson had delivered to his friend.

In his suicide note, Kurt despaired about not feeling "the excitement of listening to as well as creating music . . . for too many years now." He quoted the Neil Young lyric "It's better to burn out than to fade away." He expressed his love for Frances but emphasized that "her life . . . will be so much better without me."

The Seattle police, citing Kurt's wounds—as well as the high concentration of heroin in his system, as well as his history of depression, propensity to store weapons, and discontent with celebrity—quickly ruled the death a suicide.

In the book *Heavier Than Heaven*, Dave Reed, Kurt's former foster father, told author Charles R. Cross, "It didn't matter that other people loved him. He simply didn't love himself enough."

The public memorial to Kurt Cobain, on April 10, 1994, featured a recording of Courtney Love reading her husband's suicide note. At the end of the vigil, she arrived, handing out some of Kurt's clothes to fans. Later, she traveled to the Namgyal Monastery Institute of Buddhist Studies in Ithaca, New York, where a portion of Cobain's ashes were blessed and mixed into clay. The composite would be used to mold memorial statues.

But not every observer viewed Love's actions as sincere, particularly those insistent that the Seattle police investigation had been anything but thorough. Speaking for the cynics, Kurt's grandfather Leland Cobain announced that the singer was the victim of homicide, not suicide.

Of all the possible suspects, Courtney Love's name loomed largest. Kurt was going to divorce her, the theory went, and she needed to cash in while her name was still in the will. Tom Grant, the private investigator hired by Courtney after her husband left rehab, soon became one of the loudest proponents of this hypothesis. "Love was involved in a conspiracy in the death of Kurt Cobain," he told the New York *Daily News*, describing the Hole lead singer as both a "psychopath" and "sociopath."

She had ample assistance, according to Grant. Noting that the King County Medical Examiner delivered its suicide ruling the day after Cobain's body was found, the private investigator argued, "How can they possibly know that he committed suicide when they didn't have the toxicology report back?"

Despite Cobain's lyrics and overall gloominess, some fans contended that the rock legend hadn't been suicidal at all. Rather, it was Love who manipulated the public into believing a myth about her husband's inclinations, they said, drugging him with Rohypnol in Rome, then—when he survived the overdose—planting the story that Kurt had wanted to die.

What these critics neglected to mention was that it was Love who'd called the police in Rome, saving her husband's life.

Still, the rumors only seemed to increase. In the 1998 documentary *Kurt and Courtney*, filmmaker Nick Broomfield interviewed shock rocker Eldon "El Duce" Hoke, who said that Love offered him $50,000 to murder Kurt. Duce stated that he subcontracted the assignment to the actual killer—someone he identified as "Allen." Roundly described as unreliable, Hoke did not live long enough to elaborate. Days after the interview, the drunken performer wandered into the path of a train in Riverside, California.

Handwriting experts pored over the suicide note, with some concluding that Kurt was responsible for every word, while others reported inconclusive findings. In particular, the last four lines seemed to have been written after the rest of the missive. Did this mean that someone commissioned by Courtney Love had added to the note in order to underscore the suicide theory?

Even some of Love's defenders clung to the notion that Cobain didn't die by his own hand. Other possible perpetrators included the CIA—attempting to neuter the singer's destabilizing influence on youth—and music industry executives. The latter allegedly feared that Kurt's disillusionment with the business would lead to retirement and a general disinterest in grunge. By contrast, a dead Cobain would be immortalized for generations.

As to who pulled the actual trigger, skeptics pointed out, the fingerprints lifted from the shotgun were too smudged to allow for identification of the shooter. Although this occurs at many crime scenes, cynics wondered if powerful forces ensured that the truth about the real assassin would never emerge.

One private investigator floated the concept that the high heroin content in Cobain's bloodstream suggested that the singer was injected by someone else, then shot. "The forensic pathologist we spoke to said there's no way this guy could have injected a triple lethal dose of heroin into his system, then rolled down his sleeve, put away the drug kit, picked up the shotgun, and killed himself," Max Wallace told NBC. "He would have been incapacitated within seconds."

The inverse side of this opinion is that Cobain was a practiced addict whose high tolerance would have enabled him to execute the abovementioned tasks.

In 2014, four rolls of 35mm film from the crime scene—left behind in an evidence vault—were developed. The images were clearer than the Polaroids initially used by investigators. Some interesting details emerged. Cobain was still wearing the bracelet from the rehab facility when he died, and his foot had come to rest next to a bag of shotgun shells. But police reached the same conclusion that they had twenty years earlier.

Each year, near the home where Kurt Cobain died, fans gather in Viretta Park to pay homage to the long-deceased spokesperson for Generation X. Over time, Nirvana has sold 75 million albums internationally. In 2014, their first year of eligibility, the band—the unit that included Cobain, Krist Novoselic, and Dave Grohl—was inducted into the Rock and Roll Hall of Fame.

At least once a week, usually on Twitter, the Seattle Police Department receives a request to reopen the investigation.

But beat poet William S. Burroughs—a hero of Cobain's and a fellow addict who collaborated with the rock star on a spoken-word project—never questioned the official judgment. "It wasn't an act of will for Kurt to kill himself," the writer said in his autobiography, *William S. Burroughs: A Life*. "As far as I was concerned, he was dead already."

Selected Bibliography

In the course of researching this book, I conducted a number of firsthand interviews, perused dozens of books and read through hundreds of newspaper, magazine, and website articles. Although the following list is far from complete, it provides a window into the type of material I relied on to bring these intriguing and often contentious tales to life:

Books

Arrarás, María Celeste. *Selena's Secret: The Revealing Story Behind Her Tragic Death*. New York: Atria Press, 1997.

Boulware, Jack, and Silke Tudor. *Gimme Something Better: The Profound, Progressive, and Occasionally Pointless History of Bay Area Punk from Dead Kennedys to Green Day*. New York: Penguin, 2009.

Daniels, Neil. *The Story of Judas Priest: Defenders of the Faith*. London: Omnibus Press, 2010.

Diehl, Matt, and Derrick Parker. *Notorious C.O.P.: The Inside Story of the Tupac, Biggie, and Jam Master Jay Investigations from NYPD's First "Hip-Hop Cop"*. New York: St. Martin's Press, 2006.

Fuller, Randell, and Miriam Linna. *I Fought the Law: The Life and Strange Death of Bobby Fuller*. New York: Ricks Books, 2014.

Greenberg, Keith Elliot. *December 8, 1980: The Day John Lennon Died*. Montclair, NJ: Backbeat, 2010.

Guralnick, Peter. *Dream Boogie: The Triumph of Sam Cooke*. New York: Hachette Book Group, 2011.

Kading, Greg. *Murder Rap: The Untold Story of the Biggie Smalls & Tupac Shakur Murder Investigations*. One-Time Publishing, 2011.

Moynihan, Michael, and Didrik Søderlind. *Lords of Chaos: The Bloody Rise of the Satanic Metal Underground*. Port Townsend, WA: Feral House, 2003.

Ribowsky, Mark. *He's a Rebel: Phil Spector, Rock and Roll's Legendary Producer.* Cambridge, MA: Da Capo Press, 2006.

Ritz, David. *Divided Soul: The Life Of Marvin Gaye.* Cambridge, MA: Da Capo Press, 2003.

Spungen, Deborah. *And I Don't Want to Live This Life: A Mother's Story of Her Daughter's Murder.* New York: Ballantine Books, 1996.

Tosches, Nick. *Save the Last Dance for Satan.* New York: Rocks Books, 2012.

Trynka, Paul. *Brian Jones: The Making of the Rolling Stones.* New York: Plume, 2015.

Newspapers and Magazines

Barnes, Brooks. "A Star Idolized and Haunted, Michael Jackson Dies at 50." *New York Times*, June 25, 2009.

Burkitt, Janet, and Alex Tizon. "Zapata Slaying Suspect Called 'Predatory.'" *Seattle Times*, January 14, 2003.

Callwood, Brett. "28 Years After a Horrible Crime, Fang Singer Sammytown Still Stirs Controversy." *LA Weekly*, February 8, 2017.

Campion, Chris. "The Short Life and Mysterious Death of Bobby Fuller, Rock 'n' Roll King of Texas." *Guardian*, July 16, 2013.

Culzac, Natasha. "John Lydon: 'I Feel a Bit Responsible for Sid Vicious' Death." *Independent*, October 13, 2014.

Epstein, Dan. "Dimebag Darrell: 10 Years Later, a Look Back at the Murder of the Last Guitar God." *Billboard*, December 8, 2014.

Flanary, Patrick. "Jailed Drummer Jim Gordon Denied Parole." *Rolling Stone*, May 17, 2013.

Fong-Torres, Ben. "James Douglas Morrison, Poet, Dead at 27." *Rolling Stone*, August 5, 1971.

Glaister, Dan. "How Phil Spector Was Convicted of the Murder of Lana Clarkson." *The Guardian*, April 13, 2009.

Greenfield, Robert. "The Rise and Fall of the First Rock Star." *Playboy*, March 2010.

Horns, Ryan. "Why Did Nathan Gale Kill Former Pantera Guitarist Dimebag Darrell?" *Marysville* (OH) *Journal-Tribune*, December 14, 2004.

Hunter, Al. "The Death of Sam Cooke, Part 2." *Weekly View*, December 18, 2014.

Hutchinson, Lydia. "The Mysterious Death of Jim Morrison." *Daily Mail*, July 8, 2015.

Jones, Scott. "Has the Riddle of Rolling Stone Brian Jones's Death Been Solved at Last?" *Daily Mail*, November 29, 2008.

Lovett, Kenneth. "Mark David Chapman, John Lennon's Killer, Admits Nearly Turning Gun on Self After Infamous 1980 Shooting." *Daily News* (New York), September 16, 2016.

McPhee, Rod. "Marvin Gaye's Ex-Wife: 'I Thought He Was Going to Kill Me When He Flew into a Rage High on Drugs.'" *Mirror*, August 17, 2015.

Mitchell, Pete. "Trouble Man 30 Years On: The Secret Life and Death of Marvin Gaye." *Daily Express*, March 31, 2014.

Nelson, Sean. "Matt Dresdner of the Gits Talks About the Murder of His Friend and Bandmate Mia Zapata 10 Years Later." *Stranger* (Seattle), January 16, 2003.

Newton, Steve. "Rob Halford Forced to Defend Judas Priest's Name Against Suicide Lawsuit." *Georgia Straight*, October 25, 1990.

Paulikas, Steven. "Cantat, France Await Outcome of Murder Trial." *Baltic Times*, March 23, 2004.

Phull, Hardeep. "Jam Master Jay's Son Opens Up About His Dad's Unsolved Murder." *New York Post*, January 8, 2016.

Price, Richard. "Michael Jackson's World: He Slept in an Oxygen Tent and His Best Friend Was Bubbles the Chimp." *Daily Mail*, June 26, 2009.

Rees, Jasper. "Why Marvin Gaye's Death Was a Greek Tragedy." *Telegraph*, May 26, 2016.

Ryan, Harriet. "Jurors Visit Phil Spector's House." *LA Times*, February 20, 2009.

Samuel, Henry. "Actress in Coma After Hotel Room Row with Rock Star Boyfriend." *Telegraph*, July 29, 2003.

Schoemer, Karen. "The Day Punk Died." *New York*, October 19, 2008.

Sigel, Zack. "Old, Cold and Full of Trolls: How to Reconcile Being a Black Metal Fan Today." *Complex*, December 16, 2015.

Turner, Allan. "Devoted Fans of Selena Arrive Before Trial Starts." *Houston Chronicle*, October 8, 1995.

Wakeman, Jessica. "Flashback: Nancy Spungen Found Dead at Chelsea Hotel." *Rolling Stone*, October 12, 2017.

Winton, Richard. "20 Years Later, Notorious BIG's Killing Remains One of LA's Biggest Unsolved Homicides," *LA Times*, March 9, 2017.

Yockel, Michael. "Between Punk Rock and a Hard Place." *Miami New Times*, March 12, 1998.

Websites

All Things Crime
BBC News
Blabbermouth
CBS.com
CNN.com
Crime Watch Daily
Daily Beast
Daily Kos
Dirt City Chronicles
E! News
48 Hours
FoxNews.com
iHeartRadio
Investigation Discovery
Latino Voices
Metal Injection
MTV News
National Public Radio
OWN.com
Popdust
Rank & Review
Rock and Roll Hall of Fame
Salon
ThisDayinMusic.com
Time.com
Ultimate Classic Rock
Unsolved Mysteries
VH1
WPIX.com